#CyberDoc

No Borders - No Boundaries

National Doctrine for the Cyber Era

Editors

Timothy R. Sample and Michael S. Swetnam

POTOMAC INSTITUTE PRESS

Publisher's Cataloging-in-Publication Data

#CyberDoc : no borders - no boundaries : national doctrine for the cyber era / editors, Timothy R. Sample and Michael S. Swetnam. -- Arlinton, VA : Potomac Institute Press, c2012.

p. ; cm.

ISBN: 978-0-9852483-1-4 (cloth) ; 978-0-9852483-2-1 (pbk.) ; 978-0-9852483-3-8 (ebk.)
Discussion papers and final report from the Battelle Doctrine Project conference held at The Founders Inn, Virginia Beach, Virginia, on June 7-10, 2012, sponsored by the Battelle Memorial Institute and the Potomac Institute for Policy Studies.
Includes bibliographical references and index.
Summary: Intended to promote a debate on a national-level doctrine for the cyber era, and what it should entail.--Publisher.

1. Computers and civilization--Government policy--United States--Congresses. 2. Internet--Government policy--United States--Congresses. 3. Cyber intelligence (Computer security)--United States--Congresses. 4. Cyberinfrastructure--United States--Congresses. 5. Information warfare--United States--Congresses. 6. National security--United States--Congresses. 7. Cyberterrorism--United States--Prevention--Congresses. 8. Sabotage--United States--Prevention--Congresses. 9. Computer security--Government policy--United States--Congresses. 10. Computer networks--Security measures--United States--Congresses. 11. Data protection--United States--Planning--Congresses. I. Sample, Timothy R. II. Swetnam, Michael S. III. Potomac Institute for Policy Studies. IV. Battelle Memorial Institute. V. Title: Cyberdoc. VI. Title: National doctrine for the cyber era.

QA76.9.C66 C93 2012

303.48/34--dc23   1211

POTOMAC INSTITUTE FOR POLICY STUDIES
901 N. Stuart St, Suite 200
Arlington, VA, 22203
www.potomacinstitute.org
Telephone: 703.525.0770; Fax: 703.525.0299
Email: webmaster@potomacinstitute.org

#CyberDoc

No Borders - No Boundaries

National Doctrine for the Cyber Era

Contents

Disclaimer

The views and opinions expressed herein are those of the individual chapter authors and do not necessarily reflect the views of Battelle Memorial Institute, its affiliates, or its employees.

Authors are solely responsible for the correctness and completeness of the content of their work and any pre-publication review requirements.

The Author(s) have expressly granted rights to the chapters and manuscript to Battelle Memorial Institute and the Potomac Institute Press, including, without limitation, the copyright in the work.

List of Contributors

David Aucsmith
Microsoft Institute for Advanced Technology in Governments

Sharon L. Cardash
George Washington University

Frank J. Cilluffo
George Washington University

Gus P. Coldebella
Goodwin Procter, LLP

Randall M. Fort
Raytheon

Robert P. Liscouski
Secure Strategy Group

Ronald A. Marks
Intelligence Enterprises, LLC

Barry Pavel
Atlantic Council

Alfred Rolington
E-Side Publishing

Timothy R. Sample
Battelle Memorial Institute

The Honorable James M. Simon, Jr.
Microsoft Institute for Advanced Technology in Governments

David J. Smith
Potomac Institute for Policy Studies

Michael S. Swetnam
Potomac Institute for Policy Studies

Richard Weitz, Ph.D.
Hudson Institute

Kathryn Schiller Wurster
Potomac Institute for Policy Studies

Acronyms

ACLU	American Civil Liberties Union
ACTA	Anti-Counterfeiting Trade Agreement
ARPA	Advanced Research Projects Agency
ASIO	Australian Security Intelligence Organization
C4ISR	Command, Control, Communications, Computers, Intelligence, Surveillance and Reconnaissance
CAC	Common Access Card
CFATS	Chemical Facility Anti-Terrorism Standards
CIA	Central Intelligence Agency
CIMB	Cyber Investment Management Board
CISOs	Chief Information Security Officers
CNA	Computer Network Attack
CNCI	Comprehensive National Cybersecurity Initiative
CND	Computer Network Defense
CNE	Computer Network Exploitation
CNO	Computer Network Operations
COTS	Commercial-Off-The-Shelf
DARPA	Defense Advanced Research Projects Agency
DDoS	Distributed Denial of Service
DEPSECDEF	Deputy Secretary of Defense
DHCP	Dynamic Host Configuration Protocol
DIB	Defense Industrial Base
DHS	Department of Homeland Security
DoD	Department of Defense
DOS	Denial of Service
FBI	Federal Bureau of Investigation
FISA	Foreign Intelligence Surveillance Act
FISC	Foreign Intelligence Surveillance Court
HPSCI	House Permanent Select Committee on Intelligence

HUMINT	Human Intelligence
IC	Intelligence Community
IDSs	Intrusion Detection Systems
IO	Information Operations
IP	Intellectual Property
ISACs	Information Sharing and Analysis Centers
ISP	Internet Service Provider
LOAC	Laws of Armed Conflict
MAD	Mutually Assured Destruction
METU	Middle East Technical University
MIT	Massachusetts Institute of Technology
NAT	Network Address Translation
NATO	North Atlantic Treaty Organization
NCIRC	NATO Computer Incident Response Capability
NDAA	National Defense Authorization Act
NIST	National Institute of Standards and Technology
NSA	National Security Agency
NSL	National Security Letters
OECD	Organisation for Economic Co-operation and Development
OSI	Open Systems Interconnection
OSS	Office of Strategic Services
PLA	People's Liberation Army
PRC	People's Republic of China
SCADA	Supervisory Control and Data Acquisition
SOPA	Stop Online Piracy Act
TCP	Transmission Control Protocol
TCP/IP	Transmission Control Protocol/Internet Protocol
TIA	Total Information Awareness
WMD	Weapons of Mass Destruction

Preface

Dr. Jeffrey Wadsworth

Usage of the Internet, whether through your desktop or smart phone, is deeply engrained in the American way of life. From our personal endeavors in communications, finance, entertainment, and online commerce, to the development of advanced cyber "tools" by our military, we are touched by the cyber dimension. We may not even realize the effects that this technological transition has had on our lives, positively and negatively. By any standard, you can argue that the emergence of the Internet and the effects therein, have benefitted mankind to a great degree. But, with the development of these technologies and the explosion of their usage, new challenges have emerged that present a level of unexpected vulnerability and a level of increasing complexity. As a nation, we have tended to address individual cyber issues and challenges in a piecemeal fashion and have been focusing on other major problems that relate to our national security. These include economic instability at home and abroad, federal budgets and spending, military conflicts in Iraq and Afghanistan, and the persistent threat from terrorists' tactics.

The vulnerabilities inherent in our reliance on the Internet are rarely discussed publically in terms of our national security. As a public, we default to our reliance on the Federal Government for cyber national security concerns and solutions. However, we continue to learn of the extensive nature of the threat and of the risks facing us as other countries, groups, or individuals become increasingly adept in manipulating the cyber domain in both positive and negative ways. In a recent visit to China to attend the Chinese Academy of Engineering 11th General Assembly in Beijing, I was both impressed and concerned at the clarity and determination with which President Hu addressed the country's vision and priorities in scientific research, education, and the use of the cyber domain in China's overall stature within the world, as well as for its economic growth. Not surprisingly, they are looking decades down the road, while we are focusing on the next fiscal year.

For these and other reasons, Battelle has embarked on this project to promote a debate on a national-level doctrine for the cyber era and what it should entail. As in the very early stages of the formulation of the Containment Doctrine and its nuclear-related pieces, it was the scientists who first came forward with ideas about doctrine, as they best understood the overall impact (diplomatic and otherwise) as well as the science and technologies involved. Likewise, in this case, Battelle has a role to play. As the world's largest independent research organization, we study the science of cyber, have the ability to bring disparate areas of interest together to address the issues, and then can work with our government to encourage it to articulate and adopt a meaningful and effective doctrine. As a nation, we cannot delay. The continued issuance of strategies, policies, authorities, and legislation in the absence of such a doctrine does not ensure that our focus and actions are both sufficiently broad and tailored.

As a first step, we brought together a group of individuals who represent a broad spectrum of our society and professions, and who recognize the impact of cyber technologies in their own way. Many of these individuals either are, or have been, in government or industry in senior capacities, and represent scientists, cyber practitioners, media, and authors, among other professions. They were provided discussion papers written by a select group of experts in advance, and those papers now represent chapters in this edition. Their goal was to begin to lay out some of the challenges facing us and the areas that must be considered within the spectrum of a national doctrine, and to study a framework from which a doctrine might be constructed.

To lead the effort, we asked two individuals who have a wealth of experience inside and outside of government, and who have followed the impact of cyber technologies for a number of years. Michael S. Swetnam is the Chairman and Chief Executive Officer of the Potomac Institute for Policy Studies, and has an extensive and distinguished career in the Intelligence Community and in industry. He currently serves as a member of the Technical Advisory Group to the United States Senate Select Committee on Intelligence, has served on the Defense Science Board (DSB) Task Force on Counterterrorism, the Task Force on Intelligence Support to the War on Terrorism, and has authored and edited several books and articles on related topics. Potomac Institute has become a solid and natural partner with Battelle, as we promote our nation's continuing needs to invest in research and technology, with the requisite policies and measures that allow such technology to be adopted and effectively utilized by our government.

The second individual, Battelle's own Timothy R. Sample, has over 30 years of experience in the national security arena in government and industry, having served in senior government positions that included the Deputy Negotiator to the Strategic Arms Reduction Talks at the signing of the START Treaty, the

Executive Director of the Director of Central Intelligence's Nonproliferation Center, and as the Staff Director of the House Permanent Select Committee on Intelligence.

I thank these two individuals for their efforts and for their sustained dedication to this topic. I also thank Mr. Ronald Marks, a Battelle consultant and our Program Director for this project, Kathryn Schiller Wurster (Potomac Institute), Rhonda Ramagoz Taylor (Battelle) and Rebecca Crocker (Battelle), for their tireless work, often behind the scenes, and Jim Wolfe of the Senate Select Committee on Intelligence for assisting with the Publication Review Board process.

We are just at the beginning of this project. Over the next year, Battelle will continue to promote the debate on key topics for a cyber doctrine, and will work with our government to develop a national-level doctrine for these technologically robust times and for this era of global interaction. Above all, I hope that you will find this project useful and that you will engage with us in our efforts.

Dr. Jeffrey Wadsworth
President and Chief Executive Officer
Battelle Memorial Institute

#CyberDoc: No Borders - No Boundaries

Introduction

Timothy R. Sample and Michael S. Swetnam

In 1956, President Dwight D. Eisenhower secretly convinced Congress of the critical need to protect our ability to operate as a government in the midst of a growing nuclear threat in a developing Cold War. He then commissioned the construction of secret locations where branches of government could relocate in a nuclear crisis and effectively preserve our federal system. One of the secret locations—the one intended to house Congress itself and code-named Operation Greek Island—began construction in the Allegany mountains in White Sulphur Springs, West Virginia, at the site of one of the oldest and most well known resorts in the country: The Greenbrier. Today, the "bunker" can be toured by the public. When you begin your tour, however, you must relinquish all of your electronic devices (cell phone, smart phones, pagers, etc.), even though the "bunker's" existence has been declassified. Why? Because today the "bunker" is being used for the remote (or relocated) secure storage of information from several Fortune 500 companies. Few things speak as directly or symbolically to our transition from the Cold War to the Information Age than this.

Timothy R. Sample is the Vice President and Sector Manager for Battelle Memorial Institute's Special Programs Organization. Prior to joining Battelle, Mr. Sample served as the President of the Intelligence and National Security Alliance (INSA), a non-profit public policy and advocacy forum for intelligence and national security. Mr. Sample joined INSA after a position at General Dynamics Advanced Information Systems as the Vice President for Strategic Intelligence Strategies and Programs. Prior to General Dynamics, Mr. Sample had 30 years of intelligence and policy experience as both a supplier and user of intelligence. He served on the House Permanent Select Committee on Intelligence (HPSCI) for nine years, achieving the title of Staff Director from June 2000 to May 2003. Mr. Sample's experiences prior to Congress have included service as both an intelligence and imagery analyst in the Central Intelligence Agency. He has held senior government positions including Deputy US Negotiator for the Strategic Arms Reduction Talks (START I) when it was signed in 1991, and the Executive Director of the Director of Central Intelligence's Nonproliferation Center. His military background includes service in intelligence units within the US Air Force. Beyond his employment with General Dynamics, he has additional business experience, having worked on information processing and telecommunications technologies at GTE Government Systems and as the co-founder and first President of the Potomac Institute for Policy Studies.

Not too long ago...

In the early 1990s, we first began to hear publicly about an information revolution and about information warfare. Hollywood released the movie *Sneakers*,[1] and posited the concept of a future dominated by information, where true power would reside not necessarily in nation-states, but in individuals, corporations, or, as alluded to in the movie, organized crime, controlling information. At the time, except for those working within the secretive spaces of the government, such a reality seemed somewhat fanciful and far-fetched. Desktop computers for personal use were still something of a novelty and "dial up" service was an extravagance for most, and certainly not a necessity. Cellular telephones were scarce, generally, and few conceived of what we today call "smart phones." The equipment and services available were looked at as enhancing your access to your own information and your own circle of friends. There was no real concept whereby someone might break into your system and access data without your permission, and you could "password protect" your more sensitive files.

---

1. 1992 Copyright by Universal Studios, Inc. Courtesy of MCA Publishing Rights, a division of MCA Inc.

Michael S. Swetnam was co-founder of the Potomac Institute for Policy Studies in 1994. Since its inception, he has served as Chairman of the Board and currently serves as the Institute's Chief Executive Officer. Mr. Swetnam is currently a member of the Technical Advisory Group to the United States Senate Select Committee on Intelligence. In this capacity, he provides expert advice to the US Senate on the R&D investment strategy of the US Intelligence Community. He also served on the Defense Science Board (DSB) Task Force on Counterterrorism and the Task Force on Intelligence Support to the War on Terrorism. From 1990 to 1992, Mr. Swetnam served as a Special Consultant to President Bush's Foreign Intelligence Advisory Board (PFIAB) where he provided expert advice on Intelligence Community issues including budget, community architecture, and major programs. He also assisted in authoring the Board's assessment of Intelligence Community support to Desert Storm/Shield. Prior to forming the Potomac Institute for Policy Studies, Mr. Swetnam worked in private industry as a Vice President of Engineering at the Pacific-Sierra Research Corporation, Director of Information Processing Systems at GTE, and Manager of Strategic Planning for GTE Government Systems. Prior to joining GTE, he worked for the Director of Central Intelligence as a Program Monitor on the Intelligence Community Staff (1986-1990). Mr. Swetnam was also assigned as the IC Staff representative to intergovernmental groups that developed the INF and START treaties. He assisted in presenting these treaties to Congress for ratification. Mr. Swetnam served in the US Navy for 24 years as an active duty and reserve officer, Special Duty Cryptology.

Now...

In contrast, millions of Americans today—and billions of people around the world—view their interaction with the Internet as a normal and necessary part of life. The Internet is now considered a "utility" much like electricity, water, heating and air conditioning in our homes. The Internet, and the explosion of devices that allow its access, fundamentally altered our daily lives in ways we no longer even think about. Pay telephones are rarely seen today in major cities, as cell phones have become so prevalent in our society. Now, even laptop computers are relinquishing their mobile utility and we can access the Internet using smart phones that can seemingly do any laptop function and more. But with this access comes vulnerability.

Pick up almost any newspaper (virtual or "hard copy") today and you will likely find a story about a systems breach of some kind conducted by individuals who move with anonymity through the Internet. It might be the penetration of a government's enterprise system, or that of a major defense corporation. It might be of companies who own and control aspects of what is referred to as our nation's "critical infrastructure." It might be a credit card company or hospital, where clients' personal information is stolen. It might be a case of identity theft of an individual. In Washington, myriad organizations are hosting talks and seminars on "cyber" issues and Congress is struggling to draft and pass legislation intended to prescribe an environment where the United States is better protected from these often unseen enemies.

Today, billions of dollars are being expended by the Federal Government on defensive and offensive systems and "tools," all designed to dissuade or wage war in an environment that no one can see or feel, but is as real as the domains of land, water, air and outer space. Clearly, "cyber" issues have captured the attention of many, in and out of government; however, our government responds by addressing issues individually as they arise and in a fashion that conforms to our existing government policies and structures. Thousands of strategies, policies, and authorities are being produced at multiple levels of government intended to address various aspects of cyber activities seen today. The ultimate goal is to prepare for our engagement in a potential "war" conducted, at least in part, in the cyber dimension.

There are two fundamental problems with our nation's response thus far. First, we have yet to grapple with our role as a nation in a world that is dominated by information and governed by its control. It is a world that does not necessarily conform to our governmental structures and laws, has differing expectations of influence and privacy, and engages individuals on a global scale, unbounded by geography or borders. Until we articulate and debate our role, we will continue to address the impact of cyber challenges without consolidating our nation's overall power and intellectual resources in a fashion that can best protect our ideals and values. Historically, this is most effectively done by establishing a national-level doctrine that focuses resources inside of government and articulates our citizens' role in protection of our nation as well. It guides our priorities and development, and provides guidelines and thresholds of use for our diplomatic and military resources.

The second problem is that, in many respects, we already may well be at "war." This "war" may not neatly fit into the established norms and definitions of kinetic actions and legal definitions. As importantly, it is not bounded by existing treaties and agreements, especially those delineating military and civilian targets. It is a global information "war" that is being effectively waged by those who develop penetration "tools" and delivery systems that enter US companies' computer systems and extract intellectual property or personal data with the intent of using this information in ways that are ultimately harmful to our society and government. It may include multiple enemies with varying interests who may or may not have any relationship to each other. It may never get to the point of a "shooting war" in the traditional sense, as the battlefields are within the economic, financial, and natural resource realms. Just the same, as recently noted by General Keith Alexander, USA, Director of the National Security Agency (NSA), and Commander, US Cyber Command, "What we need to worry about is when these transition from disruptive to destructive attacks, which is going to happen. We have to be ready for that... This is even more difficult than the nuclear deterrent strategies we used to think about in the past."[2] Of significant concern is the threat of data manipulation, resulting in a lack of confidence in the data that we rely on daily.

This "war" is not new. It has been building for the past two decades. The emergence of worldwide access to the Internet, the sophistication of the tools being developed to conduct such a "war," and our overwhelming reliance (and thus our overwhelming vulnerability) on the Internet have all come together to create a threat to America that is little understood and scarcely

---

2. Josh Rogin, "NSA Chief: Cybercrime constitutes the "greatest transfer of weath in history" (July 9, 2012) *http://thecable.foreignpolicy.com/posts/2012/07/09/nsa_chief_cybercrime_constitutes_the_greatest_transfer_of_wealth_in_history.*

appreciated. At the same time, long-term outlooks and expanding interests spurred by a growing middle class in countries like China have re-introduced the prospects of dominant world superpowers whose impact and influence through attaining and controlling information are potentially equal to our own influence. Left unchecked, in the future it may be greater.

On May 29, 2009, President Obama spoke to the nation on the importance of securing the nation's cyber infrastructure. Two years later, the White House issued the *International Strategy for Cyberspace*. Without judging the specific details, we note that these efforts address implementation steps of a strategy for a doctrine that is not defined and certainly not highlighted and prioritized in a manner that evokes a nationwide response and commitment. Left open for debate is America's role in a world dominated by cyberspace.

The Call for a Doctrine

For these reasons, Battelle decided to begin a project whereby a national-level doctrine for the cyber era can be established and debated. We believe that our nation is behind the time in which a doctrine should be put forward and that it can no longer wait. In June 2012, a *Washington Post* Editorial also called for the United States to establish a cyber doctrine. It noted that, "the United States today has no overarching, open doctrine to govern an offensive cyber program, nor is there a healthy debate about what it should entail."[3] Our own interactions over the past year with several thought leaders in and out of government confirmed the long overdue need for a doctrine that would set forth a framework whereby government entities, businesses, and individuals can understand and share in their roles and responsibilities, collectively, in protecting our nation's security.

And it is more than a debate on our military might. As we note here and later in the Conference Report, General Michael Hayden, USAF (Ret.,) former Director of both the NSA and Central Intelligence Agency (CIA) said in a Strategic Studies Article in Spring 2011, "[r]arely has something been so important and so talked about with less clarity and less apparent understanding than this phenomenon." He further noted that he had been "unable (along with my colleagues) to decide on a course of action because we lacked a

---

3. Editorial, "Cyberwar secrets—Time for a more open debate on offensive cyberweapons," *The Washington Post*, June 17, 2012.

clear picture of the long term legal and policy implications of any decision we might make."[4]

Creating a doctrine is not an easy or simple task and will not happen overnight. Due to the issues surrounding cyber, the government cannot simply dictate actions, but must delicately balance roles between government and industry and be flexible enough to adjust as situations rapidly evolve. As with the first thoughts about the doctrine governing the nuclear age, scientists and practitioners must help government in developing the thoughts and foundations of a doctrine considering the impact of cyber technologies. For this reason, we began this project by commissioning several thought papers related to issues that need to be addressed within such a doctrine. These papers, which are included here as individual chapters, were intended to be jump-off points for discussion, not all-encompassing theses. Likewise, there are several other issues, such as privacy and supply chain, which were not included here, but will be addressed as this project develops.

Considerations within a Framework

Taken together, these papers provided very robust discussions of several topics of importance that addressed current and future issues, as well as their impact on our current government structures, policies, procedures, laws and operating principles. In this effort, we purposely paid particular attention to Cold War paradigms, as there are often-made comparisons between the Cyber Era and that at the end of World War II, especially in regard to the establishment and use of nuclear weapons. As our country was governed by the Doctrine of Containment for over 50 years, it seemed appropriate to start the debate by establishing whether any parallels exist between these two periods.

The first issue that has garnered much attention is "attribution." David Aucsmith establishes the groundwork of defining "attribution" and its inherent challenges. He provides a thoughtful and insightful explanation of the makeup of cyberspace, explaining why, from its roots, security and attribution are so difficult. Aucsmith rightfully notes that the success of attribution also rests on appropriate degrees of certainty that change in a

---

4.   Gen. Michael V. Hayden, USAF, Retired, "The Future of Things 'Cyber,'" *Strategic Studies Quarterly,* Spring 2011.

given situation. Preeminent in his argument is that although technology will continue to advance in refining "attribution," there likely will never be a fully attributable system. Moreover, he notes that technology alone cannot solve the "attribution" issue; instead what is required is a combination of science, diplomacy, policy, and cooperation with others. At the end, while laying out the daunting task of acceptable attribution, he also gives us hope in noting that attribution itself is asymmetric, which can favor those seeking an attacker.

Jim Simon provides insight on whether cyberspace is "defensible" and if we are now in a constant state of conflict. In other words, can we defend ourselves? Why are we so vulnerable and how can we counteract that vulnerability? He discusses risk management and the idea that we are limited in time, people and resources in our response and must look for the most effective ways to counter "attacks and vulnerabilities." Simon also discusses the state of play on the "battlefield" in terms of realistically determining who is the enemy and what type of "maximum" damage we can allow or can happen to us.

Taking off from Simon's observations, Frank Cilluffo and Sharon Cardash discuss whether "cyber war/conflict" is now the new norm. If so, what is the "spectrum" of this conflict? How can perceptions be managed in this war, if it is truly a war? Also, this leads to the question of war versus crime—what is the continuum of cyber conflict for war/military through crime/law enforcement.

Although much of the discussion of cyber tends to focus on the government, Randy Fort establishes how crucial it is to recognize the role and huge presence of the private sector in the battles of cyberspace. With large corporations having annual sales exceeding the GDP of nation-states, how do these organizations defend themselves and with what cyber barriers and protections? Is it possible that corporations could wage "war" on each other in cyberspace? Fort also looks at the overused shibboleth of "public-private" partnership. What does this really mean for businesses large and small in the United States? What do they need from the government and what should the government expect from them—and at what cost? And, finally, how should the government protect private industry from state or non-nation state attacks?

Referencing back to Simon and Fort, Bob Liscouski explains how government and private industry determine threat—how their criteria both differ and are the same. Moreover, he discusses the limits of what can be done to us in cyberspace. What real damage could be done, for instance, to the business supply chain? How are physical and cyber threats related to one another and what value should be placed on both? This then leads to the question of what role do incentives by the government play in the private sector's willingness to more than "satisfice" a solution.

In the Cold War, the response to our Doctrine of Containment was to develop a strict tactical methodology to frame our responses—the best example of which was Herman Kahn's 44 Escalation steps to Thermonuclear War. The question David Smith addresses is how far we go in "cyber battle" emulating the steps Kahn laid out in his structure. Do we need to do this— respond at the end with nuclear weapons or the threat thereof? Smith also addresses the idea of "mutually assured deception" as a parallel to the Cold War's Mutually Assured Destruction (MAD). Could it be the "thermonuclear" response necessary?

The issues of cyberspace represent an international challenge to the current nation-state structure. Barry Pavel discusses the norms that nation-states are now seeking to deal with the issues of cyberspace. Which countries are attempting to use cyberspace for their own internal political reasons by positioning themselves to outmaneuver American interests? In addition, Pavel discusses how corporations and others are viewing /dealing with these proposed new international frameworks.

Taking off on Pavel's comments, Alfred Rolington describes whether it is possible nation-states can really agree on a standard of behavior—perhaps along the lines of other treaties/agreements like the limits on use of chemical or biological weapons or the International Telecommunications Union standards. If not, can nation-states act jointly and cooperate with non-nation-state players? Can these arrangements work to the advantage of the United States? Looking forward, do we need "virtual embassies" to handle the relations of cyberspace?

Rounding out the issues brought up in Pavel's and Rolington's pieces, Gus Coldebella takes on the complex issue of legal boundaries in cyberspace. Is it possible for there to be a legal framework, given the lack of physical dimension in cyberspace? Could "boundaries" be made flexible to expand or contract based on the needs of a nation-state in times of war or emergency? And, where is the United States in this new dimension—does the sun never set on our influence, or is this truly beyond our control?

Richard Weitz addresses the very complicated issue of how a nation-state reacts to an attack or the perceived threat of an attack. When do we launch a preemptive strike against an enemy—nation-state or non-nation-state? Does "preparation of the battlefield" constitute a hostile act that is the cyberspace equivalent of a First Strike? Weitz continues to explore what counts for "tit for tat" in cyberspace. Following the Kahn model discussed earlier by Smith, what is retaliatory equivalency in cyberspace? In the language of the movie, *The Godfather*, when does the United States "go to the mattresses"? How should this be framed in international agreements, our domestic laws, and political interests?

David Smith returns and proceeds from the previous two chapters to discuss what allies the United States can build to pursue its efforts and protection in cyberspace. Does the United States have any allies or just friends of mutual convenience? Can we build a series of cyber alliances such as a cyber NATO? And, if so, how would this affect our other political ties? Will our friends in the physical space be our opponents in cyberspace? Do we need a cyber version of Interpol to handle "inter-nation-state" crime?

In the penultimate chapter, Ron Marks addresses the idea of what the responsibilities are for the Federal Government of the United States in cyberspace—how these responsibilities fit into our national security strategy and structure.

He also lays out how the government should protect itself and what actions should be directed to state and local governments, private businesses and individuals. That being said, what are the checks and balances on this Federal intrusion into a previously lightly regulated environment, and can our existing bureaucratic processes hope to keep pace with the speed of cyber activity? Marks also brings up the need for education and engagement at the individual user level, suggesting the need to establish a cyber "civil defense" that enlists our citizenry in our overall defense.

We team up with Kathryn Schiller Wurster to look at the future of cyberspace and its challenges, especially in terms of alternative realities that few want to discuss because they are difficult to address or to comprehend in today's realities. We lay out a series of policy, authority, and civil liberty issues that provoke us to think about the previous chapters in terms of how to take the disparate issues discussed and unify them into a whole doctrine reflecting America's future needs and direction in cyberspace. We also challenge the traditional power structures of nation-states with the rise of corporate presence and influence around the globe.

Starting the Debate

Once completed, these papers were given to a "core" group of individuals that represented a wide group of interests and backgrounds, including authors, editors, and several notable former policymakers and broad thinkers of our time. Their names are included near the back of this book.

In June 2012, we invited the authors of the papers and "core" group to the Founders' Inn Conference Center in Virginia Beach, Virginia, for three days of debate and discussion, to broaden the thoughts developed in the individual papers. The results were captured in a conference report that is the last chapter of this book. The goal of this conference was not to emerge with a doctrine. Instead, the goal was to debate the issues that a doctrine should consider and to begin identifying a broad framework from which a doctrine might be developed. In the process the group discussed a dozen "harsh realities and uncomfortable truths" facing our nation in addressing the creation of a doctrine and its implementation. Likewise, they established five broad points from which a framework could be considered. They are:

1. *The United States views the Internet as a critical component of its national security, and wishes to enforce a secure and peaceful cyberspace.*
2. *In doing so, the United States will take the lead internationally in cooperation with, but not subject to, other nation-states' desires.*
3. *The United States Government, in cooperation with the private sector and individuals, will work to pursue a reasonable set of rules for safe use of cyberspace.*
4. *The United States will use all offensive and defensive means to protect its citizens and interests in cyberspace.*
5. *The government of the United States will work in cooperation with its corporate sector and citizens to establish a firm understanding of citizenship in the cyber age.*

Next Steps

In his memoirs, Winston Churchill recounts, "One day, President Roosevelt told me that he was asking publicly for suggestions about what the war should be called. I said at once 'The Unnecessary War.'"[5] Churchill's point was there was so much that could and should have been done that may have possibly prevented World War II, but that governments willingly ignored the looming Fascist threat or were so slow to respond that they were forced into a reactionary mode that was nearly too late. America today finds itself in a similar situation. We do not clearly see an existential threat of the magnitude encountered during World War II or the Cold War and, therefore, are happy to believe that there isn't one. We blithely take a measured approach to our cyber activities, often relegating the debate to one of existing authorities and budgets rather than definitive actions. Successive Administrations have vested government efforts to designated coordinators or "czars" who have little real authority to direct or enact change, in order to show that our cybersecurity is important, but not the only major issue that the Administration must address. Moreover, successive senior government leaders who are or have been in charge of our key cyber activities have publicly addressed the potential of the myriad threats we face and have called for action that, in our current frame of mind, is illusive. Will history look back on a significantly weakened United States and call the cyber war we just went through the "Next Unnecessary War?"

This work is not intended to be comprehensive, complete, or final. In fact, we intend for it to be the start of a discussion on the topic that will inform and guide the development of a useful and enduring doctrine, and subsequent policies and strategies, for the United States. Over the next months, we will host several sessions and activities that work toward this purpose.

---

5.   Winston Churchill, *The Gathering Storm* (New York: Houghton Mifflin Company, 1948), electronic version, p. 45.

#CyberDoc: No Borders - No Boundaries

CHAPTER 1

The Technology and Policy of Attribution

David Aucsmith

Introduction

It is fitting that a discussion of a national doctrine considering cyberspace should begin with an exploration of attribution. Attribution is either an explicit or an implicit assumption in the definition and implementation of doctrine. Deterrence, preemption, retaliation, sanction, and prosecution all depend on knowing who has done what to whom. The certainty required of attribution depends on the nature of the act and the context of the response. Responding to criminal actions requires a degree of certainty sufficient for a court of law; those that are acts of war require a degree of certainty consistent with law, policy and public opinion. Others, such as attributing acts of espionage, may need only satisfy a very select group, but all require some degree of attribution.

Attributing acts in cyberspace to specific countries, organizations, and individuals is fraught with difficulty and, in some cases, is an unsolvable problem. The difficulty with attribution in cyberspace arises due to two distinct problems. First, the design of cyberspace itself, the nature of the technology

David Aucsmith is the Senior Director of Microsoft's Institute for Advanced Technology in Governments. He is responsible for technical relationships with agencies of the United States and other Governments, as well as on select special projects. Before joining Microsoft in August 2002, Mr. Aucsmith was the chief security architect for the Intel Corporation from 1994 to 2002. He has worked in a variety of security technology areas including secure computer systems, secure communications systems, random number generation, cryptography, steganography and network intrusion detection. Aucsmith is a former officer in the US Navy and has been heavily involved in computer security and cybercrime issues for more than 30 years. He has been an industry representative to numerous international, government and academic organizations including the technical advisory boards of the National Security Agency, the National Reconnaissance Office, the National Academy advisory board on Survivability and Lethality Analysis and the Directorate Advisory Council for the National Security Directorate of Pacific Northwest National Labs. He is co-chairman of the FBI's Information Technology

that created the computer and communications network we know as cyberspace, does not support an irrevocable mapping between individuals, addresses, routing and actions. Second, the implementation of cyberspace does not prevent someone from spoofing the origin, the route, or the accountability for such actions. These two problems make attribution in the cyber domain difficult, but not necessarily impossible.

We do attribute some actions in cyberspace, with a sufficient degree of certainty, to satisfy the requirements of law, policy, and doctrine. We do this using technologies and processes that enhance the chance of attribution. Attribution usually requires access to cyberspace components through cooperative tracing by the owners of those components, through lawful access, or intelligence tradecraft. As such, they are very dependent on the countries, organization, and people involved. They are certainly not reliable in the general case.

Cyberspace is an evolving construct. The fact that cyberspace promotes anonymity over attribution is an artifact of its design. There have been proposed changes to the design and implementation of cyberspace that would shift that balance.[1] As Lawrence Lessig notes, the architecture—the design—of cyberspace can be changed.[2] Precisely how the design of cyberspace needs to change to enhance attribution and how those changes might be effected, depends on how the need for attribution is perceived.

In the end, general attribution will never be a characteristic of cyberspace. We must shift our discussion of doctrine away from attribution and towards accountability. People, organizations, and states should have an obligation to assist in cyber investigations where their property or jurisdiction is involved. Noncooperation should be viewed as a sign of culpability. In particular, states

---

1. United States Congress House Committee on Science and Technology, *Planning For the Future of Cyber Attack Attribution: Hearing Before the Subcommittee On Technology and Innovation, Committee On Science and Technology, Congress, Second Session, July 15, 2010* (Washington, DC: US Government Printing Office, 2010).

2. Lawrence Lessig, *Code and Other Laws of Cyberspace* (New York: Basic Books, 1999), p. 20.

Study Group, a member of the Secret Service Task Force on Computer Aided Counterfeiting, a member of the President's Task Force on National Defense and Computer Technology and a member of the Department of Defense's Global Information Grid Senior Industry Review Group. Aucsmith was also US industry representative to the G8 Committee on Organized, Transnational, and Technological Crime where he participated directly in the G8 summits in Paris, Berlin and Tokyo. Aucsmith holds 33 patents for digital security.

must be held accountable for securing their national infrastructure and must assume an obligation to prevent malevolent systems from harming others.

The Nature of Attribution

Attribution in cyberspace is the ability to describe who did what to whom with the degree of certainty required by the needs of law, policy, or doctrine. Each part of the definition—*who, what, to whom,* and *certainty*—is uniquely difficult in the cyber domain.

Perpetrators "Who"

Who, the perpetrator of a cyber-act, is generally regarded as the focus of attribution. However, what precisely is the act and who is the target, are equally important and, as discussed later, in some circumstances, may actually be more important. The perpetrator can be regarded as the responsible party, but even the notion of a responsible party is complex. Depending on the act and the circumstance, the responsible party could be a person, an organization, or a nation-state.

For example, it is not necessary to identify the individual responsible for acts of war in cyberspace. The identification of the individual's state would seem sufficient. However, even this simple case becomes complicated when the individual is a "rogue actor" not acting under the authority of their state. Should a state be held accountable for the actions of its citizens in cyberspace? Was the "rogue actor" operating truly independent of the state or with tacit approval? In many cases, a true independent actor has committed a crime not an act of war.

There are real world analogies to these scenarios. In May of 1987, an Iraqi Mirage F1 attacked the USS *Stark* with two Exocet anti-ship missiles, killing 37 United States sailors and severely damaging the ship. The United States choose not to view it as an act of war. Simply identifying the individual responsible for an act is not necessarily sufficient to attribute the action to a responsible party—in this case an Iraqi premeditated act of war. The nature of attribution is bound to both the act and the policy governing the act. For example, espionage in cyberspace is frequently a case of knowing the responsible party, but being governed by a policy that dictates no direct, overt response.

Cyber Attacks "What"

The *what*, the act or attack, is important in establishing attribution. It partly defines the applicable law, policy or doctrine, which in turn partly defines the degree of certainty required. In some cases, simply knowing what occurred is sufficient; additional attribution may not be useful. For example, if there is no policy that governs any responsive action, attributing the act to a person, organization, or state serves no purpose. This is the general case of cyber attacks on commercial organizations. They are interested in removing the vulnerability or the attack vector and lack any capability or authority for pursuing the attacker.

As the nature of a cyber attack partly defines the degree of certainty required and the applicable law, policy or doctrine, it is helpful to divide cyber attacks into three different types, based on their objective and the US legal authorities that apply:

- *War*—(US Title 10) Attacks to deceive, deny, disrupt, degrade or destroy.

- *Espionage*—(US Title 50) Spying by a government to discover military and political secrets.

- *Crime*—(US Title 18) Theft, fraud, or other criminal acts.

One of the difficulties in defending against cyber attacks is that the tools, techniques, and procedures used to attack are the same regardless of the type of attack; they differ only in their objective. The objective may not be discernible until after the attack has succeeded and the damage is done. Different law, policy, and doctrine govern the certainty of attribution required of different types (objectives) of attacks and which organization has jurisdiction. A fundamental difficulty arises, such as in the case of espionage, when policy is essentially proactive yet analysis is essentially reactive.

Although in this discussion cyber attacks are described in terms of United States authorities, it should be obvious that cyber attacks are international in nature and frequently must be viewed as existing simultaneously in multiple legal frameworks, each framework having its own understanding of attribution. As attribution is generally across jurisdictional boundaries, the only way to satisfy each legal authority is to attribute at the "greatest common denominator" of the overlapping frameworks. The burden so placed on lesser-resourced jurisdictions may be large enough to doom international cooperation.

Cyber Weapons "What"

It is possible to derive information from the cyber weapons and techniques used in an attack. In some cases, this has directly led to the attribution of their maker, such as when attackers have left text strings or compiler serial numbers in their compiled attack code. It is also the case that tools and techniques have a provenance that may be of forensics value.

Victims "To Whom"

It may seem odd to speak of attributing a victim, but it is also a complicated issue. Specifically, the legal status and jurisdiction of the victim is sometimes difficult to define. For example, who is the victim in the theft of personal information belonging to a German citizen from a United States' company's database that was physically located in Singapore and the attack came through a network compromise in the company's Canadian subsidiary?

As a related problem, many cyber attacks are routed through intermediary sites, or proxies. These sites may have been attacked simply to gain eventual access of the target system. These intermediary sites are victims as well, but it may be impossible to discern the nature of the actual attack until the target victim is found and the objective understood. Thus, attributing the actual victim and the nature of the attack may not be possible by simply having access to an intermediary site.

There is also the less common case in which the victim is not known. It may be that an attack leaves evidence on an intermediary site, or through communications leakage, without sufficient information to identify the actual victim. This is particularly the case when the attack is using multi-modal communications channels, for example, having some part of the communications over a wired connection and some part over a wireless connection. Each channel may not see enough of the attack traffic to identify the victim.

Degrees of Certainty

As noted, the degree of certainty required of attribution is defined by the applicable law, policy, or doctrine, which is itself a function of the type of attack (the act), the perpetrator (who), and the victim (to whom). In some cases, attribution to the granularity of a state is sufficient, in others to an organization. Attribution may require identifying the physical location of the perpetrator or may need the identity of the specific individual or individuals, obviously, the greater the granularity of the requirement, the greater the difficulty of the task.

However, as noted earlier, the individual identified as a perpetrator may, in fact, be a victim at an intermediary attack site.

The identity of an entity in cyberspace is composed of a set of information about that entity's presence in cyberspace in terms of cyberspace's processes and protocols, such as IP address, logon time, or domain name. It is not information about the person himself or herself. It is not fingerprints or DNA. Even the most damning of cyberspace evidence must be correlated to real world identities. Unless provided with audio or video, correlation is still an imprecise process that relies on a preponderance of evidence to establish such a linkage.

The Character of the Technology that Defines the Cyber Domain

Cyberspace is unique in that it is a manmade creation. It is a virtual space. Although it occupies geographical space, it is not defined by geographical space. It is, instead, defined by the properties of the technology that created its existence. Cyberspace is the virtual environment created by the interconnected network of computing devices, communications channels, and the humans that use them. The technology that creates cyberspace imbues cyberspace with innate characteristics that define how cyberspace functions and what is and is not possible. To understand why attribution is particularly difficult in cyberspace, one first has to understand the design principles used in creating cyberspace.

The Short History of Cyberspace

Cyberspace, as we understand it today, had its genesis in the work of the Advanced Research Projects Agency (ARPA) in the early days of network computing. In 1969, their work, along with ideas contributed by both the Massachusetts Institute of Technology (MIT) and the British National Physical Laboratory, led to linking four computers together that became ARPANET— the progenitor of today's Internet.

The potential threat of a surprise attack by Soviet nuclear forces simultaneously prompted the US Air Force to fund a research project to investigate how one might build a communications network that could survive such an attack.[3] In 1964, Paul Baran, working for the RAND Corporation, published a

---

3. Manabrata Guha, *Reimagining War in the 21st Century: from Clausewitz to Network-Centric Warfare* (New York: Routledge, 2011), p. 102.

series of papers, which addressed this problem.[4] Baran's idea was to create a network of computers and/or communications devices that would be linked by transmission lines. This network of computers would have no centralized control centers, which would have been the logical targets of an attack. The network of interconnected computers would then send messages back and forth through the network by breaking the messages into small "packets," where each packet could be routed as needed. He recognized that the distributed network of computers would also need to have an "intelligence," but to survive a massive attack, the intelligence must be distributed as well. His idea was that the distributed network would have no preset routing; rather, each computer in the network would use information in the message itself to find the optimal route for the message based on the computer's understanding of the network. Each computer in the network would maintain a "routing table" that would record how much time a recently sent message packet took to reach its destination. The computers would thus be able to make intelligent decisions as to how to efficiently route their messages based on ever changing historical data. In effect, what Baran created was a network comprised of a number of unmanned digital switches, each of which possesses a self-learning capacity within a changing environment.

The Structure of Cyberspace

As cyberspace has evolved, it can be thought of as composed of computers (devices performing computation) having some degree of intelligence, which are linked together by a network of communications channels, and used by people to transmit, manipulate, or receive information.

Computing Devices

The computing devices that create cyberspace come in many forms and perform many tasks. They share the ability to take information as input, manipulate that information according to an embedded logic or program, and then output information. Examples of such computing devices in cyberspace include sensors, routers, switches, personal computers, controllers, output devices, or the myriad of other components. What is important is that the computing devices of cyberspace have "intelligence," due to their programming,

---

4.   Paul Baran, *On Distributed Communications: I. Introduction to Distributed Communications Networks* (Santa Monica, CA: Rand Corporation, August, 1964), *http://www.rand.org/pubs/ research_memoranda/RM3420.html*, accessed June 3, 2012.

and they respond to input based on that programming. They may have state. That is, they may keep a history of prior input or computational results, which they use to inform future outputs. Different inputs or different histories of inputs may generate different outputs.

Channels

Communications channels connect computing devices in cyberspace. They carry information from one component to another component. All that is required to substantiate a communications channel is the ability to deliver information, regardless of the means. Examples include fiber optic cable, microwave beams, light, or even mailing a disk drive from one point to another. Communications channels may be one-to-one, one-to many, or many-to one. They may be static or dynamic or they may be unidirectional or bidirectional. All that matters is that they pass information.

People

People are a component of cyberspace—perhaps the least reliable component. They generate, manipulate, and consume information according to highly variable "programing." Their contribution to the characteristics of cyberspace, which impact attribution, is mostly as a component of Clausewitzian friction. That is, humans contribute mostly to the unpredictability of attribution.

Implications of Cyberspace Structure

Starting with simple goals and an elegant simplicity, cyberspace has evolved into a domain whose total structure is too complex to be completely understood or analyzed. The structure of cyberspace, the consequence of its architecture and components, gives cyberspace inherent properties that are important in considering attribution. Among these are:

- Self-organization—Components of cyberspace (computing devices, communications channels, and humans) can be added or removed. They can be moved or modified and cyberspace will autonomously recognize them and reorganize accordingly. An important concept for attribution is that there is no requirement for cyberspace to keep any information regarding previous organizations.

- Historical learning—Each node or computing device in cyberspace routes packets based on the aggregate efficiency of the communications channels that were used to route previous packets. That is, when routing a new packet, a cyberspace computing device routes it through the historically most efficient path to its destination. The actual efficiency of the newly routed packet's channel is then used to update the historical understanding for future routing. For the purposes of attribution, a computing device cannot tell you how a packet was routed, only how it will route a future packet.

- Scale-free network—Unlike the distributed network that was originally envisioned, cyberspace has organized itself around nodes or hubs of high connectivity.[5] Any attempt to trace a path back through such high-density nodes may be impossible.

- Recursive organization—Cyberspace is organizationally recursive. That is, subsets of cyberspace have the same general features and organization as cyberspace in whole. One can think of cyberspace as being composed of systems of systems.[6] The complexity of the overall structure is masked by the abstraction of subsets. For simplicity, subsets do not necessarily present information up to the next level. Some information for attribution may not be presented to upper levels. For example, user names local to a subset (e.g., a company's network) of cyberspace are not forwarded to the next level (e.g., Internet Service Provider).

- Local knowledge—Cyberspace operates globally based only on local knowledge. Each component of cyberspace makes decisions based solely on its own local knowledge. The overall behavior of any given subset of cyberspace is the aggregated result of the effects of each component's local decision.

- Ephemeral knowledge—Knowledge in cyberspace components is local and may be ephemeral. That is, the information used by a given component of cyberspace to make a local decision may not be available to other components and may not be kept after the decision is made. For example, the user/address mapping information of protocols like Network Address Translation (NAT) is not generally retained when no longer needed.

- Good faith effort—The design of cyberspace assumed component failure, but not component duplicity. Security of cyberspace operations was not a requirement of the design. Intermediary nodes may manipulate information in unanticipated ways.

---

5. Albert-Laszlo Barabasi and Eric Bonabeau, "Scale-Free Networks," *Scientific American* 288, no. 5 (May, 2003): 50-59.

6. William A. Owens, *Lifting the Fog of War* (Baltimore: The Johns Hopkins University Press, 2001), p. 98-102.

The last property is, of course, directly related to the security of cyberspace in general and attribution in particular.

Problems with Attribution in the Cyber Domain

As noted, attribution in cyberspace is the ability to describe who did what to whom with the degree of certainty required by the needs of law, policy, or doctrine. However, the structure of cyberspace itself has features that make attribution either difficult or impossible. The impact of these features on attribution can be broken into seven areas.

Identification and Authentication

The fundamental design of cyberspace has no assumption of either identification or authentication. Cyberspace only requires that messages, that is packets, be addressed so that communications may take place. Both identification and authentication are properties, layered onto the design of cyberspace to meet the needs of economics or control. Providers of various components and services of cyberspace have made an investment for which they desire a return. Users must identify and authenticate themselves to the providers of those components and services to use them. Thus, a user must log into an account of their Internet Service Provider (ISP) in order to have access to the computing devices and communications channels owned by the ISP. The technology and rigor required for identification and authentication solely reflect the business needs of the ISP.

Similarly, organizations implement identification and authentication schemes consistent with their operational requirements for the protection of their property, reputation, or legal obligations. Identity is an assertion of responsibility. It may be the assertion of a real world person, but may also be a group of real world people, a device, or a software program, depending on the needs of the environment.

Cyberspace has no standards for either identity or authentication. For many business arrangements, identity to a real person is not required. Rather, it is the identity of the ability to pay. Pre-paid phones and calling cards are examples of this. Even if the identity is a real world person, the rigor in establishing the original claim of identity varies greatly. What documents were presented and how thoroughly was their authenticity verified? Very secure identity documents such as the United States military's Common Access Card (CAC), which support very strong cryptographic authentication and anti-counterfeiting protocols, are based on the initial presentation of forgeable documents (birth certificates and driver's licenses, which are also based on birth certificates). Without a thorough background check, all assertions of identity are suspect.

Authentication is a proof of the assertion of identity. There are only three bases against which assertions of identity can be authenticated: *something you are, something you know,* or *something you possess.* Each has problems for their use in cyberspace. Something you are, biometrics, relies on the unique biological features of a person, such as fingerprints or iris patterns. In cyberspace, authentication of biometrics requires a sensor to sample and communicate the trait. If the sensor, which must be located with the person, is compromised, then the authentication can be compromised. In addition, no biometric trait is secret. By definition they are observable and, thus, available for all to record and attempt to spoof.

Basing authentication on something one knows, such as a password, requires that only that person know the information. Clearly, passwords are the most common authentication mechanism in cyberspace. This is primarily due to the relatively inexpensive cost of implementing them. However, there is plenty of data to suggest that they are a poor method of authentication. Problems with the use of passwords include the fact that easily remembered passwords are frequently also easily guessed passwords, the same password is frequently used by a person on many sites, and there are techniques to observe and record password use. One's mother's maiden name is rarely known only by the person of which it is requested.

Authentication based on something one has is a common method in the real world, such as the key to a lock. In cyberspace the proof that one has something is more complicated, but can be done using challenge and response cryptographic protocols. Smart cards and secure tokens are good examples of such systems. However, they are not widely deployed and there are still risks associated with them. If the computing device through which the user authenticated is itself compromised, there is no way for the user to know what messages are being authenticated on their behalf by the compromised computer.

Attribution in cyberspace is ultimately limited by the rigor of the identification and authentication process through which the person, organization, or state, asserted their identity to cyberspace. It is important to note here that even if given perfect trace back of an act to the identity of person, that identity is only as good as the assertion and authentication of that identity in the first place. It could easily be a case of stolen identity.

IP Addresses and Binding

The basic foundation upon which cyberspace rests is the Open Systems Interconnection (OSI) Transport Layer and Network Layer protocols known as TCP/IP. The OSI model is a standard reference model for communication between two end users in cyberspace. Layer 3, the network layer, handles the routing and forwarding of the data. In cyberspace, this is almost exclusively done with the Internet Protocol (IP). Layer 4, the transport layer, manages the end-to-end control and error checking. It ensures complete data transfer. In cyberspace, this is mostly done through the Transmission Control Protocol (TCP).

In cyberspace, every node has an Internet Protocol address so that the Internet Protocol can route TCP packets from node-to-node, from start to finish. However, unlike telephone numbers and street addresses, IP addresses are easily changed, or hidden. There are two mechanisms that do this, *Dynamic Host Configuration Protocol* (DHCP) and *Network Address Translation* (NAT).

In the early days of the Internet, IP addresses were allocated to organizations in blocks and the organization would assign addresses, from its block of addresses, to individual components. These addresses were "statically allocated" to the component and did not change. Over time, it was realized that this method had many drawbacks, so DHCP was introduced. With DHCP, when a device joins an organization's network, the organization's DHCP server "dynamically allocates" an address, from its pool of addresses, to the component. The next time the component joins the network, it may be allocated a different address. This is a common practice of both ISPs and large organizations.

DHCP allows the same computer to attach to networks having different blocks of addresses. However, from the view of authentication, there is no requirement for the DHCP server to keep track of allocations over time. Usually the address allocations—the addresses' leases—are kept for some short period to allow a component to be allocated its previous address after a sudden interruption, but the lease information is not kept for an extended time. Thus, knowing the IP address of a TCP packet that comprised part of an attack several days ago, may not give you any information as to which component within an organization sent that packet.

NAT is a different problem. A device that performs NAT modifies the IP address of packets that pass through it. It may simply substitute one address for another, a one-to-one translation of IP addresses. It is more common to hide an entire IP address space, usually a private, non-routable IP addresses, behind a single IP address (or in some cases a small group of IP addresses) in another (usually public) address space. This may be done for a number of reasons. It may be that an organization does not have enough addresses for all of its devices. NAT allows many devices to share a smaller number of given addresses. For example, an ISP may only allocate one address for an organization to use in connecting to the Internet. A NAT device would allow many different devices in the organization to share the one allocated address.

NAT can also be used to enhance security. The true IP address of the devices behind a NAT device are not available to an adversary, only the address assigned by the NAT device. Obviously, the NAT device has to be able to reassign the devices IP address back to inbound packets. To do this, a NAT device assigns different ports to packets from different IP address and maintains a translation table so that return packets can be correctly translated back. This translation table is generally not maintained past session termination. In attempting to attribute an IP address, only the IP address assigned by the NAT device is available. The real IP address of the device behind the NAT device is known only to the NAT device and only known for as long as needed to perform address translation for the session.

IP addresses in cyberspace are mainly IPv4 addresses (IP version 4 style addresses). IPv4 provides approximately 4.29 billion possible addresses and all addresses have been allocated. To add new devices to the Internet, one must use NAT. IPv6 is the successor to IPv4. IPv6 has a larger address space, approximately 3.4×10^{38} addresses. The thought has been that the use of IPv6 addresses would give every possible device in cyberspace (and all future devices) their own address. Neither DHCP nor NAT would be used in the future. However, while IPv6 addresses will be used, it is unlikely that either DHCP or NAT will disappear. DHCP will continue to be used so that devices can move between blocks of addresses and NAT will continue to be used for its security properties.

For the purposes of attributing Internet addresses to real people, cyberspace does not support, nor will it support, irrevocable mapping between people, devices, and their actions.

Ephemeral Data

One of the key assumptions in the design of the Internet is that there is no point of central control. Each component makes its routing decisions based on the local information that it has. This information may be the historical latency data for various communications channels, the NAT mapping tables, or user authentication results. However, nowhere in cyberspace is there a requirement to log and save such information beyond the time for which it is immediately useful, nor would it be feasible to do so. The pure volume of such data in any given segment of cyberspace would be prohibitive to store for a period of time useful for future forensics. Most data about the structure of cyberspace is ephemeral; it is transient.

Even if it were kept, how could it be accessed and under whose authority? The fundamental design of cyberspace did not make provisions for attribution or forensics aside from logging specific data. However, as one does not know what data will be necessary in the future, it implies logging everything—which is impractical.

Network Access

In the previous discussion, it was shown that the IP address within a network may not actually identify the perpetrator's actual device. It is also the case that having the address of the network from which an attack originates, may not be sufficient in identifying the network of the attacker. The attacker may have gained access to the network surreptitiously, without the knowledge of the network's owner. This is particularly a problem with wireless networks. Many such networks have minimal or nonexistent security. It is a simple matter for the attacker to simply be in radio range of the network wireless access point and join the network.

There are a number of criminal examples that illustrate this point. Attribution, in the case of surreptitious use of wireless access, to a network address may provide a valid geographic area and nothing more.

Multi-modal Communications

Multi-modal communications refers to the simultaneous use of multiple access points into cyberspace. For example, a device may use two differ-ent wireless modes to connect to cyberspace to achieve greater aggregate bandwidth. There are devices capable of both Wi-Fi and 4G wireless network access. It is reasonable to use both. The effect on the forensics of an attack is that there would be multiple sets of packets with different addresses associ-ated with a single act, complicating both the analysis and the attribution.

Network Egress

The above cases illustrate the difficulty of associating a network address with the attacker. It is possible for the attacker to not have a network address associated with the act. This is best explained with an example. Suppose that a device has already been compromised, but the attacker now needs to exfiltrate data. A common way to attribute the attack is to "follow the data," the cyberspace equivalent of "following the money." Suppose the attacker has compromised a second device. However, the second device can be reached by a wireless communications channel. The compromised target device then sends the desired data to the second compromised device. Any attribution will lead to the second device, but the attacker has simply eavesdropped on the wireless communications channel. The attacker has the data and has not revealed themselves to any cyberspace protocol. Attribution by following the exfiltrated data in this case is essentially impossible.

Duplicity of Nodes

Attribution depends on retrieving protocol and device information from the computing devices in cyberspace. Though it should be obvious, any compromised device can lie. It is impossible to create a secure system that will remain secure forever. Therefore, one must view as suspect any information retrieved from a device that has been attacked or any other device to which the attacked device had access.

The design and implementation of cyberspace is based on technology and protocols that set fundamental limits on the reliability of attribution.

Attribution in the Cyber Domain

The previous section described the aspects of the design and implementation of cyberspace that make attribution difficult. However, attribution is accomplished in many cases. With rare exceptions, attribution requires collecting information at the site of the attack, the compromised device, to recreate the actions or the communications of the attacker. Clues may be found in the attack code (the weapon), the nature of the act (such as information stolen of manipulated), and the communications channels used for both the attack and exfiltration—if any. This usually simply points to some other node earlier in the attack sequence. The investigation then starts anew at the next node. As attacks may cover many different infrastructure providers and jurisdictions, the question is what information is available and how does one get access to it.

Attribution by Cooperative Efforts

Particularly for criminal acts and nuisance behavior such as financial fraud, spam and distributed denial of service attacks (DDoS), the various infrastructure providers cooperate to provide the data they have available and piece together a picture that can support attribution. Here the limit is the data available. If the infrastructure providers are sufficiently forewarned, they may be able to log and save ephemeral data.

Attribution by Lawful Access

Failing cooperation, if the act and the jurisdiction warrant, law enforcement may assert their lawful right to access the nodes and collect, or cause to be collected, what data is available. The advantage that state resources have over completely cooperative efforts is the access to additional, non-cyber information that may be germane to the investigation. Indeed, many cases of attribution hinge on the additional data used to focus an investigation, such as physical surveillance, wiretap, or criminal histories. Law enforcement may remove the last vagaries of attribution by the physical seizure of the attacker's devices or monitoring the attacker's action in real time. Obviously, attribution by a state's law enforcement organization is only relevant to attacks that take place within the state's jurisdiction or another jurisdiction with which the state has agreements or treaties.

Attribution by Intelligence Tradecraft

Particularly for cyber warfare and espionage, the only way to obtain reliable attribution may be by using "close access" intelligence techniques. That is, by planting monitoring capabilities on nodes within the attackers network or attack path. This technique can produce some of the most reliable attribution but is extremely difficult as it involves attacking the attacker's devices without their knowledge and exfiltrating data supporting attribution. It is, in essence, an espionage attack in its own right. It is more effective the closer to the source of the attack it can be.

Looking Forward: How Might Attribution Be Achieved

As noted earlier, there have been many different proposals for changes in the design or implementation of cyberspace to increase the probability of attributing attacks, war, espionage, or criminal. None is a "silver bullet," for the reasons already covered, but all of them can be put into one of three categories.

Strong Identification and Authentication

There are proposals for requiring or allowing stronger identity and authentication of people, computers, and packets. As described earlier, this is not a panacea but does provide a level of assurance. However, one must understand that such a technology is likely to be more useful to authoritarian regimes that wish to monitor their citizens than it would be in combating cyber warfare or cyber espionage, as it would not force noncooperative regimes to utilize it.

Persistent Data

As noted, the design of cyberspace has no requirement to maintain state information, the ephemeral data discussed earlier, beyond the time needed by the protocols. There are a number of proposals that would require, or allow for, selective parts of this data to be logged and saved for some length of time. Examples of such information would include routing tables, NAT translation tables, and DHCP leases. The hope is that this information would be available for forensics examination after an event.

Proximity

The most useful data for attribution is data collected close to the attacker. There are proposals for monitoring the characteristics of data entering network segments and analyzing some portion of the data. For example, it is possible to spoof the source IP address in a TCP packet. This is a technique used in DDoS attacks. The egress verification of source addresses would eliminate such techniques. The same could apply to spoofing email addresses. The outbound mail server could verify that the address was legitimate.

Doctrinal Ramifications of Attribution

From the forgoing, it should be obvious that complete and reliable attribution will never be accomplished. The design and implementation of cyberspace do not support reliable attribution in the general case. Although we cannot necessarily attribute actions, we can hold people, organization, and states accountable for the actions of those over which they have authority. If attribution points to the attack having originated within a nation-state, then the information supporting attribution should be given to that state. That state should have the responsibility to investigate and produce its findings. Noncooperation in investigating cyber attacks (cyber warfare, espionage, or crime) should be taken as a sign of culpability. States must take the responsibility of policing their national infrastructure and they must assume an obligation to investigate and stop attacks originating in their jurisdiction.

Lastly, there is a curious property of attribution and the asymmetric nature of cyber attacks. In the balance between cyber attacks and cyber defense, it is frequently asserted, correctly, that cyber offense is far easier than cyber defense.

Cyber attacks are highly asymmetrical. That is, one can attack anywhere from anywhere. This creates an asymmetry between offense and defense. Offense is free to attack anywhere and defense must defend everywhere. This naturally leads to a quotation from Frederick the Great, "He who defends everything, defends nothing." Defense in cyberspace is inferior to offense. However, attribution is also highly asymmetric, but in the other direction. Those who wish to remain anonymous must do so everywhere, while those wishing to identify them need do so only once.

CHAPTER 2

Toward a General Understanding of Cyber Safety

The Honorable James M. Simon, Jr.

In our time, it is commonplace to say that the industrial age is dead and that we now live in the information age.

> *"I wish it need not have happened in my time," said Frodo. "So do I," said Gandalf, "and so do all who live to see such times. But that is not for them to decide. All we have to decide is what to do with the time that is given us."*[1]

In this "time" of cyber, Gandalf speaks to government leaders with a special significance; especially to those leaders for whom computers and social networking are an interesting fad; rather than a given state of being.

Once, weapons were so expensive, so complex, and required so many resources that only nation-states could build them. Banalities aside, the industrial age arsenals of national defense have been superseded by the information age garage and the Internet café. Once, the design and production of weapons was the province of craftsmen, or scientists, with years of study and training honed by constant practice. In history, this single fact alone restricted advances in weapons technologies to relatively few places where scientific knowledge, engineering technology, and key resources all came together to meet a need. In today's cyber world, the ingredients necessary are available on a truly global scale and talent so common that children have successfully

---

1.   J.R.R. Tolkien, *The Fellowship of the Ring* (Boston: Houghton Mifflin, 1965), p. 60.

Mr. Simon is presently CEO of Intelligence-Enterprises, LLC and formerly was Microsoft's Chief Strategist for its Worldwide Public Sector, head of its Institute for Advanced Technology in Governments. Mr. Simon served in the CIA for nearly three decades and was an analyst before becoming a bureaucrat.

created cyber weapons. Governments have reserved to themselves the right to wage large-scale violence but they no longer have a monopoly on the means.

Many years ago, a famous American bank robber was asked why he robbed banks. His answer: "Because that's where the money is."[2] Today that money is in cyber-crime. 2011 appears to have been the first year in which the proceeds from cyber-crime surpassed that of the drug trade—with a lot less risk for its practitioners. To oversimplify only a bit, if a target has a valuable secret that can be monetized, it'll be stolen. Entire new enterprises, like the late Russian Business Network, arose to serve the needs of criminals, but quickly found new customers and became available to do "out-sourced" work for governments; or anyone else with money. The consequence is that cyber conflict is in the reach of even the most technologically incompetent—if they have money.

Once, money was in vaults and theft required a measure of organization and competence. Today, bank robbery is the province of the unskilled. Credit cards and electronic banking have spread the money around to repositories rather less secure than a bank vault. Significantly, it is now worthwhile for organized crime to steal from the non-rich. Theft from many can match or exceed theft from the few. Indeed the ubiquity of the Internet means that citizens, or rather their computers, can be easily enlisted into cyber conflict regardless of the intent of the owners. Few countries let its citizens drive cars or fly airplanes without some form of safety regulation: training and licensing, brake lights, seatbelts, and so on. Any idiot can own and operate a computer and many do.

Traditionally, we depend on governments to protect us and our rights—to keep us safe. In human history, governments were, next to God, the most powerful entities in our experience. Families and tribes and allegiance to football teams matter as they always have, but even the "power of the people" was ultimately only expressible in the collective notion of government.

When man first went into space, it was government that led the way—in reality, it was the only way into space. Governments monopolized the means to get into space and no one "went" without their permission.[3] None of this is true of cyberspace. Here, the sinews of power have changed and the

---

2.   Attribute to Willie Sutton, but, alas, apocryphal.
3.   Governments had, and still have, considerable control on the rules and uses of space. That space is no longer a realm of excitement and progress is testimony to governments' effect on technological innovation and risk—even on imagination.

exclusivity enjoyed by governments around large, consequential technologies has been altered in ways that are profound.

Indeed, companies, criminals, and informal, self-organizing groups invest more people and money than any single government. It is my observation that more money is spent on cyber with effect[4] by companies, criminal enterprises, and self-organizing groups than by governments. Talent, with notable exceptions, resides with companies, criminal enterprises, and self-organizing groups. Governments rise near the top, second only to criminal enterprise in only one area: technology devoted to attack and even then, their status is threatened by self-organizing groups.

With determination and thoughtful leadership all of these weaknesses can be overcome, but one. Governments have many sterling qualities, but agility is an uncommon one. Governments are on the sideline in main because they are too slow, too rigid, and too unimaginative to play in a realm dominated by individual talent, business imperatives, and rapid technological change.

Nearly all-modern governments are products of the industrial age. They possess industrial age procurement practices designed for major, end-item procurement with an accompanying incremental modernization and maintenance system in turn intended to ensure the purchased item would last years and even decades. Obsolescence came slowly and product improvements and modifications allowed one to use used, aged weapons long past their predicted date of replacement. Because technology and the means to make weapons of it matured slowly, the five-year plan mode of planning and contracting made sense. The US B-52 bomber is the poster-child for this acquisition model. In turn, this heavy industrial system required a multi-year R&D model accompanied by a multi-year planning and budget cycle. In today's parlance, we call it: "The Industrial Base."

A second complication is that government budgetary practices also value maintenance and sustainability ahead of innovation and modernization. Unfortunately for governments, in the Age of Information Technology, the speed of change is such that throw-away-and-replace is the norm in commercial enterprise and the imperative for a successful cyber defense. Obsolescence happens in months and years, not decades and centuries.

---

4.   An unsupported assertion to be sure without, reliable or even obtainable, data; but one informed by personal observation.

Figure 2.1. Defense and Companies

The Defense Industry	Commercial Companies
Knows government customer	Knows everyone else
Business processes mirror customer	Processes target consumer purchasing rhythm and desire for something "new,"
Structured, government-driven requirements	Unstructured market-driven requirements
Customer needs known to all competitors	Customer needs "invented" by proprietary interests and marketing
Poor agility with long attention span	Agile with short attention span
Effectiveness oriented	Efficiency oriented
Low margins, ROI, employment rates	High
Stable, predictable customer	Fickle
Multi-year revenue model	Quarterly
Select nations as customers	Global customers
Full security regime	Only IP protection
National law	Laws of many nations
Industrial base	Somebody's garage
Enduring revenue: long life cycle, training & support	Low cost, ease of use, throw away & replace
Acquisition to increase government market share	Acquisition to expand revenue/ acquire new markets
Citizens able to acquire a clearance	Citizens and non-citizens; clearance?
ITAR	What?

For governments, the avoidance of risks, especially legal and audit risks, through budgetary program management has been and continues to be the key skill. The entire procurement system is in itself a barrier to entry for small companies or those focused on the commercial arena as opposed to the world of large defense contractors. For large industrial-base procurement programs for equipment like tanks and bombers, this is a useful model but one that is foolish in a technology realm dominated by small, commercially oriented companies.

Indeed the traditional corporate partners of government, the large defense systems integrators, have become part of the problem. Too many are prisoners of the past and while some few have begun to evolve, it is a long and painful process and too many have not yet begun. Figure 2.1 admittedly is an over-simplified cartoon, but is a generally accurate description of the gulf between the defense industry and the commercial sector.

In the Age of Information Technology, talent is more critical than any other aspect of the R&D chain. A final blow to the industrial age perhaps is that the globalization of the Internet has also meant the globalization of talent, making single-nation efforts in this domain almost quaint. Because talent is global, no single country, however rich and powerful, can monopolize the intellectual capital necessary to dominate the cyber realm. Even though assertive lip service is paid to this proposition, no country behaves as if it is true.

The Internet, with its global connectivity, anonymity, lack of traceability, and rich set of targets, is a great place to play. And, thanks to low cost computer technology, widespread connectivity, and the technical ease of creating or obtaining malware, almost anyone can play. Almost everyone does.

Kto kogo: A Russian phrase popularized in the Soviet era by Lenin, it is literally "Who, Whom." For Lenin, this was the central question of politics and was intended to convey that to understand any occurrence; one had to know who was doing what to, or for, whom. In the "good old days," nations had the comfort of having well-known or, at least, strongly suspected adversaries. In 1983, when KAL-007 was shot down by the Soviet Union, there was no doubt that the perpetrator was a nation-state because only nation-states flew jet fighters. Even today's reoccurrence of piracy is localized and the perpetrators known or readily identifiable.

The cyber world is different in important respects. First, and with enormous consequence for governments' attempts to cope, the cyber world does not exist on land, at sea, in the air or in outer space, but in a new domain.[5] This fact alone poses enormous challenges to traditional military establishments everywhere as each try to figure out what service ought to be in charge. All agree it is a new "domain" but someone still must be in-charge with all the attendant complications. Worse, most cyber attacks are criminal acts that do not fall into the old definitions of national security. Human beings reason by analogy and some thoughtful government leaders, like Mike Rothery,[6] argue persuasively that the very search for one—cyber war, cyber crime, et al.—has helped hide the novelty of a new domain of human activity. Even worse, in his view, these comfortable phases have allowed governments to focus on the bureaucratic aspects of response rather than on the reality of the challenge as policemen and soldiers argue over who ought to be in charge. For now, let's just term it cyber conflict.[7]

There are many more sources of attack than the purposeful actions of nation-states. They range from routine human error with misconfigured installations that look a lot like attacks, to the individual nut-case, to vandals seeking their bit of fame, to "hactivists" anxious, like the anarchists before them, to demonstrate their moral superiority over everyone else, to criminals (individuals to syndicates) out for money, to terrorists out to cause indiscriminate harm, and finally to nation-states with all these motives and a few more.

Motives range from the traditional areas of criminal activity (fraud, theft, the distribution of child pornography), economic espionage, military espionage, reconnaissance, to full-scale cyber conflict. All these motives mean an action that may deter one group and may be ineffective against another.

In history, governments have tended to seek to safeguard their spheres of interests through prevention, deterrence, retribution, and occasionally pre-emption.

Prevention encompasses a number of efforts. Law, regulation, rules and standards are all designed to normalize behavior to make the detection of

---

5. Some military thinkers know this, for example, see Arthur K. Cebrowski, Vice Admiral, USN and John H. Garstka, "Network-Centric Warfare—Its Origin and Future," *US Naval Institute Proceedings* 124, no. 1 (January 1998) and William J. Lynn, "Defending a New Domain," *Foreign Affairs* 89, no. 5 (Sep/Oct 2010).

6. Personal conversation with the author. Mike Rothery is First Assistant Secretary, Australia Attorney General's Department. For those interested in why Mike likely is correct, see Daniel Kahneman, *Thinking, Fast and Slow* (New York: Farrar, Straus & Giroux, 2011).

7. An articulate defender of this term is Professor Ahmed Chazali Abu-Hassan of Malaysia's National Defence University who ably argued its usefulness at the Cyber Security Malaysia Conference in October 2010.

deviation easier. These measures tend to be inter-locking, so that a law against running red lights is supplemented by police presence and surveillance cameras. In addition, to secure a license, an individual—and their vehicle—must meet minimum standards for a host of things, but most emphatically safety. In the cyber realm, individuals, not actively malicious, are relieved of any government-mandated responsibility for the consequence of their negligence upon others. Botnets, for example, would be far less effective without irresponsible and unwitting foot soldiers.

Deterrence and its implied comrade-in-arms, retribution, still matter; although their application has become confused in a time when one is not always sure who is the aggressor, what their motive is, or even where they might be.

Pre-emption is more complicated in that the attacker, their motive, their status (citizen, criminal, foreign entity,) their location and the range of unforeseen consequence is mostly unknowable and perhaps even undiscoverable. It is true that serial attackers develop signatures than can potentially warn an alert defender and all such groups are susceptible to age old espionage techniques as well as a few new ones.

Because the motive for an attack is not always evident; neither is the response. We do know that counter-attacks can cause collateral damage. Because the Internet is a shared and integrated domain used by citizens, businesses and governments, responses to a specific threat are extremely complicated. Collateral damage can be high and even unacceptable. Worse, because we cannot even be sure we have correctly identified the attacker, a too-rapid counter attack may harm the innocent, even an ally, or even one's self.

In this time, the best place from which to attack a nation-state is from an allied capital, or even from within a country's own borders. For many nations, especially democracies, this poses a special complexity because the origin of the attack determines who responds: local law enforcement, national law enforcement, or the military.

We cannot even be sure if we have been attacked. For example, nearly all problems reported to software vendors involve either incompatible device drivers, components like video cards, or simple user-error. Real attacks are quite varied. The most publicized is the remote attack. Remote attackers take advantage of product errors and vulnerabilities, system misconfigurations, and social engineering. Because different actors may use similar techniques, the nature of the attack may not yield reliable clues about the identity of the attacker or the attacker's motives. This fact, combined with anonymity and lack of traceability, means that attributing attacks is very difficult, and punishment for malicious activity is rare.

Conversely, the "hacktivist" movement does seek publicity for their point-of-view, but they are the exception that proves the rule. The history of anarchist movements tells us that, sooner or later, the ethical and moral intent of hactivists activities (however debatable) will cause loss of life or enable commonly agreed evils, such as interfering with the political rights of others, or enabling child predation or human trafficking. This is already happening and the hactivists' social cachet can be expected to decline as violence, hatred, and purely criminal endeavors become the hallmark of their efforts. The decline of the social cachet will reduce the size of the problem, but individual acts will continue.

To think about being "safe," we must start with trying to perceive the potential attacker. Serious attackers start with reconnaissance. As Sun Tzu said: "What is called 'foreknowledge' cannot be elicited from spirits, nor from gods, nor by analogy from with past events, nor from calculations. It must be obtained from men who know the enemy situation."[8]

This is still true and the serious attacker seeks knowledge of the target before the attack. Prediction is possible, but even then, I have found a useful law of analysis to be: "One may not use rational means to predict irrational events." Please note that the "rational actor" model so long favored by defense theorists remains dependent on your opponents sharing your definition of rationality. Recall Osama bin Laden's expectations of the consequence of a terror attack on the United States or Hitler's expectation of the response to his invasion of Poland. Nonetheless, from the perspective of a "rational" would-be cyber attacker, the creation and testing of weapons has to be done with care—otherwise an alert defender can predict the attack vector and potentially pre-emptively counter weapons' effects.

One novel aspect of the cyber realm is that the use of any weapon immediately exposes it to targets and competitors and allows them to re-create the weapon though copying or reverse engineering or mutate it to yet another level of virulence. Aircraft carriers and intercontinental missiles are not easily cloned even if you see them and experience their power. Cyber weapons can be, and are, quickly copied and evolved and their use in one context in no way precludes their use in yet another. This fact alone will, as it

---

8.   Sun Tzu, *The Art of War*, trans. Ralph D. Sawyer (San Francisco: Westview Press, 1953), p. 231.

becomes understood, be a major impediment for offensive cyber conflict for many countries as the moral and ethical potential of action and reaction will counsel inaction.

Some attacks resemble reconnaissance rather than direct action. Network scans or unauthorized access to a system may be a prelude to information theft, a data integrity breach, or a disruption of service. Moreover, the complex interrelationships between systems suggest that there may be unanticipated cascading effects, some which may be more severe, or have wider effect, than what was intended. A simple reconnaissance might morph into a major attack, almost by accident.

Finally, while some attacks may be obvious (e.g., a denial of service attacks against a critical infrastructure) and generate a quick response; other attacks may be harder to detect. For example, the exfiltration of data from sensitive systems is a constant concern, but more damaging may be an alteration of critical data. Not only may this be hard to detect, but it may be difficult to discern when the data was changed without authority, thus making it difficult to "roll back" to a known good state. Creating doubt as to validity of one's own knowledge can easily lead to inefficiency and even paralysis.

Remote attacks, despite all the press attention, are trivial to a well-defended government or an enterprise when compared to either the suborned insider or the supply chain attack.

No commercial enterprise expects to keep a high-value secret from organized crime, or even determined competitors.[9] There is no civilian ability to deal with theft and, especially, extortion where the adversary is known to kill to achieve their ends. A good example is the drug barons that may kill a family to make an example and, more recently, are effectively able to frighten-off would-be hacktivists.[10] This is not new under the sun. Businesses, and the rest of us, rely on civil society as part of the social compact with those who hold the monopoly on force and violence—government. In our lawless cyberspace, costs and losses are high and will remain so until governments find a means to ensure that retribution, or justice, occurs in the real world.

Governments have a more complex problem in that would-be attackers have a longer-term view than attackers motivated only by a "return on

---

9. Mark Clayton, "Report: Chinese Hackers Targeted Big Oil Companies, Stole Data," *Christian Science Monitor* last modified February 10, 2011, *http://www.csmonitor.com/USA/2011/0210/Report-Chinese-hackers-targeted-big-oil-companies-stole-data.*

10. Report: "Anonymous Mexico" last modified November 5, 2011, *http://www.zimbio.com/Mexico+Drug+War/articles/Mj3XEc_qtp4/Anonymous+Mexico.*

investment." An attacker of nation-states has unique objectives and practices. Ease and certainty of success in an attack is the most highly prized attribute. It is easier to go through an open door than to scale a wall. This next desired objective is making an undetectable attack, and failing that, one that cannot be attributed to the attacker or, better yet, blamed on someone else. Remember, professional attackers want to attack repeatedly, again and again. Nor do they want their preferred means of attack, or weapons, to be usable only once. So they have every incentive to select the easiest attack that delivers the desired result.

Precision also matters. Attackers have incentives to choose the most precise attack that strikes the specific target—and no other. Promiscuous attacks raise unwanted alarm and risks unpredictable collateral damage or even counter-attacks. Precision strikes also allow valuable cyber weapons to be re-used against less-capable targets, even within the same entity. Perhaps of even greater import, known attacks can be reverse-engineered and become available to all: opponents and competitors. Keeping one's "intellectual property" for one's own use is a thesis that appeals to many, but especially to governments and criminals.

The scale of attack is itself a policy decision of enormous significance. Any cyber act that caused large-scale property damage, loss of life or significantly diminished military capability could be viewed as an act of war and the response could likely not be cyber. This leads to a cost-benefit analysis that is the essential prelude to a decision to launch a large-scale attack. Secondly, while cyber attacks are highly asymmetric—giving the attacker the advantage, anonymity is asymmetrical in the opposite direction. That is, for the attacker to remain anonymous, he must do so everywhere and the defender need only identify him once. This fact weighs heavily on the risk side of the cost-benefit equation.

Generic, broad attacks like denial of service attacks are the equivalent of a punch in the face. They gain attention, create anger, but do not end the fight. They invite, almost demand, a response. The professional attacker launches no attack without a careful assessment of the balance between risk and reward. Special attention must be paid to the ability and will of a target to counter-attack.

Other forms of attack are more deadly in that they can have the purpose of seeking decisive consequences—from the tactical to the strategic.

There are various means to launch such attacks, but by far the easiest, is to suborn someone in the targeted organization or who supports it. No one can reliably check tens-of-millions of lines of customized code, making it quite profitable to suborn a programmer. And, after all, the code does indeed perform as expected, when tested for what it was supposed to do—at least for now. Out-sourcing for customization with its multiple layers of sub-contracted work eases the attacker's way. An attack is most effective when there is no consistent code-base to compare and observe changes. Continued customization and modification necessary to avoid obsolescence guarantees this to be an insoluble problem for procedural redress.

The second easiest means is through the supply-chain. Lax procedures for the procurement of hardware or software by the defender or the widespread use of pirated components make this both the easiest, but more importantly, the least risky avenue. In the latter instance, piracy involves criminals who are easily susceptible to monetary incentives or physical threat. All that is necessary for an attacker is to identify the target, their point of purchase and act accordingly.

Lax procedures are not, in themselves, an indication of an easy attack. First, an adversary must insert themselves into the proximate delivery system—difficult when legal, normal commercial procurement practices are followed. Even then, commoditized products use installation and registration procedures that add enormous complexity to the insertion of harmful sub-systems or software. Unusual, or corrupt, procurement practices or the use of purpose-built software offer the attacker the best opportunities to take advantage of lax procedures.

With hardware, the simpler the device, the easier it is for an adversary to make a modification. USB drives, for example, did not, until lately, receive the scrutiny that servers and routers do. By far the easiest way to make a supply chain attack is to suborn a member of the manufacturer's local delivery and installation team.

Software, at least proprietary software, is less vulnerable to that sort of attack than hardware because of the inaccessibility of the core programming as well as the complexity of the core's relationship with its native applications. Worse yet for a would-be attacker, advanced vendors of proprietary software add security layers and registration procedures that are, so far, impossible to defeat once the product has passed its software assurance tests.

But to play offense, one must understand defense and the relationship between the two missions is complicated. The history of signals intelligence is one of alternating dominance with offense usually having the upper hand. This made a lot of sense when government and military communications were both segregated and unique. In the Internet world where private citizens and economic interests share a common domain with governments and the military, the defense must be dominant. No state or enterprise can afford to suffer a seriously debilitating attack, thus the goal for the defended is to predict and forestall successful attacks.

The IT department's set ways and negligence is usually blamed for all successful cyber attacks. Scapegoats are convenient and do often share some guilt, but a word in defense of the IT shop is in order. Too often, they are given money and schedule that are defined by budget goals rather than mission. This means that there is not enough time, nor money for the extra-ordinary. One consequence is that IT shops manage for efficiency instead of effectiveness leading to a system run for schedule convenience rather than active defense. Funding, only in the name of efficiency, is antithetical to the possibility of a successful cyber defense. In short, a plan dictated by those who plan and mandate budgetary and procurement practices. Here it may useful to recall Immanuel Kant's observation on planners:

> *"Making plans is too often the occupation of an extravagant and boastful mind. It thus obtains the reputation of creative genius by demanding of others what it cannot itself supply, by denigrating what it cannot improve, and by proposing what it knows not where to find."*[11]

The necessary, but not sufficient, solution is that IT, at least where it affects cyber defense requires financial reserves and special procurement authorities. In the event of an attack, or better yet in anticipation of an attack, the IT department needs the resources for the extreme—change-out of the compromised software or hardware within a time period that is effective rather than efficient. To make this change possible, most countries will require their executive and legislative authorities to become creative. Organisms learn from experience only if their disposition to react changes in the course of time. Can government learn in time?

---

11.   Immanuel Kant. *Prolegomena*, trans. Paul Carus *http:///webexhibits.org/causesofcolor/ref/Kant.hmtl.*

A solid defense has three main components: the perimeter, the inside, and awareness. The first is well understood and exhaustively written about, although rarely in the context faced by governments.[12] The second, deliberate penetration of one's own organization by an adversary is the most serious and has been a threat since the dawn of human history. This paper focuses on the last, awareness, as the most decisive and most critical in the cyber age; for without it, there is no knowledge of either attack or defense.

Awareness has a number of simple components. First, there must be absolute knowledge of all hardware and software resident in one's system. Second, there must be an absolute knowledge of each aspect of all hardware and software, total configuration control, and, especially, complete knowledge of each component's base (normal) state. Finally, there must be a system of error recognition and reporting that alerts the defenders of any potential change in the normal state. For any of this to be effective, there needs to be a dedicated, professional analytic effort devoted to understanding normality, detecting and understanding deviance, and enabling the detection and prosecution of rogue insiders. Only in this way, can reconnaissance be detected and the defense alerted.

Business, having given up on effective policing, focuses on patching as needed and paying attention to software and hardware security assurance practices. Government has a more immediate and inescapable problem. But the key tool remains the same—analysis. Part of the analytic effort is heavily technical, but an equal part is to understand and identify key individual and institutional actors. This requires a serious effort at attribution—knowing or being able to deduce who did it. Cyber conflict, like art, is a craft where the individual qualities of the practitioners are paramount. Knowing the intellectual leaders as well as the clever and, not so clever, foot soldiers is a key ingredient for a successful and purposeful defense.

Clausewitz taught that the introduction or elimination of friction could be decisive in war.[13] It follows that the defender has every incentive to increase

---

12. Some with "isolated" systems think they are immune—actually all they have done is make themselves an easy target for the insider threat, ensure progressive and certain obsolescence, while creating an ideal target for a decapitation attack. The attacker's dream is to limit the attack, and its consequences, to the specific target and no other.

13. Carl von Clausewitz, *On War*, trans. Michael Howard and Peter Paret (Princeton, NJ: Princeton University Press, 1989). For an insightful look at Clausewitz's concept of *Friktion*, see Barry D. Watts, *Clausewitzian Friction and Future War*, *McNair Paper 52* (Washington: Institute for National Strategic Studies, National Defense University, 1996).

the friction incurred by a would-be attacker while the attacker naturally seeks the path of least resistance.

From this, it follows that there are a number of defensive operating principles to increase, through complexity, the friction for the attacker. The most important general principle is to defeat the targeted attack. A thief or a hostile power prefers its success to be without risk. Generic attacks raise the alarm, prompt countermeasures, and may even lead to violence. By far, the best attack succeeds while keeping the target in ignorance.

In cyber war, as all other war, deception must always be considered. False flags are an age-old feature of deception in warfare and a common ploy in the cyber domain. Thus, defense needs active intelligence, which, in turn, requires knowing the order of battle for the cyber domain. A primary aim must be to gain enough insight to allow the anticipation and, ideally, the ability to forestall attack vectors. Clearly, for governments, certain knowledge of who is the attacker is central to the selection of counter-measures and a thoughtful response as well to provide a guide for the development and creation of effective strategies.

Attackers can be expected to choose attack strategies that confuse or mislead the defender. Confusion is always helpful and "cry wolf" attacks and feints may lead the target to ignore, or be blind to, more advanced, and more valuable attacks. This is a particular problem when defending a complex system that span entities (like alliances) or intra-governmental efforts. Attackers can be expected to select the weakest link. Sowing distrust in a cooperative system or among allies can multiply the effectiveness of other attacks.

To pick just one aspect, the inter-related nature of coalition warfare and the need for inter-operability among allies are well known. The newest complexity is that the least secure member of a coalition (for example, aimed at combating piracy or UN peace keeping operations) becomes a liability instead of an asset. Thus cyber defense is no longer a technical one for experts but a policy issue for the highest levels of government.

A few immediate suggestions as to what to do to be "safe:"

- Go to IPv6; Now. To still use IPv4 is indefensible in all the implications of that word.

- Use the newest software and hardware. As systems age, it is certain that attackers have found whatever holes there are. New systems, like new weapons, require more effort than the familiar for an attacker to understand

and exploit. The attacker has the latest technology; the defense should have no less. Do not be penny-wise and pound-foolish.

- Pay attention to technological changes. In addition to the obvious, technological change occasionally risk the viability of an attacker's most advanced weapons. When this circumstance is foreseen, attackers can be expected to consider immediate use against the highest-value targets. High-value targets need to be alert.

- Patch. Now. Attackers are quick to reverse-engineer patches for attack purposes. To not patch is to presume one is intrinsically safe, knows more than anyone else, or is technically superior to everyone else. Invincible ignorance is always dangerous. When the IT shop complains that a new release will break existing systems and thus the risk of cyber penetration is acceptable, what they are really saying is that "I would rather be insecure than inconvenienced." The exceptions tend to be large, complex operational systems, but even there patch testing is too often wrongly treated as a nice-to-have and not the urgent necessity that it is.

- Establish strict control over the introduction of hardware and software into one's system. Pirated software and hardware offer an easy entre for both the malicious and the stupid.

- If possible, allow no customization of any system that touches, in any way, one's enterprise—money or secrets. When not possible, insist on total knowledge of the base system, know who did it, why it was done, and establish a rigorous crosscheck of all changes. Next to pirated attacks on the supply chain, the easiest attack means is to suborn your programmer. Firm configuration control offers some chance of risk mitigation but, if done well, tends to be expensive and time-consuming. If done poorly, it is a disaster waiting to happen—or one that has already happened, but then you will be the last to know.

- Especially where secrets or money are at risk, use commoditized hardware and software. The sheer complexity of subverting widely sold commercial products with targeted attacks, coupled with manufacturers' internal security assurance procedures and evolutionary updates make these products difficult, but not impossible, to attack for a specific purpose.[14] In time, attackers will develop testing methods that are contained and reduce the warning time available to an alert defender. Even then,

---

14. Despite the fantasies of conspiracy theorists, no global vendor of software or hardware can afford the financial consequences of assisting any one to harm another.

commodity products have the inherent advantage of rapid change driven by large-scale, global commercial markets.

- Log all usage of all machines. Create an internal entity to search for deviant behavior in employee sub-groups. Identify group dynamics and cross-group linkages so that if something happens, a damage assessment can be quick and accurate. In the event of an attack, absent this knowledge, triage and rapid recovery are certain to be ineffective.

Government needs to solve three serious problems if they are to keep us safe:

1. In an inter-connected cyber realm, how to keep the least capable, the least aware among us from posing the larger community a threat; even if one of ignorance, not purpose,
2. How to change law and process so that government can enlist the active participation of companies without stifling business and killing creativity and thereby empowering less cooperative entities, and
3. How can they cooperate with other governments—but only some, not all? Cyber warriors are disproportionately in states where the rule of law, or its' application, is a sometime thing. How can the few learn to work together across their various national legal and commercial differences to create an international "coalition of the willing" that could learn to a new, enforceable standard?

To solve these problems, government should create a defensive policy that assumes attacker initiative and defender reaction, but focuses energy and resources on establishing an agile defense.[15] Deterrence is enabled by the certainty that a government has both the means and will to respond. But, no defense, whatever the doctrine, can expect to be agile without the effort to learn to monitor, predict, and pre-empt potential attacks—a policy decision of national consequence, if only because of the inescapable nexus between defense and civil liberty.

---

15. Three studies worth a look are John Blackburn and Gary Waters, *Optimising Australia's Response to the Cyber Challenge: Kokoda Paper 14* (Canberra: The Kokoda Foundation, 2011); Fred Schreier, Barbara Weekes, and Theodore H. Winkler, *Cyber Security: The Road Ahead: DCAF Horizon 2015 Working Paper No. 4* (Geneva: The Geneva Centre for the Democratic Control of the Armed Forces, 2011); Barbara Fast, Michael Johnson, and Dick Schaeffer, *Cyber Intelligence...Setting the Landscape for an Emerging Discipline.* (Arlington: The Intelligence and National Security Alliance, 2011).

Acknowledgement/Disclosures

This chapter is the personal view of the author and is not endorsed by employers, past or present. This chapter focuses on governments, rather than on enterprises or individuals, and is intended for laymen; not technologists. The concerns of technical experts are important, even critical, in many ways for addressing the problems of cyber conflict. But, the pace of technological change makes the concerns of the technicians transitory and ephemeral for the rest of us. In the spirit of "my time," I bear no responsibility for error but only note that others—Dave Aucsmith, John Manferdelli, Tony Oettinger, and George Spix, are more culpable, if only because they mentored the unqualified to pontification.

CHAPTER 3

Defining "War" in the Cyber Era

Frank J. Cilluffo and Sharon L. Cardash

The cyber era is synonymous with speed. Operations take milliseconds or less, and can be conducted with considerable precision. Expectations have adjusted accordingly, with patience in relatively short supply. Actions too are undertaken hastily, often with the intent of limiting damage, be it to national security, corporate financial standing, or individual personal reputation. In this swirl of point and counterpoint, terms and concepts are tossed about readily. Think "cyber war" or "cyber attack." Though ubiquitous, the precise meaning and contours of these terms remain unclear. While it may not be surprising that, in the age of the here and now, the need and demand for instantaneous response has heretofore relegated definitional clarity and thoughtful analysis to a subordinate position, there are consequences. Action and reaction, particularly in the context of war, are at their sound best if and when guided by fundamental principles in the form of doctrine, which serves as framework to execute strategy, and inform tactics, techniques, and procedures. Thinking first, and then acting, will save lives, protect property, and contribute to stability in the affected area, if not also beyond.

Frank J. Cilluffo has served as Director of the Homeland Security Policy Institute since joining The George Washington University in April 2003. He is also an Associate Vice President and leads GW's homeland security efforts on policy, research, education, and training. Before joining GW, he served at the White House as Special Assistant to the President for Homeland Security. Shortly following the September 11, 2001 terrorist attacks on the United States, Mr. Cilluffo was appointed by the President to the newly created Office of Homeland Security, and served as a principal advisor to Governor Tom Ridge. Prior to his White House appointment, Mr. Cilluffo spent eight years in senior policy positions with the Center for Strategic & International Studies (CSIS), a Washington-based think tank. At CSIS he chaired or directed numerous committees and task forces on homeland defense, counterterrorism, transnational crime, and information warfare and information assurance.

Our aim therefore is to explore, or at least begin to, what "cyber war" really means. In doing so, we adopt an expansive interpretation of national security that incorporates an economic security dimension. We also proceed according to the understanding that cyberspace, in addition to serving as a force multiplier relative to all other domains, is itself a distinct domain that transforms the prosecution of war and the conduct of defense. Cyberspace as domain extends the battlefield to incorporate all of society: vulnerabilities in our systems reach across sectors, and effective defense requires a whole-of-society approach.

Pre-Digital Conflict Behavior Is No Longer the Norm

War in the pre-digital world was generally understood to be "the organized use of violent force by groups to forward a political goal."[1] The laws of armed conflict, and international law as reflected in the Charter of the United Nations, specifically Articles 2(4) and 51 which speak respectively to the use of force and the right to self-defense, together with the 1974 General Assembly resolution defining "aggression"—collectively developed and interpreted in the analog era, and still in effect today—invoke and apply the concepts of armed attack, and breach of territorial integrity, by the armed forces of one state against another. Formal "combat and actual deaths" have been thresholds used to distinguish what is and is not war. These constructs emerged as a function of their times, and the defining features thereof. That world was ordered

1.   Charles Billo and Welton Chang, *Cyber Warfare: An Analysis of the Means and Motivations of Selected Nation States* (Institute for Security Technology Studies at Dartmouth College, November 2004, Revised December 2004), p. 140.

Sharon L. Cardash has served as Associate Director of the Homeland Security Policy Institute (HSPI) since joining The George Washington University in 2005. She has also acted as Senior Advisor to GW's Center for Preparedness & Resilience. Before joining GW, she served as Security Policy Advisor to Canada's Minister of Foreign Affairs. Ms. Cardash has served as principal or contributing author for numerous reports, articles and testimonies on a range of homeland security issues. Prior to 9/11 she worked at the Center for Strategic & International Studies in Washington, DC. There for two years, she managed task forces on terrorism and cyber threats, and co-authored multiple publications including on transnational crime. She holds a Law degree (J.D.) from the University of Toronto, a Master's degree (M.Phil.) in International Relations from the University of Cambridge, and clerked for Justice Joseph T. Robertson, then of the Federal Court of Appeal of Canada.

by physical/geographic boundaries, and the primacy of state actors and their sovereignty. The cyber era, by contrast, is quintessentially porous. The power of borders and territory as organizing principles is diminished, compared to what it once was. As a corollary, non-state actors and even individuals have gained currency as the bar to entry has been lowered, and their Internet-enabled empowerment has given rise to demonstrable capacity to affect state behavior and influence geopolitical calculus.

These developments have given rise to new phenomena, categories, and nomenclature, including conventional warfare (and special operations) that incorporate a cyber component, and cyber war. Regarding the former, the US military today makes extensive use of advanced information technologies, evidenced for example in US use of drones and intelligence, surveillance, and reconnaissance at the tip of the spear in hot spots across the globe. Our adversaries likewise employ networked technology to advantage. Consider the war in Iraq. Insurgents and extremists there used the Internet to conduct and refine operations against US and allied forces, such as by sharing continually updated knowledge and lessons learned about the effective creation and deployment of deadly improvised explosive devices.

Cyber war, on the other hand, by its very name suggests the "pure" use of bits and bytes to achieve an end-state akin to what bullets and bombs would produce. Consider Libya in the period immediately prior to Qaddafi's capture and death, as NATO intervention took shape. It has been reported that the Obama Administration contemplated cyber action designed to "sever [Libyan] military communications links and prevent the early-warning radars from gathering information and relaying it to missile batteries aiming at NATO warplanes." In the end, however, the United States used "conventional aircraft, cruise missiles, and drones."[2]

An effort to define cyber war and associated rules of engagement is reportedly underway within the US Department of Defense (DoD).[3] Multiple relevant terms of art, with elaborated meaning and a certain degree of overlap between and among them, already exist. These include Information Operations (IO), Computer Network Defense (CND), Computer Network Exploitation (CNE), Computer Network Attack (CNA), and Computer Network Operations (CNO).

---

2.   Eric Schmitt and Thom Shanker, "US Debated Cyberwarfare in Attack Plan on Libya," *New York Times,* October 17, 2011, *http://www.nytimes.com/2011/10/18/world/africa/cyber-warfare-against-libya-was-debated-by-us.html?_r=1&pagewanted=print.*

3.   Federal News Radio, "DoD Hammering Out Rules of Cyberspace," (October 21, 2011), *http://www.federalnewsradio.com/?nid=398&sid=2602063.*

IO is an umbrella term encompassing activity aimed at "disrupting or influencing an adversary's decision-making processes." CND refers to activities "that are designed to protect US forces against IO attack from adversaries." CNE "involves intelligence collection...to prepare the IO battle space," and "is usually performed through network tools that penetrate adversary systems to gain information about system vulnerabilities, or to make unauthorized copies of important files." CNA seeks to "disrupt or destroy information resident in computers and computer networks."[4] CNO is a component of IO and an overarching term meaning the sum of CNA, CND, and CNE taken together.[5]

In practice however, the bright line between offense and defense that exists in theory is blurred, especially where "active defense" is concerned. Particularly in a hyperlinked world, in which time is of the essence, a reactive posture is problematic. A more robust defensive stance would "incorporate predictive, active, and pre-emptive measures...to prevent, deflect, or minimize the efforts of the attacker."[6] This begs the question: "When does a cyber reconnaissance become an act of war?"[7] Alternatively, what is the cyber equivalent of "intelligence preparation of the battlefield"? Other classification schemes are also subject to possible leaks in their facially watertight character. For instance, might the volume and/or nature of certain acts of cyber espionage or cyber crime be adjudged to rise to the level of an act of aggression? A brief survey of selected real-world events illustrates the depth and breadth of activity underway, and helps to place these key questions into relief.

The most sensitive sectors of the US Government—the Departments of Defense, Homeland Security, Energy, and State—have been victim to cyber espionage on a grand scale involving the extraction of "terabytes of data" (operation "Titan Rain"), as discovered in 2004, and attributed to computers

---

4. CRS Report for Congress, "Information Operations, Electronic Warfare, and Cyberwar: Capabilities and Related Policy Issues," Clay Wilson (Updated March 20, 2007), pp. 2, 4, 5. See also Department of Defense (DoD) Directive, "Information Operations—Revision One," Number 3600.1 (October 2001), *http://www.iwar.org.uk/iwar/resources/doctrine/DOD36001.pdf*; and Changes Incorporated (May 23, 2011), *http://www.dtic.mil/whs/directives/corres/pdf/360001p.pdf*.

5. Office of Counterintelligence, Defense Counterintelligence and Human Intelligence Center, Defense Intelligence Agency, "Terms and Definitions of Interest for DoD Counterintelligence Professionals—Unclassified Glossary" (May 2, 2011), *http://www.ncix.gov/publications/ci_references/docs/CI_Glossary.pdf*. See also DoD Directive (October 2001), *http://www.iwar.org.uk/iwar/resources/doctrine/DOD36001.pdf*; and Changes Incorporated (May 23, 2011), *http://www.dtic.mil/whs/directives/corres/pdf/360001p.pdf*.

6. Clay Wilson, "Information Operations, Electronic Warfare, and Cyberwar," p. 11.

7. James A. Lewis, "Thresholds for Cyberwar" (Sept 2010) *SIS* p. 8. *http://csis.org/files/publication/101001_ieee_insert.pdf*.

located in China. The United States is not alone. Cyber espionage operation "Shady RAT," initiated in 2006 and reported in 2011, pilfered sensitive data from dozens of targets including multiple international organizations such as the United Nations, companies in at least nine countries in Europe and Asia, several governments including that of the United States, and more than a dozen US defense contractors. Further, in 2009, "a massive electronic spying network ['GhostNet'] that had infiltrated 1,295 computers in 103 countries" was discovered. It was ultimately determined that "[m]inistries of foreign affairs and embassies in Iran, Bangladesh, Indonesia, India, South Korea, Thailand, Germany, and Pakistan were…affected." Though China is the "alleged source" of all three episodes, the Chinese government has "denied responsibility."[8]

Finding the Attacker

Pinpointing the perpetrator in cyberspace is generally a challenge because "attackers can hide their identity, cover their tracks. Worse, they may be able to mislead, placing blame on others by spoofing the source."[9] Imposing accountability and executing a response is thereby complicated. Yet some practitioners have suggested that they "can identify Chinese hackers just by the way they work. 'They have quirks, maybe even the way that they type, the way that they select commands [and] the way that they build their software… There's probably 20 or more characteristics you can use, none of which involve an IP address'."[10] Notably, some Chinese sources have taken few pains to conceal: consider the 1999 book "Unrestricted Warfare" by two Chinese Army colonels who urge consideration of alternative means to defeat an opponent, distinct from traditional direct military action.[11]

8.   Joshua E. Keating, "Shots Fired: The 10 Worst Cyber Attacks," *Foreign Policy*, Feb 27 2012, *http://www.foreignpolicy.com/articles/2012/02/24/shots_fired?page=full*. See also Dmitri Alperovitch, "Revealed: Operation Shady RAT," McAfeeWhite Paper (August 2011), *http://www.mcafee.com/us/resources/white-papers/wp-operation-shady-rat.pdf*; and Information Warfare Monitor, "Tracking GhostNet: Investigating a Cyber Espionage Network," (March 29, 2009), *http://www.scribd.com/doc/13731776/Tracking-GhostNet-Investigating-a-Cyber-Espionage-Network*.

9.   Richard Clarke, "War From Cyberspace," November/December 2009, *The National Interest*, p. 33. See also: Statement of Frank J. Cilluffo Before the US House of Representatives, Committee on the Judiciary, Subcommittee on Technology, Terrorism, and Government Information, "Cyber Attack: The National Protection Plan and Its Privacy Implications," (February 1, 2000) *http://www.gwumc.edu/hspi/policy/testimony2.1.00_cilluffo.pdf*.

10.   Tom Gjelten, "US Not Afraid To Say It: China's The Cyber Bad Guy," citing Richard Bejtlich, MANDIANT's chief security officer (February 18, 2012) *http://www.npr.org/2012/02/18/147077148/chinas-hacking-of-u-s-remains-a-top-concern*.

11.   Qiao Liang and Wang Xiangsui. Published by China's People's Liberation Army, Beijing.

Regarding China, former senior US officials have spoken out, in categorically blunt terms. In a January 2012 op-ed published in *The Wall Street Journal*, Vice Admiral Mike McConnell, former Director of National Intelligence and the National Security Agency, together with Michael Chertoff, former Secretary of Homeland Security, and William Lynn, former Deputy Secretary of Defense, wrote: "The Chinese government has a national policy of economic espionage in cyberspace…. Evidence of China's economically devastating theft of proprietary technologies and other intellectual property from US companies is growing." That assessment, together with the co-authors' proposed prescription—"to respond with all of the diplomatic, trade, economic, and technological tools at our disposal"[12]—came in the wake of a report released by the Office of the National Counterintelligence Executive.[13] The head of that Office summarized the report's contents thus: "The nations of China and Russia, through their intelligence services and through their corporations, are attacking our research and development….This is a national, long-term, strategic threat to the United States of America." Among the areas hardest hit has been "military technology."[14]

In testimony before the Senate Armed Services Committee in February 2012, the Chairman of the Joint Chiefs of Staff, General Martin Dempsey, stated that he "'believe[s] someone in China is hacking into our systems and stealing technology and intellectual property, which at this point is a crime." When asked "if it could be proven that the PLA [People's Liberation Army, meaning China's military] was behind a hacking of the defense infrastructure, whether it would be considered a 'hostile act'," Dempsey responded not necessarily. When pressed to specify "what he would consider a hostile act," he indicated that "'attacking our critical infrastructure' would be "a[n] act worthy of a

---

12. "China's Cyber Thievery Is National Policy—And Must Be Challenged" *Wall Street Journal*, January 27, 2012, See also: Homeland Security Policy Institute, Policy & Research Forum Series Special Event, "A Conversation on Cybersecurity Legislation with Mike McConnell, Michael Chertoff, and Senior Congressional Staff" (February 22, 2012), *http://www.gwumc.edu/hspi/events/cyberPRF413.cfm*.

13. "Foreign Spies Stealing US Economic Secrets in Cyberspace." Report to Congress on Foreign Economic Collection and Industrial Espionage, 2009-2011. (October 2011), *http://www.ncix.gov/publications/reports/fecie_all/Foreign_Economic_Collection_2011.pdf*.

14. Siobhan Gorman, "China Singled out for Cyber Spying," *Wall Street Journal*, November 4, 2011, citing Robert Bryant. *http://online.wsj.com/article/SB10001424052970203716204577015540198801540.html#ixzz1ckLNwAJX*.

similar response."[15] Largely owned and operated by the private sector, critical infrastructure is that deemed by the Department of Homeland Security (DHS) to be "essential to the nation's security, public health and safety, economic vitality, and way of life."[16]

The 2010 Stuxnet worm presented the scenario that Dempsey described, though with Iran as apparent target. Malicious software designed to disrupt and disable "a particular type of industrial control system…infiltrated Siemens systems at Iranian nuclear power plants and caused centrifuges to malfunction."[17] While arguably a clever means of disrupting Iranian nuclear activity, other countries were also affected, though less acutely, including China, Germany, India, Indonesia, Pakistan, and the United States.[18] Former Director of both the National Security Agency and Central Intelligence Agency, General Michael Hayden, has suggested that disrupting Iran via Stuxnet was "a good idea," although he has also acknowledged that others may "attempt to turn it to their own purposes" in future.[19] As one analyst notes, "[m]any… view…the Stuxnet worm as the best example of cyber warfare, because it caused *physical* damage to infrastructure vital to national security."[20] Stuxnet has been called "the world's first 'precision-guided cyber-munition'[21]," as well as "'a game-changer'," because "'we have not seen this coordinated effort of information technology vulnerabilities and industrial control exploitation completely wrapped up in one unique package."[22] Likewise, the Executive

---

15.   Adam Levine, "Joint chiefs chair: Chinese hacking not necessarily a hostile act" (February 14, 2012) CNN *http://www.cnn.com/2012/02/14/us/dempsey-china-hacking/index.html*. See also p. 40 of hearing transcript—US Senate Committee on Armed Services, "Hearing to Receive Testimony on the Defense Authorization Request for Fiscal Year 2013 and the Future Years Defense Program (February 14, 2012) at *http://armed-services.senate.gov/Transcripts/2012/02%20February/12-02%20 -%202-14-12.pdf*.

16.   DHS website, Critical Infrastructure *http://www.dhs.gov/files/programs/gc_1189168948944.shtm* [webpage]. Accessed March 4, 2012.

17.   Jonathan Masters, "Confronting the Cyber Threat," Council on Foreign Relations (Updated May 23, 2011) p. 4: http://www.cfr.org/technology-and-foreign-policy/confronting-cyber-threat/p15577.

18.   Paul K. Kerr, John Rollins, Catherine A. Theohary, "The Stuxnet Computer Worm: Harbinger of an Emerging Warfare Capability" (December 9, 2010) CRS Report for Congress, p. 4.

19.   CBS News, "Fmr. CIA Head Calls Stuxnet Virus 'Good Idea'," (March 1, 2012) 60 Minutes. *http:// www.cbsnews.com/8301-18560_162-57388982/fmr-cia-head-calls-stuxnet-virus-good-idea/*.

20.   Masters, "Confronting the Cyber Threat," p. 4.

21.   Paul K. Kerr, John Rollins, Catherine A. Theohary, "Stuxnet" CRS Report, p. 5, citing Rodney Joffe, "Hunting an Industrial-Strength Computer Virus Around the Globe," PBS Newshour, (October 1, 2010) *http://www.pbs.org/newshour/bb/science/july-dec10/computervirus_10-01.html*.

22.   Paul K. Kerr, John Rollins, Catherine A. Theohary, CRS Report, p 6, citing Sean McGurk, then DHS's Acting Director of the National Cybersecurity and Communications Integration Center, as

Director of the European Network and Information Security Agency charac-
terized Stuxnet as "'a paradigm shift...Not only for its complexity and sophistication...the fact that perpetrators activated such an attack tool can be
considered as the 'first strike'...'[23]."

Others cast the significance of Stuxnet rather differently. Consider Farwell
and Rohozinski's evaluation: "Stuxnet is less sophisticated or advanced than
billed....less stealthy than much of the more advanced malware that criminals use...Nor particularly innovative." The authors conclude: "Stuxnet's core
capabilities and tradecraft...render it more of a Frankenstein patchwork of
existing tradecraft, code and best practices drawn from the global cybercrime community...". And therein lies the rub. As the authors further observe:
"Nearly every significant cyber event reported since 2005 involves tradecraft,
techniques and code tied to the cyber-crime community."

The Emerging Model In Cyber War

Viewed through this lens, the 2007 attacks against Estonia and the 2008
attacks against Georgia (both commonly discussed when the subject of cyber
war arises), "epitomize the emerging model." As Farwell and Rohozinski explain: "'Botnets' harnessed by Russian criminal operators effected the denial
of service that disrupted Estonia's national networks [including the websites/
operations of the President, parliament, ministries, banks, and other entities]
in May 2007. Botnets played a key role during the 2008 Russia-Georgia war,
serving Moscow as a strategic multiplier for its military campaign through
distributed denial of service (DDoS) attacks. Commercial-grade botnets originating from Russian cyberspace silenced Georgian government websites and
independent media, and disabled the government's ability to communicate to
its population. The DDoS attacks helped create an information vacuum that

---

quoted in Rob Margetta, "Stuxnet Could be a Harbinger of Threats to Come for US" *Congressional
Quarterly—Homeland Security*, November 17, 2010, *http://homeland.cq.com/hs/display.do?docid=3
764486&sourcetype=31&binderName=news-all.*

23. Paul K. Kerr, John Rollins, Catherine A. Theohary, CRS Report, p 8, citing Dr. Udo Helmbrecht,
as quoted in "EU Agency Analysis of 'Stuxnet' Malware: A Paradigm Shift in Threats and Critical
Information Infrastructure Protection," Press Release initial comment and brief, high level analysis
of the recent 'Stuxnet' attacks," October 7, 2010, *http://www.enisa.europa.eu/media/press-releases/
eu-agency-analysis-of-2018stuxnet2019-malware-a-paradigm-shift-in-threats-and-critical-informa-
tion-infrastructure-protection-1.*

paralyzed Georgia's civil administration. In each case, Russia denied official involvement. Yet the botnet attacks directly supported Russian state policy."[24]

The New Normal

If ubiquity is any indicator, then cyber war, conflict incorporating a cyber component, and antagonistic activity conducted by cyber means, are now the new norm. Bear in mind, too, that the examples discussed above represent a selected collection rather than a comprehensive survey. Perhaps the more fitting tool to make sense of these relatively recent developments may be a continuum or spectrum, rather than a series of hard and fast categories with little, if any, opportunity for bleeding between and among them. Of course the shades of gray inherent in a continuum render the matter of response more complicated, making it highly case-specific and circumstance-dependent, and thus requiring the careful exercise of judgment and discretion.

In any conflict situation, perceptions and perception management are crucial. As Lewis notes, the "calculus for deciding upon an attack is based on…perception of risks and rewards."[25] The ability to shape those perceptions forms the foundation of the capacity to deter, as well as compel, specific behaviors and actions on the part of adversaries. During the Cold War diverse constructs emerged, such as mutually assured destruction and arms control regimes, and functioned so as to lend a degree of stability to the international system. Signaling mechanisms and confidence-building measures, developed and refined over time, served this same end. Translating and transposing these features into and onto the cyber era is challenging, because a one-to-one correspondence between the two realms does not exist. For instance, the verification principle that underlay conventional arms control (and continues to do so) is far more vexing in the cyber context, which begs the question whether arms control could even "work in cyberspace." A further trenchant question is: "How does deterrence work in cyber war when our capabilities are secret and our own weapons undemonstrated?"[26] Indeed the present situation is a

---

24.   James P. Farwell and Rafal Rohozinski, "Stuxnet and the Future of Cyber War," *Survival: Global Politics and Strategy,* 53, no. 1 (2011) 23-40, at pp. 25-26. Reprinted above and in subsequent references by permission of the publisher, Taylor & Francis Ltd., *www.tandfonline.com.*

25.   Lewis, "Thresholds for Cyberwar," p. 6.

26.   Clarke, "War From Cyberspace," p. 36.

curious one, in that the US Government has specifically "called out" China and Russia (in the context of cyber espionage that rises to the level of strategic threat to the US national interest[27]) while at the same time choosing not to elaborate upon US cyber capabilities. It could be argued that this is in fact the worst of all worlds, in that the threat is specified—but it is not clear what the United States is doing about it. This relative absence of signaling is germane for reasons and purposes beyond the named parties, of course. Consider also Iran and North Korea, for example, which "are presumed to have access to sophisticated cyber capabilities[28]." Disincentives to future nefarious action on the part of the foregoing actors are needed to hold in check behaviors that could, and in some cases already do, significantly and negatively affect US national and economic security.

The US Government Draws Lines of Action and Behavior

Drawing clear lines in the silicon, in the form of a fulsome exposition of US redlines concerning actions, behaviors, and outcomes that simply will not be tolerated, could help render a measure of order unto a decidedly disorderly frontier. Still, the approach assumes that the adversary is a rational actor, who is in fact susceptible to deterrence. Yet that assumption may not hold. As Michael Singh writes with respect to Iran (though not specifically in connection to cyberspace), "even otherwise rational actors are prone to the occasional—and sometimes very consequential—irrational decision. And in an authoritarian state with an aging and increasingly isolated leader, this risk goes up exponentially."[29] Just because the system would be less than foolproof does not mean that the effort is not worth making, however, (indeed, the same could be said of the Cold War-era deterrence framework which likewise offered no iron-clad guarantee), as evidenced by certain steps that the United States has already taken in the proposed direction. As reported in November

---

27. NCIX Report, "Foreign Spies Stealing US Economic Secrets in Cyberspace".

28. Farwell, Rohozinski,, "Stuxnet and the Future of Cyber War," p 35. See also: "Google Admits Iranian Superiority in Cyber Warfare," *Radio Zamaneh* (December 18, 2011), *http://www.payvand. com/news/11/dec/1189.html*; and "Iran Among 5 States with Cyber Warfare Capabilities: US Institute," *Payvand News*, May 3, 2009, *http://www.payvand.com/news/09/may/1020.html*.

29. Michael Singh, "Is the Iranian Regime Rational?," *Foreign Policy*, February 23, 2012, *http://shadow. foreignpolicy.com/posts/2012/02/23/is_the_iranian_regime_rational*.

2011, DoD stated in a report submitted to Congress (in answer to legislators' queries posed earlier) that, "if directed by the President, it [DoD] will launch 'offensive cyber operations' in response to hostile acts. Those hostile acts may include 'significant cyber attacks directed against the US economy, government or military'[30]." Declaratory policy, supported by a strong and visible offensive capability, can help bring us closer to halting bad actors in their tracks.[31]

The *International Strategy for Cyberspace* issued by the White House in May 2011 reinforces the importance of clearly specified (and commonly agreed) notions of what is, and is not, acceptable behavior in cyberspace. In the section titled "Stability Through Norms," the Strategy states that the "United States will work with like-minded states to establish an environment of expectations, or norms of behavior, that ground foreign and defense policies and guide international partnerships." The Strategy speaks also to the criticality of resilience at both the domestic and international levels, meaning the ability to reconstitute quickly and effectively after an attack.[32] To the extent that a given system proves resilient, the attacker's goals (disruption, destruction, etc.) will be thwarted.[33] Resilience thus alters the "perceived benefits" portion of the equation, as conceived by potential future adversaries, and thereby holds a measure of capacity to deter them, presuming they are rational, meaning susceptible to cost/benefit analysis and logic.[34]

30. Ellen Nakashima, "Pentagon: Offensive Cyber Attacks Fair Game," *Washington Post*, November 15, 2011, citing "the report, obtained by *The Washington Post*." *http://www.washingtonpost.com/blogs/checkpoint-washington/post/pentagon-offensive-cyber-attacks-fair-game/2011/11/15/gIQAxQl-cON_blog.html?hpid=z3.*

31. Nick Hopkins, "Militarization of Cyberspace: How the Global Power Struggle Moved Online," *The Guardian*, April 16, 2012, *http://www.guardian.co.uk/technology/2012/apr/16/militarisation-of-cyberspace-power-struggle.*

32. White House, *International Strategy for Cyberspace: Prosperity, Security, and Openness in a Networked World*, May 2011, 9, 19, *http://www.whitehouse.gov/sites/default/files/rss_viewer/international_strategy_for_cyberspace.pdf.*

33. Statement of Frank J. Cilluffo before the US Congress Joint Economic Committee, "Wired World: Cybersecurity and the US Economy," (June 21, 2001) *http://www.gwumc.edu/hspi/policy/testimony6.21.01_cilluffo.pdf.*

34. Lt Col Scott W. Beidleman, USAF, "Defining and Deterring Cyber War" (2009) US Army War College, Strategy Research Project ("submitted in partial fulfillment of the requirements of the Master of Strategic Studies Degree"), p. 16, citing Robert H. Dorff and Joseph R. Cerami, "Deterrence and Competitive Strategies: A New Look at an Old Concept," in *Deterrence in the 21st Century*, ed. by Max G. Manwaring (London: Frank Cass, 2001), p. 111.

DoD released its own Strategy for Operating in Cyberspace in July 2011.[35] The unclassified version of the document was notably devoid of reference to offense, however, focusing instead (as we wrote at the time) on "the use of sensors and other means to support 'active defenses' intended to detect and disrupt cyber attacks."[36] With this in mind, then-Vice Chairman of the Joint Chiefs of Staff, General James Cartwright, commented to reporters: "the Pentagon currently focuses 90% of its cybersecurity effort on defense and 10% on offense. A better balance for the US Government as a whole would be 50-50."[37] Calibration in this sense relates to whether the US posture is robust enough vis-à-vis the full spectrum of operations on the cyber conflict continuum. The question of preparedness is not limited to DoD either, given the confluence between cyber crime and other antagonistic activity in cyber-space, up to and including war—which brings in a civilian dimension, incorporating law enforcement authorities and other non-military US Government entities as well as the private sector, in whose hands the majority of US critical infrastructure lies. Against this complicated background, a strategy of layered defense led by US Cyber Command and executed in partnership with DHS, the Department of Justice, and others, is sound practice.

The animating principle of layered defense is to identify and neutralize threat(s) as far away from US shores as possible. The outermost layer relies upon "government intelligence capabilities to provide 'highly specialized active defenses'."[38] As General Cartwright explained in a February 2012 speech, active defense includes (but is not limited to) "real-time updates about attacks," "immediate pushback," and "possibly shutting off your network until it's safe to be on." One related, essential but presently unresolved, question he noted is: "how active will we allow ourselves to be?" Put bluntly, the National Security Agency (NSA) possesses powerful monitoring capabilities that, for reasons of

---

35. Department of Defense, *Department of Defense Strategy for Operating in Cyberspace*, July 2011, *http://www.defense.gov/news/d20110714cyber.pdf*.

36. Frank J. Cilluffo and Sharon L. Cardash, "Commentary: Defense cyber strategy avoids tackling the most critical issues" July 28, 2011, *http://www.nextgov.com/nextgov/ng_20110728_3046. php?oref=topnews*.

37. Lolita C. Baldor, "Pentagon to publish strategy for cyberspace war" *The Associated Press*, July 14, 2011, *http://www.navytimes.com/news/2011/07/ap-pentagon-publish-strategy-cyberspace-war-071411/*.

38. Michael Stevens, "Defense Department's Cyberwar Credibility Gap," (August 30, 2010) citing then-Undersecretary of Defense, William J. Lynn. *http://www.securityweek.com/defense-departments-cyberwar-credibility-gap* "Recent Developments in Cyber Warfare." Event hosted by The Hudson Institute, Washington, DC (February 13, 2012).

policy and law, have been directed abroad. Intelligence Community support for active defense, moreover, by definition involves a measure of "intermixing" between the intelligence and national defense functions. The "challenge" inheres in the fact that "the two have different missions," yet are each dependent upon the other.[39]

On the law enforcement side, there is an expressed recognition of the gravity of the problem. FBI Director Robert Mueller stated in March 2012 that, "in the not too distant future, we anticipate that the cyber threat will pose the No. 1 threat to our country."[40] In earlier testimony he stated further that, "[w]e will increasingly put emphasis on addressing cyber threats in all of their variations…The personnel in the bureau have the equipment, the capability, the skill, the experience to address those threats."[41] The Justice Department's Inspector General begged to differ, though, concluding in a report issued almost concurrently that "many FBI field offices do not have the training, skills, and support to investigate cyber attacks." More specifically, "[t]he audit found that 36% of the FBI's cyber squad agents interviewed 'reported that they lacked the networking and counterintelligence expertise necessary to investigate national security [computer] intrusion cases'." The report went on to suggest that this skills deficit was linked "in part to the FBI's rotation policy, in which agents are transferred among field offices without assessment of their cyber skills. As a result, a cyber agent may be transferred to a field office and perform work not related to his or her expertise. And the agent replacing the cyber agent may have no special cyber knowledge or training."[42]

As the principal interface between the private sector and US Government in this context, DHS occupies a pivotal position. The manner in which that role will continue to evolve remains somewhat unclear as of the time we write this chapter. Competing bills before Congress were principally at odds

39. General Cartwright, remarks at Hudson Institute.
40. Michael Cooney, "FBI Says Cyber Attacks Will Soon be Top Threat to US Security," *Network World US*, Mar 5, 2012, *http://www.computerworlduk.com/news/security/3342007/fbi-says-cyberattacks-will-soon-be-top-threat-to-us-security/*.
41. "Cyberwar: Pentagon takes on Cyber Enemies, Other Agencies," (Nov 8, 2011), citing Director Mueller's testimony before a Senate Judiciary Committee hearing, in June 2011, to extend his term in office. *http://www.defenseindustrydaily.com/cyberwar-department-defense-doctrine-response-06931/* Used with permission of Watershed Publishing; permission conveyed through Olivier Travers.
42. "Cyberwar: Pentagon takes on Cyber Enemies, Other Agencies," citing "The Federal Bureau of Investigation's Ability to Address the National Security Cyber Intrusion Threat," US Department of Justice, Office of the Inspector General, Audit Division, Audit Report 11-22 (April 2011), *http://www.justice.gov/oig/reports/FBI/a1122r.pdf*.

over whether DHS should be accorded the power to regulate privately owned critical infrastructure by developing—together with industry—and enforcing compliance with minimal cybersecurity standards designed to reduce vulnerabilities and thereby protect against "catastrophic damage to life, the economy or national security."[43] It may be that the business case alone (for implementation of the requisite best practices) has failed to incentivize or persuade, or perhaps that case has not been made and thoughtfully considered by all relevant parties. Either way, we would submit that this is an area where market failure is an unacceptable outcome, and thus DHS should be given the chance to help move the ball forward. Raising the bar through the careful creation and implementation of standards—ideally initiated and driven by the private sector—that could save lives, and help maintain trust and confidence in the system should that "very bad day" materialize, is an important aspect of layered defense. It could also be argued that we owe it to DoD to make best efforts before the fact, since steps taken to mitigate damage could correspondingly reduce the need for risk-laden response measures after the fact that could put members of the US military in harm's way. Bear in mind, too, that DoD depends on civilian infrastructure to project power and deploy forces. DHS, furthermore, has produced its own strategy, Blueprint for a Secure Cyber Future, as a companion piece to the International Strategy and DoD's own. The Blueprint reinforces the need for resilience, and envisions the twin advancement of economic interests and national security.[44]

Cyber Conflict—Looking Ahead

Looking ahead, the challenge is to determine how best to balance the many and varied competing equities in the cyber domain: the public versus the private sector, the military versus the non-military sector, war versus crime, offense versus defense, attack versus exploit, the domestic versus the international dimension—and of course the multiple points of intersection between the elements in each dyad, as well as the intersections between and among the dyads themselves. There are no easy answers. For instance, some contend

---

43. Tim Starks, "Senate Cyber Bills Split at Security Standards," *CQ Today Online News,* Mar 2, 2012, *http://homeland.cq.com/hs/display.do?docid=4039478&sourcetype=6&binderName=news-all.*

44. "Blueprint for a Secure Cyber Future: The Cybersecurity Strategy for the Homeland Security Enterprise," (Nov 2011), pp. 6-7. *http://www.dhs.gov/xlibrary/assets/nppd/blueprint-for-a-secure-cyber-future.pdf.*

the best defense is a good offense,[45] whereas others would argue that offensive measures generate a significant risk of blowback—think Stuxnet, now out in the wild for all to see and potentially use, being turned back on its creator(s).[46] What seems clear, though, is that airing these difficult issues in the public square, with an eye to elucidating options and exposing their respective consequences and implications to sunlight, is itself a productive step forward. After all, cyber attacks are intended to undermine trust and confidence in the system, so perhaps one way to effectively fight fire with fire is to call the key questions, discuss and debate them transparently, and then proceed to implement those consensus goals that emerge. Rhetoric translated into action, and backed up by resources, builds credibility as well as capability and capacity. All would serve the United States well in this context.

Granted, some would argue that the threat in and from cyberspace has been overstated[47]. Reporting on the 2012 RSA security conference, Zetter noted panelists' skepticism: "Despite recent rhetoric…that Anonymous, Iran, Al Qaeda and others are bent on destroying US critical infrastructure in a cyber attack, they lack the capability to do so…". Conversely, panelists suggested that those with capability (China for example) "lack the intent" as they are aware of their own matching vulnerability.[48] The line between exploit and attack is thin, however, with the two being distinguishable only by intent. In other words, the exploit provides the tool(s) for attack, which may be held in reserve until the adversary deems the time is ripe for use. At least one RSA panelist conceded the point: "'We don't want to make the mistake of underestimating our opponents, in particular the high-end opponents…They're doing the reconnaissance and they have capabilities'."[49]

---

45. See for example Isaac R. Porche III, Jerry M. Sollinger, Shawn McKay, A Cyberworm that Knows no Boundaries, RAND Occasional Paper, Prepared for the Office of the Secretary of Defense, 2011, at p. xi: "The best defense includes an offense."

46. James Farwell and Rafal Rohozinski, p. 36: "Strategies for using cyber weapons like Stuxnet need to take into account that adversaries may attempt to turn them back against us." Citing Mark Clayton, "Stuxnet 'Virus' Could Be Altered to Attack US Facilities, Report Warns," *Christian Science Monitor*, Dec 15 2010.

47. See for example Thomas Rid, "Think Again: Cyber War," *Foreign Policy* (Mar/Apr 2012), contending that "[v]irtual conflict is still more hype than reality." *http://www.foreignpolicy.com/articles/2012/02/27/cyberwar?page=0,0.*

48. Kim Zetter, "DHS, not NSA, Should Lead Cybersecurity, Pentagon Official Says," *Wired*, March 1, 2012, *http://www.wired.com/threatlevel/2012/03/rsa-security-panel.*

49. Zetter, "DHS, not NSA, Should Lead," citing Jim Lewis, Senior Fellow and Program Director with the Center for Strategic and International Studies.

Under the circumstances that prevail, we think it better to err on the side of caution. Now is the time to reflect upon fundamental operating principles, formulate and implement doctrine (for defense and offense), and work our way through these challenging issues together. The nation deserves, and should demand, as much. This is not to say that we can, or will, attain perfection. The adversary must only succeed once—this, in a context where DoD alone has been facing tens of thousands of attacks per year. An ambitious yet attainable goal may, therefore, be "the 80% solution," which would entail raising standards and implementing best practices across government and critical industries so as to deny or at least minimize benefit to would-be attackers, while at the same time freeing up resources (human, technological, and capital) to focus on the most advanced and persistent threats, and tailor responses accordingly, including to specific actors. The latter exercise will require the United States to draw on a multiplicity of instruments, to meet and defeat the variegated nature of the threat. Cyber defense and offense are two sides of a single coin, and unless both sides are solidly crafted, the structural integrity of the whole will suffer. In addition, cyber capabilities should be smartly and deeply integrated into the larger portfolio of US capabilities. As General Cartwright has suggested, "don't come at the adversary with just one trick. Instead create the opportunity for surprise/advantage."[50] Cyberspace may be a boon for asymmetry and newly empowered non-state actors, including individuals, with hostile or malicious intent—but it is worth remembering that even actors like "al Qaeda, Hamas, Hezbollah, and other terrorist groups" have a "decision calculus" that "could be changed by creating expectations that cyber aggression might be an uncertain or costly act."[51]

Postscript

Since the time of initial writing the cyber terrain has continued to evolve and rapidly. Press reports suggest that the Pentagon is ramping up the development and acquisition of cyber weapons,[52] and that Cyber Command may become

---

50. General Cartwright, remarks at Hudson Institute.
51. Richard L. Kugler, "Deterrence of Cyber Attacks," chap. 13, pp. 309-340 at pp. 326, 338. In *Cyber Power and National Security,* edited by Franklin D. Kramer, Stuart H. Starr, and Larry K. Wentz, (Center for Technology and National Security Policy, National Defense University, NDU Press, Potomac Books, Inc: Washington, DC, 2009) 1st edition.
52. Ellen Nakashima, "Pentagon to Fast-track Cyber Weapons Acquisition," *Washington Post* (April 9, 2012) *http://www.washingtonpost.com/world/national-security/pentagon-to-fast-track-cyberweapons-acquisition/2012/04/09/gIQAuwb76S_print.html.*

a combatant command.[53] Further reports have identified the United States and Israel as partners who allegedly worked together on Stuxnet—a digital weapon intended to disrupt Iran's efforts to acquire a nuclear weapon—said to have been part of a larger initiative (dubbed "Olympic Games") to thwart that very end.[54] Against this background, editorial boards have begun to argue that there is a distinct need for a national conversation on the guiding principles that will inform US cyber policy and practice.[55] We echo that call. The cyber challenge requires a whole-of-society response. Even the most powerful country is only as strong as its weakest link in this context. The need for doctrine and frameworks to govern and guide actions and behaviors in this area is recognized also by others. Indeed, even Russia and China, despite the challenges that they pose in present context, have engaged in discussions with the United States recently—respectively on a possible cyber hotline which would take the Cold War era's nuclear hotline as model,[56] and in military talks focused on cyber war issues.[57] Airing and working through these crucial and difficult matters with key actors internal and external to the United States is the first step toward deliberate and deliberative policy and practice. These conversations must continue in earnest if we as a nation are to get where we need to be.

53. Ellen Nakashima, "Military Leaders Seek Higher Profile for Pentagon's Cyber Command Unit," *Washington Post*, May 1, 2012, *http://www.washingtonpost.com/world/national-security/military-officials-push-to-elevate-cyber-unit-to-full-combatant-command-status/2012/05/01/gIQAUud1uT_print.html*.

54. David E. Sanger, "Obama Order Sped Up Wave of Cyber Attacks against Iran," *New York Times*, June 1, 2012, *http://www.nytimes.com/2012/06/01/world/middleeast/obama-ordered-wave-of-cyberattacks-against-iran.html?pagewanted=all*.

55. Editorial Board, "What is America's Cyber War Policy?" *Washington Post*, June 16, 2012, *http://www.washingtonpost.com/opinions/what-is-americas-cyberwar-policy/2012/06/16/gIQAkxgnhV_story.html?tid=wp_ipad*.

56. Ellen Nakashima, "In US-Russia Deal, Nuclear Communication System May be Used for Cybersecurity," *Washington Post*, Apr 26, 2012, *http://www.washingtonpost.com/world/national-security/in-us-russia-deal-nuclear-communication-system-may-be-used-for-cybersecurity/2012/04/26/gIQAT521iT_print.html*.

57. Jane Perlez, "Unease Mounting, China and US to Open Military Talks," *New York Times*, May 1, 2012, *http://www.nytimes.com/2012/05/02/world/asia/unease-mounting-china-and-us-to-open-military-talks.html?_r=2*.

#CyberDoc: No Borders - No Boundaries

CHAPTER 4

The Role of the Private Sector in Cyber

Randall M. Fort

One of the most challenging aspects of cyber is the appropriate role for the private sector. One of the first challenges is to understand that the private sector is not a monolith; one can, in fact, reasonably divide the private sector into a number of constituent groups, including the commercial, (both large-cap companies and small businesses), government-regulated, the government contractor (including, notably, the Defense Industrial Base [DIB]), the academic, the non-profit, and the individual. The private sector can be further divided by relevant sector of function or activity—in fact, the US Government has identified 18 specific sectors, e.g., Banking and Finance, Communications, Chemical, and so forth.[1] Each of those groups has different views, concerns and needs regarding cyber, which may or may not align with all the other groups. For the purposes of this chapter, we shall define the private sector as

---

1. United States Department of Homeland Security, "Homeland Security Presidential Directive 7: Critical Infrastructure Identification, Prioritization, and Protection," December 17, 2003.

Randall M. Fort is Director of Corporate Programs Security for Raytheon. He joined the Engineering, Technology and Mission Assurance leadership team in July 2009. In his leadership role, Fort is responsible for partnering with Raytheon's customer community to elevate programs security as a strategic business enabler. Fort's enterprise guidance ensures the integration of information, systems and people with customers so that our products and capabilities provide value worldwide. He is knowledgeable in the essential coordination of physical and cyber security, a key discriminator for delivering comprehensive solutions for customers and for protecting Raytheon products and systems. Prior to Raytheon, Fort was employed at the US State Department as the assistant secretary of state for Intelligence and Research, from 2006 to 2009. He managed the production and dissemination of all-source intelligence analysis for the secretary of state and other senior policymakers. Fort headed the department's Cyber Policy Group and the Bureau of Intelligence and Research. Before his US State Department appointment, Mr. Fort was director of Global Security for Goldman

those companies comprising the "Fortune 500" list of publicly traded companies. This is not to dismiss the cyber concerns and requirements of the other groups listed above; it is rather, an attempt to circumscribe the issue to a reasonable set of entities and focus on the most salient issues.

A second challenge is to describe the cyber issue in a way that explains both government and private sector perspectives. A first step is to define cyberspace, which can be described as follows:

> "Cyberspace exists solely as lines of communication. It has no other expression. Through cyberspace travel the command, control, communications, intelligence, surveillance, and reconnaissance of armies and the essential trade and commerce of nations. Cyberspace is the global 'center of gravity' for all aspects of national power, spanning the economic, technological, diplomatic and military capabilities a nation might possess. Cyberspace has become, as Clausewitz said regarding a center of gravity, *'the hub of all power and movement on which everything depends'*" (emphasis added)[2].

Thus, the government and private sector find their interests and equities inextricably intertwined—national security and corporate security, military operations and business operations all coexist in the same cyberspace.

---

2. David Aucsmith, "A Theory of War in the Cyber Domain: An Historical Perspective," paper, February 12, 2012, p. 17.

Sachs, from 1996 to 2006, where he was responsible for all aspects of physical security risk management, including investigations, travel safety, executive protection, risk analysis, access control, perimeter protection and security technology. He also served as chief of staff to the president and co-chief operating officer of the firm. From 1993 to 1996, Mr. Fort was director of Special Projects at TRW, Inc. for two of the corporation's Space and Defense operating groups. Fort's private sector experience was preceded by 11 years of additional service in the US Government. He served as the deputy assistant secretary for Functional Analysis and Research in the Bureau of Intelligence and Research at the US Department of State from 1989 to 1993. He was also the special assistant to the secretary for National Security and director of the Office of Intelligence Support at the US Department of the Treasury from 1987 to 1989. Prior to moving to Treasury, he served as a professional staff member, first as assistant director and subsequently as deputy executive director, of the President's Foreign Intelligence Advisory Board at the White House from 1982 to 1987. (The views expressed herein are solely those of the author and do not in any way represent an endorsement by his current or previous employers.)

Unlike many national security issues, however, the private sector finds itself on the "front line" of the cyber challenge, for a host of reasons. The first is ownership—there are no authoritative figures, but estimates are frequently cited that the private sector owns between 80-95% of the infrastructure that comprises cyberspace: the routers, servers, cables, software and other elements that are the sum and substance of the Internet. While no one knows for sure just how much of cyber infrastructure is in private hands, it is clearly the preponderant share. It is the private sector that owns and therefore controls the technological foundation upon which all functions of modern society, including essential government responsibilities like national security, are utterly dependent.

With ownership comes significant fiduciary responsibility on the part of all companies, both those that own or control significant cyber infrastructure, such as Internet Service Providers or telecommunications companies; as well as companies that have created and/or acquired cyber capabilities to serve their own needs. Their responsibility to shareholders is legally very clear and financially very compelling. In contrast, their responsibility to take on cybersecurity requirements outside their immediate needs to protect their assets, intellectual property (IP) and shareholder value is vague and uncertain. While certain cybersecurity standards may be considered good public policy, they may or may not constitute good business practices.

Third, the private sector is the source of the creativity, innovation and investment that is driving the technological growth and use of cyber capabilities. While the US Government may have been the original "inventor of the Internet"—albeit with active collaboration and assistance from private sector companies like BBN—today it is the private sector that leads in developing cyber products, tools and applications as well as the infrastructure to support them. And that leadership has been astonishingly successful—smart phones, smart pads and a host of other mobile devices; applications created by the millions and downloaded by the tens of billions; digital storage available to individuals by the gigabyte and to companies by the terabyte; comprehensive search engines; cloud computing; and many others. The pipeline for these technological developments is global and immense, relentlessly proving the essence of "Moore's Law" (that a microchip will double in capacity every ~18 months at constant cost).

The private sector is not altruistic—it has developed and implemented these cyber technologies for the purposes of making a profit. In doing so, untold billions, likely trillions of dollars of value, as measured by sales, profits, and market capitalizations, have been created. For example, companies with names few had scarcely heard of less than a decade ago—Facebook, Google—or which didn't even exist—Twitter, Groupon, Zynga, among many others—have gone or soon will go public creating tens of thousands of jobs and significant wealth for shareholders. Apps are being written, data is being aggregated and analyzed in new ways, social media channels are being created and exploited, all at market or "Internet speed."

That track record of extraordinary market creativity, speed and agility stands in stark contrast to the US Government's information technology (IT) competence and capability. Former Deputy Secretary of Defense (DEPSECDEF) William Lynn stated that, "On average, it takes the Pentagon 81 months to make a new computer system operational after it is first funded."[3] That's 6.75 years, or 4.5 Moore's Law cycles to complete an acquisition for even simple, commercial-off-the-shelf (COTS) IT equipment. By contrast, Lynn pointed out in his article that it took Apple only 24 months to develop the iPhone.[4] Further, Director of National Intelligence James Clapper noted in Congressional testimony that "We currently face a cyber environment where emerging technologies are developed and implemented faster than governments can keep pace."[5]

To be sure, there are pockets of IT excellence in the Federal Government; there are also some special authorities which allow some government agencies, especially in the Intelligence Community, to circumvent the slow, onerous acquisition rules under which most elements of the US Government labor. Moreover, DoD is seeking to reform its IT development and acquisition rules to allow for more expedient purchase of IT equipment and capabilities, according to a recent announcement by current DEPSECDEF Ashton Carter.[6] In addition, DoD has recently established a "Cyber Investment Management

---

3. William J. Lynn, "Defending a New Domain," *Foreign Affairs* 89, no. 5 (Sept/Oct 2010), p. 107.
4. *Ibid*, p. 107.
5. James R. Clapper, Director of National Intelligence, "Unclassified Statement for the Record on the Worldwide Threat Assessment of the US Intelligence Community for the Senate Committee on Armed Services," February 16, 2012, p. 7.
6. Amber Corrin, "DOD restructures oversight of department-wide IT," *Federal Computer Week*, February 17, 2012, *http://fcw.com/articles/2012/02/17/dod-memo-restructures-it-governance.aspx*.

Board" (CIMB) to oversee a more rapid acquisition process for cyber capabilities.[7] But those are exceptions, and the contrast remains between a private sector acutely responsive to competitive market pressures, constantly at the cutting edge of technology, with rapid delivery of new capabilities; and the government, burdened by onerous rules and a sclerotic acquisition process, inevitably lagging behind state-of-the-art technology by many generations.

Then there is the nature of cyber itself—that it is a separate domain. There has been some debate about whether cyber is a fifth "domain," after land, sea, air and space; DoD certainly considers it as such, with former DEPSECDEF Lynn declaring in 2010, "As a doctrinal matter, the Pentagon has formally recognized cyberspace as a new domain of warfare."[8] Accepting that definition, it is the only artificial domain, and it is the only one which has infrastructure presence and uses in all the other domains. Moreover, cyber is a very crowded domain—government and private sector, corporate and non-profit, nation-state and individual, foreign and domestic all share the common infrastructure for their respective purposes. If the military considers cyber to be an operational domain, then they will be undertaking their missions in the very same space and as part of the same infrastructure as private sector activity. When one thinks of sea battles or air-to-air warfare, one doesn't think about those engagements occurring in New York Harbor or in the airspace over LAX, but that would be one way to think about cyber engagements that used common infrastructure to conduct military operations.

The private sector may also serve as a useful harbinger for future cyber threats to military systems. Air Force Chief Scientist Mark Maybury recently stated that "there are linked parallels among cyber attacks on civilians and military aircraft, ships and ground vehicles."[9] Attack tools and techniques may first be used on civil systems that employ similar technical architectures and hence vulnerabilities, so the government can learn useful lessons from private sector experience.

To the degree that cyberspace is contested ground, either for conducting espionage ("Computer Network Exploitation," or CNE) or warfare ("Computer Network Attack," or CNA), then there are no secure rear areas or safe harbors—everyone is on the front line. And it really doesn't matter if the "attackers" are

---

7.   "DOD Establishes Senior Board, Dual Track for Rapid Cyber Acquisition," *Inside Defense*, April 12, 2012.

8.   Lynn, "Defending a New Domain," p. 101.

9.   "Civilian Cyberattacks Could Foreshadow Military Threat," *Aviation Week*, March 28, 2012.

foreign nation-states, criminal groups, terrorists of ideologues; the tools and techniques are similar and the lack of easy attribution of those attacks makes intent unclear. In any event, cyber attacks have targeted both government and private sector computer systems, and both have shown themselves to be vulnerable to such attacks. But the perspectives of the government and the private sector are different. For the government, cyberspace is a channel to conduct routine business and communications functions, as in the private sector; but it is also an operational domain for collecting intelligence or conducting and/or facilitating military operations. In addition, the government looks at the entirety of our nation's cyber infrastructure and dependencies, and thinks strategically about the threats to that capability. In particular, they are worried about a proverbial "Pearl Harbor," a surprise attack that damages, degrades or destroys critical national cyber infrastructure, and hence military capability.

The private sector is not structured or incentivized to take a national or strategic view of cyberspace. For most companies, cyber offers the platform, tools and channels for efficiently conducting business. Their chief concern is to protect and maintain their key business functions. Also, since most information is digital and accessible via cyber, that means it is vulnerable. As we have seen, there is a massive effort by nation-states, criminals and activist groups to access and steal, disrupt or expose data from any and all entities that own and control data. The private sector in particular has strong interest in protecting their proprietary IP and other sensitive information, both to preserve the value of that information, as well as to preserve their reputation as a reliable and trustworthy steward of sensitive customer data. But the private sector is as challenged as the government in balancing utility vs. security—as DNI Clapper noted, "owing to market incentives, innovation in functionality is outpacing innovation in security, and neither public nor private sector has been successful at fully implementing existing best [security] practices."[10]

Confusion about the appropriate balance between the government and private sector's cyber roles and responsibilities is reflected in the current vigorous debate in Congress. As of June 2012, there were at least 43 pieces of pending legislation dealing with some aspect of cyberspace, including education, privacy, data handling, information sharing and regulation. There may or may not have been any final legislative decision by the time this book is

---

10. Clapper, "Unclassified Statement for the Record," p. 7.

published. The confusion is understandable given the uncertainty about the impacts and effectiveness of many of the proposed laws.

That uncertainty is also exacerbated by the volatility of the underlying technology. Congress is confronted with rapid increases in cyber capabilities, computer speeds, new products and social media tools and techniques for which is there is no clear understanding in policy and doctrine, let alone the law. But the continuing deluge of reports of cyber hacking by both private groups such as Anonymous and LulzSec and nation-states against a wide range of government and private sector data bases has created political pressure for the Congress to do something to mitigate the considerable and growing cyber threats.

Two general legislative approaches or perspectives have come into focus: regulation vs. information sharing. Proposed Senate legislation, the "Lieberman-Collins" bill (S.2105), requires a more intrusive regulatory regime on key sectors of the US economy, to be monitored and controlled by the Department of Homeland Security (DHS). Alternatively, the House Permanent Select Committee on Intelligence (HPSCI), among others, has proposed an alternative approach (H.R.3523)—more fulsome information sharing between the government and the private sector.

As of now, there is no clear consensus about the correct approach. For its part, the private sector is concerned about an overly-intrusive or specific regulatory regime. This concern is larger than just government regulation of cybersecurity: "…no corner of information technology is safe from what Joseph Schumpeter famously called 'creative destruction.' That, in turn, should remind us that the public policy governing what is acceptable to do in the marketplace and what's not is based on assumptions that rarely apply to the industries powering innovation and growth in advanced industrial economies."[11] That's true in spades in the cyber arena. The technology and hence the threat changes too fast to allow for exact, prescriptive rules and regulations for cybersecurity standards. Even now, the previously effective "signatures based" defenses—that is, defenses against the "signature" of known malware or cyber intrusion capabilities—have become obsolete. The most sophisticated cyber operators are already *inside* their target networks, and hence cause or leave no particular signature for their nefarious activities. Mandating protection against specific signatures will be fighting yesterday's battle, to little or no

---

11. Robert Hahn, "Google's Turn to Quake?" *Wall Street Journal*, April 5, 2012, p. A-13.

avail. The government has acknowledged their more reactive cybersecurity approach—in budget testimony before the Senate Armed Services Committee, Gen. Keith Alexander, commander of US Cyber Command and Director of the National Security Agency (NSA) spoke of the need to become more proactive, saying "Today we are in the forensic mode. I think we should be in the prevention mode."[12] In other words, the government should be less a forensic pathologist explaining why the patient died and more a doctor treating the disease and helping the patient get well.

A more novel cyber defense strategy that is evolving is to assume that cyber hackers will gain access to a system, and then develop measures to limit their ability to exfiltrate information they are seeking to steal—a sort of cyber "roach motel." This approach holds significant technical promise, but is not a topic of current general debate—most cybersecurity discussions still revolve around a signatures-based defense. In any event, it is the private sector that is at the forefront of developing those new cybersecurity techniques.

A cyber regulatory regime may serve only to drive affected companies to configure their cybersecurity efforts not to address the real threat, but to comply with the formal regulations. And those regulations will likely be ineffective in defending against cyber attacks—the government simply will be unable to identify a threat and define and implement a regulatory standard fast enough to keep up with the speed of the threat. The regulatory response will almost certainly be obsolete and therefore ultimately futile at securing the cyber activities of the regulated. Private sector companies could be in complete compliance with the government-imposed regulations and still be seriously vulnerable to cyber intrusions.

Moreover, there is great uncertainty about how much the proposed cybersecurity legislative mandates will cost, both for the government and the private sector. Cost-benefit studies of the impact of cybersecurity measures have been problematic, and there is apparently no agreement on any particular methodology for conducting such studies.[13] Cybersecurity runs the risk of becoming another in a long line of "unfunded government mandates." There is ultimately a concern that onerous government regulation of the Internet and cyber technology will stifle and retard the creation and realization of new

---

12. William Jackson, "DOD vs. DHS: Who Should Mind the US' Cyber Defense?" *Defense Systems. com*, March 27, 2012.

13. Jody Westby, "Cyber Legislation Will Cost Businesses and Hurt Economy," *www.forbes.com*, February 27, 2012, *http://www.forbes.com/sites/jodywestby/2012/02/27/cyber-legislation-will-cost-businesses-and-hurt-economy/2/*.

information technologies. An overly restrictive cybersecurity regime could "kill the goose that lays the golden eggs," causing deleterious economic impacts, including the loss of jobs, investment, and the US lead in developing and deploying new technologies.

Information sharing between the government and the private sector has been offered as a better alternative to regulation, but it is not an easy or straightforward process, and it is certainly not a panacea to solve all cybersecurity threats. There is, after all, a historic tension between the government and private sector—taxation, regulations, and oversight all combine to create a certain skepticism when the private sector hears, "Hi, we're from the government and we're here to help." Moreover, unlike typical national security issues, this is a two way street—the private sector's knowledge of the threat is substantial and effectively equal to the governments. Those private sector firms most targeted by cyber intruders have considerable independent knowledge of those threats and long experience dealing with them. Financial firms in particular have been dealing with cyber intrusion attempts for as long as they've been online—the "Willie Sutton Rule" (robbing banks because that's where the money is) applies in cyberspace as well as in the real world. So the private sector brings considerable experience, information and expertise to the table in any cyber sharing relationship.

Information sharing with the private sector is not an easy process for the government, as well. The US Government tends to classify or over-classify just about everything in the national security area, including information on cyber intrusions and/or attacks, especially so-called "zero-day exploits" (that is, cyber attacks that are being used for the very first time). The government has good reason to keep secret some of what it knows about zero-days and other malware, as it does not want to compromise its own offensive cyber capabilities (those capabilities have only recently been acknowledged[14]). But logically, the "bad guys" already know about the zero-day exploits or other malware sets—they are already using them to conduct their cyber intrusions; so not sharing that information means only the victims will be ignorant about how they were attacked. In addition, the government will need to think carefully about the "business model" for sharing information with the private sector; if the government attempts to package threat information and sell it to private

---

14. Department of Defense, *Department of Defense Cyberspace Policy Report—A Report to Congress Pursuant to the National Defense Authorization Act for Fiscal Year 2011, Section 934*, November 2011, p. 5.

sector entities for a fee, many of the latter will likely reject the proposition, especially those companies which make an active contribution to the cyber threat knowledge base.

In any event, it's not clear that government-provided information about cyber vulnerabilities is particularly unique. In 2011 the Department of Defense conducted a pilot information sharing program with a number of companies that comprise the DIB. An independent review of that project by Carnegie Mellon University reported that the project achieved only mixed success; apparently, "only one percent of the attacks were detected using 'NSA threat data that the companies did not already have themselves'…the value of the threat signatures 'was not conclusively demonstrated.'"[15] But at the least, DoD did establish a format and process for sharing information with the private sector, and it's likely that the quality and utility of that information sharing—in both directions—will improve with time and experience. In fact, DoD has indicated that they will soon complete a set of rules to expand the number of participating companies from 37 to 200.[16]

What does the private sector need from the government for improved cybersecurity? Large companies with significant technology infrastructure and exposure have a good understanding of the cyber threat, because they routinely are confronted by that threat. Companies with less investment in cybersecurity will require greater levels of threat warning information from the government and/or other private sector entities to focus their defensive measures. All companies, however, would benefit from having access to what the government knows about cyber threats, and that information would need to be detailed and timely to be effective. Additionally, to ensure effective and timely sharing, the private sector would appreciate having clear legal protection for active cooperation among businesses, especially if they are in the same industry—the anti-trust issues arising from cybersecurity cooperation are unclear. The private sector would also benefit from liability protection for taking actions based on shared information to respond to cyber threats that may impact operations or lead to the disclosure of personal or proprietary information.

Can there be a genuine public-private partnership for cybersecurity? There have already been a number of useful steps in that direction. Informally,

15. Jason Healey, "Cyber Security Legislation Should Force US Government to Listen Less and Speak More," *The Atlantic*, March 23, 2012, *http://www.theatlantic.com/technology/archive/2012/03/cybersecurity-legislation-should-force-us-government-to-listen-less-and-speak-more/254491/*.

16. Jim Wolf, "US Eyes Broader Cyber-threat Pact with Companies," *Reuters*, April 24, 2012, *http://www.reuters.com/article/2012/04/24/us-cyber-usa-companies-idUSBRE83N18D20120424*.

there has been considerable interaction between Chief Information Security Officers (CISOs) on both sides, and that cooperation will likely continue. But that is limited to a relative few major companies in the DIB or other key industries with the patience and wherewithal to develop those government relationships. Also, the government has sponsored a number of Information Sharing and Analysis Centers (ISACs) since 1999, and they have evolved into a productive two-way channel for "sharing critical, authoritative information across a range of industry players...instantly."[17] The ISACs have proven to be a good model for sharing information and discussing cooperative measures in key sectors of the economy.

There have also been suggestions to establish a non-government "clearing house" to serve as a secure repository of cybersecurity information that could be contributed to and shared among both the government and private sector.[18] By operating outside of official government channels, concerns about government intrusion into private networks or having unauthorized access to private information could be mitigated. There have even been proposed technical solutions that would provide high levels of privacy assurance for shared information.[19] Such an effort would be an extension of the existing sharing mechanisms, and would continue to build trust and confidence between the interested parties.

Even without formal laws or government regulatory prescriptions, the private sector is already taking steps to improve the safety and security of cyberspace. For example, there was the IT company coalition that formed to counter the "Conficker botnet" (a collection of compromised computers connected to the Internet) in 2009.[20] In early January of this year, email service providers united to back a joint effort to reduce "phishing" emails (which attempt to trick recipients into thinking the emails originate from a legitimate source).[21] Microsoft also led efforts to shut down servers controlling a

---

17. Financial Services Information Sharing and Analysis Center homepage, *www.fsisac.com*, March 30, 2012.

18. "Recommendations of the House Republican Cyber Security Task Force," October 2011, p. 10.

19. J.C. Smart, "Privacy Assurance," *Georgetown Journal of International Affairs*, special edition, Fall 2011, pp. 216-223.

20. Adam O'Donnell, "Microsoft Announces Industry Alliance, $250k Reward to Combat Conficker," February 19, 2009, *http://www.zdnet.com/blog/security/microsoft-announces-industry-alliance-250k-reward-to-combat-conficker/2572*.

21. Ben Worthen, "Email Giants Move to Slash 'Phishing,'" *Wall Street Journal Online*, January 30, 2012, *http://online.wsj.com/article/SB10001424052970204652904577191360158848618.html*.

particularly massive botnet called "Zeus,"[22] and US Internet service providers have agreed voluntarily to undertake new cybersecurity measures recommended by a Federal Communications Commission advisory committee.[23] The private sector is also exploring insurance coverage for cyber events, such as was just announced by Travelers—new coverage options for costs arising from cyber attacks, to accompany existing cyber liability policies.[24] Insurance may hold significant potential as a cybersecurity catalyst: cyber risk would be calculated by market forces, companies would make decisions about coverage based on those risks, and the insurance companies would enforce compliance with their particular standards—all without government intrusion. All of these initiatives are likely only the "tip of the iceberg" of cooperative private sector cybersecurity efforts.

The confusion about the appropriate role for the private sector in cyber is part of the confusion surrounding the entire cyber issue. The government has made policy pronouncements only slowly, e.g., the Comprehensive National Cybersecurity Initiative (CNCI) in January 2008, and then demonstrated little concrete follow-up. Many key areas of cyber policy are uncertain or unknown, with no specified doctrine or regulations; some key issues are only just now being publically articulated. For example, after many years of massive nation-state-directed cyber intrusions into both US private sector and government computer systems, the government finally named the principal culprits—Russia and China—only in October 2011.[25] In addition, the government just acknowledged for the first time their offensive cyber capabilities, as well as their cyber intelligence mission, in November 2011.[26] Those disclosures are useful in understanding the cyber threats and government capabilities for defending against those threats, but there are numerous policy issues left unresolved. If cyber is indeed a domain, then how will the military use it in a war? How do the Laws of War and Laws of Armed Conflict (LOAC) apply in

---

22. Byron Acohido, "Microsoft Shuts Down 2 Servers for Zeus Botnet," *USA Today*, March 27, 2012, p. 3-B.

23. Grant Gross, "US ISPs Commit to New Cyber Security Measures," *PC World*, March 22, 2012, *http://www.pcworld.com/businesscenter/article/252358/us_isps_commit_to_new_cybersecurity_measures.html*.

24. "Travelers Launches Enhanced CyberFirst® Product with New First Party Coverage Options," *www.marketwatch.com*, April 16, 2012.

25. Office of the National Counterintelligence Executive, *Report to Congress on Foreign Economic Collection and Industrial Espionage, 2009-2011*, "Foreign Spies Stealing US Economic Secrets in Cyberspace," October 2011, p. i.

26. DOD Cyberspace Policy Report, pp. 6-7.

cyberspace? (While the United States has stated that the LOAC would apply in cyberspace,[27] China has reportedly decided that they would not accept such limitations.) What are accepted norms of behavior for collecting intelligence in cyberspace as compared to conducting offensive cyber operations (that might cause degradation, corruption or destruction of information or capabilities)? Have we completely considered the consequences of offensive cyber operations, including possible "collateral damage" and second and third order effects of those operations? Reportedly, "the United States would use cyber weapons against an adversary's computer networks only after officials at the highest levels of government approved...because of the risks of collateral damage,"[28] clearly, the government is thinking about the consequences of cyber warfare, but the policies remain inchoate. Because of the interdependencies described above, segregating the "battle space" from the "business space" in cyber warfare will be a considerable challenge. To be sure, the private sector has some very real interests in the answers to these and many other policy questions.

One key question may become especially pertinent as the policy issues evolve: does the US Government have the responsibility to protect private sector entities—the "dot com" world—from cyber intrusions, especially CNE, leading to theft of valuable intellectual property? The government has turned to NSA to take the lead in securing their networks in the .mil and .gov domains, which is appropriate given that that agency has the greatest cyber resource base in the government. However, the Department of Homeland Security (DHS) has been designated as the focal point for securing the .com domain, and that is problematic for two reasons: first, DHS lacks the deep cyber resources and capabilities of NSA; and second, DHS will be attempting to secure a domain that it does not control. There are concerns about NSA's involvement in providing cybersecurity assistance to private sector infrastructure in the .com domain, especially involving privacy issues, that do not pertain with the .gov and .mil domains. But any initiative to secure the preponderance of the nation's cyber infrastructure that does not include leveraging the government's most capable cyber experts is likely to fail. At least one US Senator

---

27. Keith Alexander, General USA, "Statement for the Record, Commander, US Cyber Command," before the House Armed Services Committee, September 23, 2010, p. 4.

28. Richard Lardner/AP, "Official: Cyber Attacks Need Top-Level Approval," *MilitaryTimes.com*, April 24, 2012.

agrees: Sen. John McCain (R-AZ) stated in a letter to Gen. Keith Alexander: "I do not understand why you believe DHS can more effectively protect our nation's critical infrastructure better than US Cyber Command or the National Security Agency."[29] The private sector can only hope that the Congress finds a reasonable balance between security and privacy, and appropriate divisions of labor among government entities, as new cybersecurity laws are legislated.

If the US Government cannot offer competent cyber protection, then another critical question arises: can the private sector take active, offensive measures to protect itself? Banks, for example, can employ armed guards and use lethal force to protect assets and persons in their business from robbers—can banks, or other businesses, use the cyber equivalent of "lethal force" against cyber intruders? As of now, all private sector victims of cyber attacks have been able to do is publically announce their victimization; for example, Google and the "Aurora attack" from China disclosed in January 2010, and RSA and their Chinese attack reported in March 2011. Technology may allow the most sophisticated firms to track their attackers to the latter's "home base," and if so, offer the prospect of responding offensively to the intrusion and theft. If private sector entities are being attacked, and they are, then they may assert the right to conduct their own active defense, especially if the government is unable or unwilling to effectively defend their interests. Interestingly, the government has signaled they may be willing to consider novel security arrangements: DHS Secretary Janet Napolitano indicated "she would consider having tech companies participate with the government in 'proactive' efforts to combat hackers based in foreign countries."[30] It will remain to be seen how forthcoming the government will be in sharing responsibilities to "combat hackers."

The Preamble to the Constitution requires that the US Government "provide for the common defense," and that would seem to include in cyberspace. Moreover, the government has asserted that "the President reserves the right to respond using all necessary means to defend our nation, our allies, our partners, and our interests from hostile acts in cyberspace. Hostile acts may include significant cyber attacks directed against the US economy, government or military."[31] What is unclear in that statement is what cyber intrusion

29. Letter, from Sen. John McCain to Gen. Keith Alexander, Director NSA, March 29, 2012, publically released.

30. Steve Johnson, "Homeland Security Chief Contemplating Proactive Cyber Attacks," *San Jose Mercury News*, April 17, 2012, *www.mercurynews.com*.

31. DOD Cyberspace Policy Report, p. 4.

would rise to the level of "significant," and whether mere CNE or theft would constitute a "hostile act". In other words, will the US Government take action to defend actively Google or any other private sector firm from having their IP stolen? This issue becomes even more complicated if there should be indications and warning (likely from US Intelligence Community sources) that a foreign cyber attack against a private sector target was imminent—would the government contemplate or actually execute a preemptive strike in defense of private sector equities? In the physical world, when law enforcement becomes aware of a threat to a person or entity, they are obligated to provide warning; that seems to be a reasonable standard to apply in cyberspace as well. Government preemption to neutralize a cyber threat would seem to be a more challenging policy issue, but one for which the private sector would appreciate some clarity.

There are other policy and political complexities that will require consideration and resolution. For example, how should the government respond if the imminent attack on the private sector was being directed from a non-state actor (e.g., Anonymous)? FBI Director Robert Mueller said in open testimony to the Senate Select Committee on Intelligence that "down the road, the cyber threat will be the number one threat to the country…it will be tomorrow."[32] As cyber technology grows and proliferates, the ability of non-state actors and groups in particular to inflict great damage increases, and the need to anticipate future crises and plan for the necessary capabilities and policies to address that non-traditional threat becomes ever more acute.

Since much of the threat is based outside of US sovereign territory, there are a range of international issues that must also be assessed: for example, are US business subsidiaries based overseas to be protected by US Government cybersecurity measures? The President has declared his intent to defend, *inter alia*, "interests," as stated above, but their location was not specified. Moreover, the statement included "allies," but will the United States be willing or obligated via alliances such as NATO to protect foreign private sector interests in member states? The complexities of private vs. government interests and responsibilities become replicated across the international landscape; just as the network is global, so are the policy challenges. The US Government has

---

32.   J. Nicholas Hoover, "Cyber Attacks Becoming Top Terror Threat, FBI Says," *Information Week*, February 1, 2012, *http://www.informationweek.com/government/security/cyber-attacks-becoming-top-terror-threat/232600046.*

many tools at its disposal to address national security threats from whatever quarter, including bilateral and multilateral diplomacy, economic sanctions and, ultimately, military force, both kinetic and cyber. Finding a balance between government and private sector responsibilities to defend the latter's interest will be a difficult but necessary cyber policy challenge.

Technology is not slowing down or waiting for the Congress or the Executive Branch to decide these key policy issues regarding cyberspace. It continues to develop with Moore's Law speed and efficiency, and it will create new and unknown challenges as it progresses. According to technology estimates, there will be 35 zetabytes (one zetabyte is 10 to the 21th, or a sextillion) of digital data[33] and 22 billion Internet-connected devices by 2020.[34] Computers have already reached "petaflop" speeds (quadrillion operations per second) and will reach "exa-scale" (quintillion operations per second) within the next half decade or so. These technology developments are rapid and relentless. The private sector will almost certainly not wait for the government to decide many of the policy issues described in this chapter; it will move forward at "market speed" to develop entirely new areas of technology and products for which the government will have little or no policy control, or even understanding. If the government cannot improve its acquisition and assimilation of technology, they may not even be able institutionally to fully comprehend the technologies as they are developed and sold in the marketplace. It will be in the private sector's interest to insure that the government not fall too far behind the technology curve, so that the interests of both can be weighed and balanced to achieve a stable and secure cyberspace. And it will be in the government's interest to create a policy and legal framework sufficient to allow dynamic and substantive cooperation with the private sector to facilitate a more secure cyberspace.

Disclaimer

The views expressed herein are solely those of the author and do not in any way represent an endorsement by his current or previous employers.

---

33. IMS Research, *www.imsreasearch.com*, 2010.
34. IDC Digital Universe Study, "Big Data is Here, Now What?" *www.chucksblog.emc.com*, 2011.

CHAPTER 5
Political and Economic Coercion in the Cyber Era

The Honorable Robert Liscouski

Introduction

The United States faces mounting insecurity in cyberspace that has and will continue to compromise critical government and corporate networks and in turn exploit vulnerabilities to expansive critical infrastructure and our economic security. Our current approach to cybersecurity puts the government and the private sector more at risk every day. Pundit talk of a cyber-Armageddon only exacerbates the lack of action instead of stimulating it, because business and government leaders either do not know how to respond or believe that an effective response is neither practical nor affordable. In practice, good cybersecurity is achievable and affordable, but a coherent and

Robert Liscouski is a partner and co-founder of Edge360, LLC, an enterprice risk management and technology solutions firm, and a partner in Secure Strategy Group, LLC, a New York and Washington DC based investment bank dedicated to backing and building market leaders in the security and defense technology sectors. He is also co-founder and Managing Director of Edge360 an enterprise risk management and technology solutions firm and a founder of Steel City Re, a firm specializing in reputation risk and intangible asset risk management. Previously, he served as Director of Information Assurance, The Coca-Cola Company and President and CEO of Content Analyst Company, LLC, a developer of text analytics software. Prior to this, Mr. Liscouski was appointed as the first Assistant Secretary for Infrastructure Protection, when the Department of Homeland Security was founded in 2003 and served in that position under Secretary Tom Ridge until 2005. As Assistant Secretary for Infrastructure Protection, Mr. Liscouski led the development and implementation of the nation's efforts to protect its critical infrastructure from terrorist attacks and natural disasters. He also led the development of the National Infrastructure Protection Plan, the nation's risk management framework to protect its national infrastructure. Under Mr. Liscouski's leadership, the Department created the National Cyber Security Division and the US CERT, the US Government's effort to identify and counter cyber security threats. Mr. Liscouski led the Department's efforts to create legislation (CFATS) to protect the US Chemical Sector and was the executive manager of the National Communications Systems (NCS).

implementable strategy with common government and private sector goals needs to be developed to incent businesses and help governments (federal, local and state) lead.

While the focus of this chapter is on cyber security, one cannot consider protecting from cyber attack without considering the parallel risks from physical vulnerabilities and those related to insider threats. Regrettably, most enterprises, both private sector and government, are still managing the protection of physical and cyber assets with little coordination between the two functions within their organizations, contributing to the vulnerabilities of the organization as well increasing costs and inefficiencies. The current national strategies for Infrastructure and Cybersecurity are two ships passing in the night rather than an armada with a common destination. Government cannot lead and the security industry is more interested in proposing single point technologies to address vulnerabilities rather than rational and scalable solutions. The challenges we face are not a lack of technology but a lack of leadership and responsibility in government and industry. For the United States to achieve a goal of securing its infrastructure, both physical and cyber, the focus needs to change from a Federal Government dominated approach to one that is community oriented in order to build capacity and sustainability that protects our country's future for generations to come. This chapter will examine how that goal might be achieved.

Cyber Threats and Potential Damage

The rapid modernization and reliance of our nation's critical infrastructure, including the energy, finance, and transportation sectors, on the Internet and information systems has created a target that cyber attackers continuously exploit.[1] In terms of economic losses, in 2010, an FBI/McAfee study estimated that cybercrime costs the United States $400 billion annually, and cyber security incidents can cost companies between $17 and $28 million per incident, causing severe tangible and intangible damage.[2]

The unprecedented rise in the frequency and scale of cyber attacks and the lack of a comprehensive and actionable national strategy for cyber security

---

1.   Barbara Fast, Michael Johnson, and Dick Schaeffer, "Cyber Intelligence...Setting the Landscape for an Emerging Discipline," *Intelligence and National Security Alliance*, (2011): 10, *https://images. magnetmail.net/images/clients/INSA/attach/INSA_CYBER_INTELLIGENCE_2011.pdf.*

2.   Ashish Garg, Jeffrey Curtis, and Hilary Halper, "The Financial Impact of IT Security Breaches: What Do Investors Think?" *Information Systems Security*, (2003): 22-33, *http://www.auerbach-publications.com/dynamic_data/2466_1358_cost.pdf.*

leaves the United States vulnerable to a host of information security challenges that current legislation is attempting to address. In a statement introducing, "The Protecting Cyberspace as a National Asset Act of 2010," Senator Joe Lieberman stated, "The future security of the American way of life depends on passage of comprehensive cyber security legislation that will provide the Federal Government with modern tools to secure and defend the nation's most critical networks and assets."

The majority of our critical infrastructure was created before the advent of the digital age, and some sectors are slow to modernize due to cost concerns, a false sense of security, or a limited understanding of the threat.[3] Also, some sectors may be modernizing too quickly, creating additional vulnerabilities. Although there is increasing awareness of cyber threats, many companies "do not take advantage of available [cyber security] technology to secure their systems".[4]

Control systems that are vital for the proper functioning of our critical infrastructure have not developed quick enough to keep up with the growth of IT systems over the last two decades.[5] If a cyber criminal exploited this vulnerability, we could be subject to a prolonged disruption of vital assets, affecting every infrastructure sector and causing significant physical destruction, because IT systems also control GPS, air traffic control, railways and traffic systems.[6] While it is easy to imagine a doomsday scenario, a cyber attack that targets our critical infrastructure, or intellectual property for that matter, can easily go unnoticed and lay dormant for prolonged periods of time. Also, as successful viruses gain notoriety they can be adopted, downloaded and enhanced by others, causing severe economic and physical damage. Security and technology experts now fear that the Stuxnet and Flame viruses used to disrupt Iran's nuclear program are proliferating on the Internet and could be

---

3. Margaret E. Grayson, Gregory Peters, and George Conrades, "Final Report and Recommendations By The Council," *The NIAC Convergence of Physical and Cyber Technologies and Related Security Management Challenges Working Group,* (2007): 9, *http://www.dhs.gov/xlibrary/assets/niac/ niac_physicalcyberreport-011607.pdf.*

4. Internet Policy Task Force, "Cybersecurity, Innovation And The Internet Economy," *The Department of Commerce,* (2011): 1, *http://www.nist.gov/itl/upload/Cybersecurity_Green-Paper_ FinalVersion.pdf.*

5. Grayson, Peters, Conrades, "Final Report and Recommendations" p. 10.

6. "Securing the Supply Chain," *Transportation and Logistics 2030,* Vol. 4, SMI (2011): 22, *http://www. pwc.com/en_GX/gx/transportation-logistics/pdf/TL2030_vol.4_web.pdf.*

"repurposed" to attack our infrastructure.[7] That being said, our rival economic powers have an interest in masking their intellectual theft cyber activities and capabilities in order to preserve their financial interests. For a nation like China, armed conflict with the United States is bad for business.

Dealing With Actual or Potential Economic Cyber Coercion

The major issue in dealing with cyber coercion, economic or otherwise, is attribution. The fact that there are no physical boundaries in cyberspace and that attackers can disguise operational locations makes the process of identifying an attacker and pinpointing the actual origination of an attack difficult. The consequence of misidentifying the origin of an attack could have significant diplomatic, political and military ramifications should the targeted country mount an active defense and retaliate for an aggression in cyberspace. However, active defenses initiated against an on-going attack may be the only method of engagement to ensure that an attack is stopped.

The complexity of ensuring attribution for attacks in cyberspace can make our national defense efforts difficult. As an example; a terrorist group operating outside of the United States engages in a cyber attack on the US electric power infrastructure, in which SCADA (control) systems, are actively attacked and begin to fail. This tactic is typically used to deny command and control capability in preparation of a follow on attack using physical force. The US defense community would have the authorization to mount a counter attack against the adversary *if* it could identify the origin of the attack and assure attribution.

Our experience after September 11, 2001 redefined the actions a nation may take as a right of self-defense. As Jeffrey Carr points out in his book, *Inside Cyber Warfare: Mapping the Cyber Underworld*, US military action in Afghanistan was internationally accepted, by and large, as an act of self-defense, regardless of whether the Taliban government or the nation of Afghanistan had control over Al Qaeda.[8] US action was internationally justified because the Taliban government took no steps to prevent the terrorist attacks. Under the right circumstances we can define when we are legally

---

7. Ricardo Bilton, "Malware writers could adapt Flame for future attacks, Microsoft Warns," June 4, 2012, *http://venturebeat.com/2012/06/04/malware-writers-could-adapt-flame-for-future-attacks-microsoft-warns/*.

8. Jeffrey Carr, *Inside Cyber Warfare: Mapping the Cyber Underworld*, (Toronto: HarperCollins Publishers Ltd., 2011), p. 249, Kindle edition.

justified to take offensive action, even if it doesn't conform to traditional laws of war. It is generally accepted that a state must take appropriate measures to prevent terrorist attacks emanating from their soil, and cyber coercion and attacks are beginning to be seen as another form of terrorism. UN Resolution 1373, passed after September 11th, directs states to "refrain from providing any form of support" to terrorists through act or omission, to "deny safe haven" to those who commit terrorist acts."[9]

The lack of a clear US Cyber Doctrine creates ambiguity in drawing a line between what "active defenses" are permissible by law enforcement compared to the corporate sector. There are a number of scenarios in which the possibility of a US-based corporation (either US or foreign-owned) could, because of its sophisticated information security posture, mount an active defense resulting in political or military ramifications to the United States.

Scenario I

The target is a large US multi-national financial institution coming under attack from cyber criminals conducting extortion. The criminals demand $10 million in exchange for halting the attack. The company doesn't respond and a denial of service cyber attack continues to its main servers, degrading its ability to conduct institutional financial transactions and provide services to its customers. The US institution acting in its own defense would then mount aggressive cyber retaliatory measures, resulting in the destruction of the attacker's cyber capability.

An April article from the online edition of *The Atlantic* magazine discussed this scenario in the framework of a "Stand Your Ground" law. The idea is based on the basic right of self-defense and that private companies have been the primary victims of cyber attacks by foreign entities, and therefore, should have the right to defend themselves if they perceive or are subject to a cyber attack. In the physical world this precedent already exists. *The Atlantic* compares this notion with piracy on the open seas,[10] explaining that if commercial ships are attacked by pirates or perceive an imminent attack they are authorized to shoot and kill the pirates. However, this scenario can

---

9. UN Resolution 1373, *http://daccess-dds-ny.un.org/doc/UNDOC/GEN/N01/557/43/PDF/N0155743. pdf?OpenElement.*
10. "Stand Your Cyberground Law: A Novel Proposal for Digital Security," *The Atlantic*, April 30, 2012, *http://www.theatlantic.com/technology/archive/2012/04/stand-your-cyberground-law-a-novel-proposal-for-digital-security/256532/.*

have severe repercussions when discussing cyber defense if a company mis-identifies an attacker due to a lack of positive attribution out of the need to preserve its business, and in doing so embroils the United States in a major diplomatic incident.

Scenario II

A large US-based technology company, which maintains an index of web-sites and other online content for users, advertisers, and network members and other content providers, comes under attack by hactivists. They deface the company's website and begin a series of denial of service attacks to protest pending anti-piracy legislation.

However, one problematic scenario with this idea, in the cyber realm, is that hactivists can use sophisticated techniques to initially spoof the attack as though it came from a foreign state that had previously shut down the company's web services to censor content from its citizens during one of the Arab Spring uprisings. As a result, the company's CEO orders an immediate active defense resulting in a diplomatic demarche to the US State Department and exacerbating already tense political relations.

The Role of Incentives and Private Sector Cybersecurity

Technology, while indeed part of the solution, tends to be the easy but inef-fective answer. The real issue for the private sector and government is leadership and with that, accountability to ensure that goals are met. This harks back to the old business adage that people will do what they get paid to do. CEOs are incented to run their business; sell their goods, build shareholder value, and operate profitably. Boards of Directors are incented to provide Governance Oversight and ensure the CEO is operating the company in the shareholders' best interests. This generally works well and CEOs and Directors pay attention to those issues and matters that have a direct impact on the company and where they may be liable for malfeasance or nonfeasance. Regrettably, security has historically not been one of those issues, despite the fact that cyber attacks and disruptions can substantially decrease shareholder value

- After a cyber attack "brand and reputation can decline by 17-31% and it may take an organization more than a year to recover its corporate image."[11]

- A 2011 Aon Cyber Insurance Report stated that, "among 2,807 publicly disclosed data breaches worldwide during the past five years, the damages to target companies and victims of the breached data exceeded $139 billion."[12]

In addition to a loss of shareholder confidence, attacks such as these expose a company to embarrassment, loss of business, litigation and liability, investigations by regulators and government agencies, and significant expenses.[13]

In October 2011 the SEC imposed its regulatory authority to require public companies to report cyber security incidents that have a *material* impact on company operations, though materiality is not defined. Director and Officer Liability continues to increase and there are gaps in current risk coverage. The risk environment is further complicated by the lack of a clear understanding of what adequate protection from cyber threats really is, as well as, how to communicate to the government and shareholders that companies are adequately protected without divulging information that can be exploited or provide a competitive disadvantage. This is an environment in which fear and disincentives drive costly and ineffective solutions, however, it also creates opportunity to shape behavior at the most senior levels of a company.

Making the "business case" for cyber security remains a major challenge, because often private industry does not understand the potential economic damage of a cyber attack, the cost benefit analysis of securing critical networks or the possibility of increased market value if they take appropriate cyber security measures.[14] A 2010 McAfee study stated that overall cost was most frequently cited as the biggest obstacle to private sector implementation.[15] A

11. Jody R. Westby. "Governance of Enterprise Security: CyLab 2012 Report," *Carnegie Mellon University CyLab*, (2012): p. 11, *http://www.rsa.com/innovation/docs/CMU-GOVERNANCE-RPT-2012-FINAL.pdf.*

12. Kevin P. Kalinich, "Cyber Insurance 2011 Update—Privacy and Security Exposures and Solutions," *AON*, (2011): 2, *http://www.aon.com/attachments/Aon_Privacy_Security_031611.pdf.*

13. Westby, "Governance of Enterprise Security," p. 11.

14. "Cybersecurity: Incentives and Governance," *The Brookings Institution*, Conference Transcript, July 21, 2011, *http://www.brookings.edu/events/2011/0721_cybersecurity.aspx.*

15. Stewart Baker, Shaun Waterman and George Ivanov, "In the Crossfire, Critical Infrastructure in the Age of Cyber War," *McAfee* (2010): p. 14, *http://www.mcafee.com/us/resources/reports/rp-in-crossfire-critical-infrastructure-cyber-war.pdf.*

2012 CyLab survey, based upon results received from 108 respondents at the board or senior executive level from Forbes Global 2000 companies, exposed the following:

> *"For the third time, the survey revealed that boards are not actively addressing cyber risk management. While placing high importance on risk management generally, there is still a gap in understanding the linkage between information technology (IT) and enterprise risk management."*[16]

There are a number of incentive based models that can serve as viable cyber security incentive options. These include:

- Regulatory approaches—measures to enforce compliance through punitive measures for non-compliance.

- Regional and local government models that could create "Economic Security Zones."

- Insurance based incentive models—that build capabilities to identify vulnerabilities, liabilities, best practices, information sharing and risk transfer mechanisms.

The most practical and implementable option is one that focuses on incenting business to improve their security. The issue of cyber security has risen to the top of "national security" concerns by the US Government, which has consequently spawned an entire industry selling a wide variety of cyber security solutions to large and small businesses. There are many cyber security solutions being offered without really understanding how businesses need to be protected, what the vulnerabilities are, what the threat is and most importantly—how effectiveness is measured. The old military maxim, "He who protects everything, protects nothing" applies to the corporate environment as well. Companies cannot afford to protect everything all the time. So it raises the question—how does one know what to protect and what the right level of protection is? One answer focuses on the true value of a company particularly in the public market place—Reputation is the key asset to protect. Why focus on Reputation? Reputations result from perceptions that stakeholders have about a company's intangible assets. In today's volatile markets, reputation resilience is the dominant factor in determining a company's ability to thrive and continue rewarding shareholders with above-average returns. Intangible

---

16.   Westby, "Governance of Enterprise Security," p. 5.

asset value arises from shareholder's perceptions of future cash flows. Until the mid-1970s, the apparent competitive advantages that secured those cash flows resided primarily in a company's balance sheet—liquid assets, property, physical plant and equipment. Thirty years later, those same tangible assets have come to represent less than a third of a company's value.

Today's most valuable corporate assets are intangible (70% of the median value of publicly traded companies on the US markets).[17] These intangible assets are known by many names: intellectual capital, intellectual assets, vital assets, and the like.

These are umbrella terms for the business processes that ensure:

1. An ethical work environment,
2. Drive innovation,
3. Assure quality,
4. Uphold safety,
5. Promote sustainability and
6. *Provide security*.

These processes collectively create value. They also underlie the communication practices that signal *authentic* value to stakeholders who are the ultimate owners of a company's reputation. For that reason, intangible assets are so valuable. Companies with superior reputations deliver superior long-term shareholder returns by enabling:

1. Stronger pricing power,
2. Lower operating costs,
3. Greater earnings multiples,
4. Lower beta, and
5. Lower credit costs.

As a group, companies with higher reputation rankings have higher equity returns and lower credit costs. They have lower operating costs, and higher net incomes. In rising markets, companies with superior reputations reward their shareholders with superior returns. In down markets, companies with superior reputations are more resilient and lose less value.[18]

---

17. Nir Kossovsky, *Mission Intangible: Managing Risk and Reputation to Create Enterprise Value*, (Victoria, BC: Trafford Publishing, 2010).

18. Kossovsky, *Mission Intangible*.

Risks to Reputation

These are challenging times for top and senior management at all companies public and private. Scandals and crises are ubiquitous and they present material financial risks.[19]

- The 835 public companies that announced a supply chain disruption between 1989 and 2000 experienced ROI that was 33-40% lower than that of their industry peers. In addition,

- 25% of companies that experienced IT outages of two to six days during this same 11-year period went bankrupt immediately, and

- 93% of the companies that lost their data centers for a minimum of 10 days filed for bankruptcy within a year.

Business and Reputation Risk

Business depends on its networks; financial, suppliers, manufacturers, marketing, sales, customers, etc. Whether a business is a Fortune 50 with a global presence or a small business with local footprint it is highly dependent on data, information, and its business networks to survive.

- Organizations that outsource non-core functions create value through business networks.

- Business networks, however, *have inherent and often hidden* risks:

1. Ethical sourcing
2. Product safety
3. Integrity
4. Environmental sustainability
5. *Intellectual property*
6. *Security*

   When adverse events occur in the networks

- Direct damages may be covered by conventional insurances,

- But *reputational losses due to share holder loss of confidence are frequently long-term or fatal.*

---

19. Council of Competitiveness. "Resilient Enterprise Paradigm," Prepared for US Department of Commerce, Technology Administration. p. 4

The sixth processes linked to Reputation—Security—is often looked at as necessary expense in today's world of terrorist events, wars, civil unrest, escalating crime and cyber attacks. Frequently, there is little to show for the investment in security because there is no good financial measure for preventing incidents. However, when bad things do happen and they frequently do, the cost of recovery is typically orders of magnitude greater than the investment in prevention. Cyber security risk is increasing virtually daily. Businesses are exposed to risk through a variety of channels:[20]

Figure 5.1.

Business Partners	Supply Chain	Corporate Espionage
Trusted insiders	Competitors	State sponsored activities
Terrorist Groups	Organized Crime & Criminal Groups	Hackers

A cyber incident may be through any number of points; malware, virus, email spoof or phishing, data download, service disruption, etc. But the effects of the attack could be devastating to the business. The question facing CEOs today is, "I can't afford to protect everything, so how do I know what to protect and how much to invest?" The answer is: Focus on the core business processes that contribute to your greatest value and protect your *reputation*.

Cyber Security Investment to Protect a Company's Reputation and Shareholder Value

What level of investment is sufficient, and what are the financial benefits of, investing in this particular intangible asset?

First—one has to assess what needs to be protected—what is the true value of the asset (intangible and real value) and how does it contribute to the critical function of the company?

---

20.   Kossovsky, *Mission Intangible.*

Second—How best to protect? What are the best practices?

Third—How to build resiliency to loss? How to communicate resiliency to the market?

Shareholders and the market react to such signals and will reward or punish a company more rapidly than the government ever can. The cyber risk has such an immediate impact on victims that a government regulated approach can never react to the threat quickly enough to encourage companies to take the appropriate measures to protect themselves, but market-based approaches have proven to be effective mechanisms to change behavior and improve resiliency.

In 2009, US-based payments processor Heartland, revealed that it was exposed to a year and a half long breach that affected approximately 130 million payment cards.[21] Heartland's breach epitomized the far reaching effects and characteristics of a cyber attack. According to Heartland, the breach was unnoticed for 18 months and affected "hundreds of banks and credit unions,"[22] which led to costly lawsuits and a loss of shareholder confidence. While the breach was extremely damaging to the company, Heartland quickly implemented best practices mechanisms that have improved the company's resiliency and set a standard for the industry.

According to Heartland CEO Bob Carr, Heartland overcame the breach because the company had "open communications" with its stakeholders and other affected companies, and "took responsibility" for the breach, recognizing that the security breach may have spread to other companies' systems.[23]

Ensuring that a company has implemented cyber security best practices and an effective response following a breach such as Heartland's is an area that the cyber insurance industry has focused on. By encouraging the use of cyber insurance, the government can make the case for private sector cyber security. Cyber insurance provides privacy and security liability, data breach crisis management, Internet media liability and higher reputation ranking, providing higher equity returns and lower credit costs. While the benefits and potential growth of the cyber insurance industry are difficult to refute, 57% of

---

21. Tracy Kitten, "A Tale of Two Breaches, What Heartland's Story Says About Global Payments' Future," *Bank Info Security*, April 6, 2012, *http://www.bankinfosecurity.com/tale-two-breaches-a-4658/op-1.*
22. Kitten, "A Tale of Two Breaches, What Heartland's Story Says About Global Payments' Future".
23. Tracy Kitten, "Breach Response: The CEO's Story," *Bank Info Security*, April 27, 2012, *http://www.bankinfosecurity.com/breach-response-ceos-story-a-4714/p-3.*

boards of Forbes Global 2000 companies are not reviewing insurance coverage for cyber related risk. 65% of boards were doing so in 2010. According to Carnegie Mellon CyLab, 89% of boards review risk assessments, but less than half of them hire outside expertise to assist with risk management.[24] The cyber insurance industry can also be utilized by the private sector as a tool to drive the proliferation of cyber security best practices and in doing so curb federal regulations and oversight.

The Government's Model—Compliance Through Regulation—The Carrot & Stick Approach

The government and the private sector are finding that a risk-based approach to determine and protect against cyber threats is the most efficient cyber security method. As is the case in private industry, a "one size fits all approach" to cyber security cannot be applied to the various federal sectors. Currently, federal regulatory entities within the various sector segments issue specific risk-based cyber security requirements.[25] An area or sector that makes up critical national infrastructure, or private industry for that matter, "comprises a large number of organizations and systems," therefore, focusing protection on one sector or developing identical regulations for each is useless.[26]

In 2010, the National Institute of Standards and Technology (NIST) issued guidelines for Smart Grid cyber security that advocated a multi-layered security approach. NIST's approach was to determine risk and to quantify the threat, vulnerability and potential consequences of an attack.[27] A risk-based approach, such as the one advocated by NIST, is the most appropriate way for both the government and the private sector to address cyber threats. This tactic works with the diverse cyber security environments that define private industry and various government sectors such as critical infrastructure, finance, energy and telecommunications.

As mentioned earlier, the very nature of cyber threats poses a formidable problem for the government in securing the cyber realms that crisscross into

---

24. Westby, "Governance of Enterprise Security," p. 24.

25. "Critical Infrastructure Protection—Cybersecurity Guidance Is Available, but More Can Be Done to Promote Its Use," *Government Accountability Office*, GAO-12-92, (December 2011), 16, *http://www.gao.gov/assets/590/587529.pdf*.

26. Gabi Siboni, "Protecting Critical Assets and Infrastructures from Cyber Attacks," in *Military and Strategic Affairs*, Vol. 3, no. 1 (2011): 96, *http://www.inss.org.il/upload/(FILE)1308129638.pdf*.

27. Richard J. Campbell, "The Smart Grid and Cybersecurity-Regulatory Policy and Issues," *Congressional Research Service*, (2011): 5, *http://www.fas.org/sgp/crs/misc/R41886.pdf*.

the private sector. While the majority of the United States' critical infrastructure is owned and operated by private industry, the government still has an obligation to ensure the safety and security of its citizens and that critical infrastructure is adequately protected and operating. The challenge, currently being played out in Congress, is for the government and private sector to reach a mutual understanding on cyber security. The Government's primary concern is the security of the nation's critical assets and infrastructure. This is not to say that private industry is solely focused on protecting reputation, business competitiveness and privacy. The private sector is composed of American citizens who share deep concerns for the protection of the nation's infrastructure and security, but they also must take business considerations into account.

The Democratic Party's approach to the issue advocates the general stance of government, while most proposed Republican legislation sides with the concerns of private industry. The stark differences between the two imply that a passable piece of legislation will find a middle ground, reflecting the reality of today's cyber security challenges. The private sector will have to concede some freedoms when it comes to the most critical sectors of the nation's infrastructure. Some regulation is inevitable. At the same time, it has become abundantly clear that private sector cooperation necessitates not only that the government make a "business case" for cyber security but also that the government allow the private sector to play a major role in formulating cyber security standards that both sides must adhere to. Just as the government will never convince private industry to disregard business concerns, it will also never bridge private industry's intrinsic distrust of federal authority without major private sector contributions to cyber security standards.

There is a foundation for this lack of confidence. The parallel to the risk based cyber security approach can be found in the legislation enacted for the Chemical Facility Anti-Terrorism Standards (CFATS). DHS' implementation of the CFATS legislation included a risk based methodology, which ranked chemical storage facilities into a tiered system. Unfortunately, poor program management failed to disclose that there was an error in the risk analysis software, which incorrectly ranked chemical storage facilities into higher risk categories resulting in significant over investment (estimated in the tens of millions of dollars). The mistake was ultimately revealed only after the investment was made and significant reputation damage was suffered by DHS, as was a significant loss of confidence in DHS by the private sector. While the initial CFATS strategy was sound, the execution was so poor that it has tainted the risk based approach for other domains including cyber. Distrust of the government's ability to provide oversight and governance on its own programs by the private sector is significant.

Economic Security through Good Governance

Threats to the various states and regions cover a wide range of hazards both natural and man-made. While there are commonalities for threat preparation (to include resilience) and response overall, there are specific policies and actions that require some degree of tailoring depending on the region and the type of business (ie. chemical manufacturing & storage vs. a shopping mall—one is a target to create a WMD effect, the other is a target of the WMD or lesser incident). Neither the state nor the private sector can afford to protect against all threats and risks, so careful risk analysis (with input from the federal and local governments and the private sector) is required to ensure that the regional strategies are rational and achievable. The premise is that if the regions or zones can focus on driving actions in the private sector to better secure themselves against the major threats, it will contribute to resilience and survivability of those businesses, and therefore, ensure economic viability of the region and the state. This Security and Economic Regional (or Zone) strategy should be applied to the cyber sphere. Public and private sector awareness of this strategy will serve to attract and sustain business opportunities and growth.

This is not hypothetical—immediately after 9/11, some major businesses moved their operations from New York City across the Hudson River to Jersey City and other New Jersey cities with access to New York City. Subsequently, every time there is a major threat to New York City, the remaining businesses worry that their employees will not come to work for a period of time or will decide to find employment elsewhere resulting in lost productivity. Even if the businesses were not targeted directly (as in the case of CitiGroup in August 2004), disruption in the supporting networks; transportation, communications, schools, etc. would have significant ramifications to business and the psyche of the population. Most urban regions are not as high profile as New York City, but because they are the hub of the local government's business and its supporting infrastructure, they offer highly attractive targets. This strategy is predicated on a framework of best practices for cyber and physical security. It also has to take into account telecommunications and Internet communications networks, transportation, electrical grid, and other critical infrastructure, as well as key government facilities, major businesses, universities, and the general population areas. Incentives to the business sector beyond branding the specific areas as "Security & Economic incentives" could include:

- Tax or other economic incentives for meeting goals;
- Assistance to businesses and communities from the state to implement best practices and share information;
- Insurability or lower insurance costs due to the benefits of business resilience;
- Educational incentives.

Conclusion

The government and private industry must find a common ground to secure our nation's cyberspace and everything connected to it. The space separating the government and the private sector when it comes to cyber security is really not as far apart as both sides portray. Both the government and the private sector have found that a risk-based approach is the most effective cyber security solution, and the fact that both sectors are rushing to modernize their systems, to increase operational and cost effectiveness, indicates a common interest in viable cyber security standards.

The Federal Government must make the "business case" for cyber security by pushing common sense incentives such as cyber insurance, voluntary standards, public private partnerships, liability protections and leading by example through purchasing the best cyber security technology and implementing best practices. Both sides will have to concede some ground in the effort to secure cyberspace while at the same time respecting each other's interests. The price of the shared threats amassing in cyberspace towards the government and private industry are too great for either side to ignore. The flood of cyber security legislation clearly conveys that both sectors see a problem and want a solution, and the key is to constructively forge a path ahead and prepare ourselves for a more dangerous and complicated cyber landscape than we currently face.

Acknowledgement

The author wishes to acknowledge the contributions of Research Assistant, Alex Sorin to this project and chapter.

CHAPTER 6

Cold War Paradigms
Does MAD Work with Cyber Weapons?

David J. Smith

Introduction: Before the Cold War

In September of 433 BC, the fleets of Corcyra and Corinth clashed in the Battle of Sybota, which became one of the precursors to the Peloponnesian War. The Athenians, led by the brilliant Pericles, had concluded a strictly defensive alliance with Corcyra—*epimachia;* different from the traditional full alliance, known as *symmachia*—and laid an exceedingly detailed deterrent strategy. The objective was to deter Corinth without a fight and not to provoke Sparta. Instead, the Athenians were drawn into the battle, driving the sulking Corinthians to seek restored honor with their Spartan allies.[1]

"Of the hundreds of warships in their navy," writes Donald Kagan, "they sent only ten...it was clearly of more symbolic than military significance, meant

---

1. Donald Kagan, *On the Origins of War and the Preservation of Peace* (New York: Penguin Books, 2003), pp. 45-49. For a fuller treatment, see Donald Kagan, *The Peloponnesian War* (New York: Penguin Books, 2003), pp. 3-40.

Ambassador David Smith joined the Potomac Institute for Policy Studies as a Senior Fellow in 2005. In 2012, he became Director of the Potomac Institute Cyber Center. Amb. Smith has had a distinguished career in defense and foreign affairs, is an expert on international security issues, and in recent years has focused on the emerging field of cyber security. His other areas of expertise include US strategic missile defense, arms control, European security policy, and security relationships with China, Russia, and Korea. He also has in-depth expertise and experience in building stability and security in the South Caucasus region. Ambassador Smith is currently involved in a major project to assist Georgia in reforming its national security institutions, and serves as Director of the Georgian Security Analysis Center in Tbilisi. President George H. W. Bush nominated Ambassador Smith to lead the US-Soviet Defense and Space Talks on September 21, 1989. He was confirmed by the Senate and sworn in by Senator Bob Dole. He subsequently led the US team that worked to negotiate an agreement to allow deployment of defenses against the growing threat of ballistic missiles until the demise of the Soviet Union in 1991. From 2002 to 2005, Ambassador Smith was Chief Operating Officer of the National Institute for Public Policy, Fairfax, Virginia. From 1993 to

to show that Athens Meant business and to deter the Corinthians." Moreover, the Athenians contrived to appoint Lacedaemonius—the name literally means Spartan—Kagan continues, "To disarm Spartan suspicion of his mission." And Lacedaemonius was ordered not to sail against the Corinthian fleet unless it threatened Corcyra itself. It "was an effort," Kagan says, "at what is called in current jargon 'minimal deterrence'."[2]

Soon, Thucydides records, "Fine distinctions were no longer made. The situation had developed to the point where the Corinthians and Athenians necessarily had to fight one another."[3] The Corinthian admiral could not have known whether scores of Athenian ships lay in the next bay or under what orders Lacedaemonius had sailed. And if anyone was impressed with his family's ties to Sparta, there is no record of it.

In reviewing Thucydides, Richard Ned Lebow sums up:

> There is not much convincing evidence of general and immediate deterrence success. Policy makers nevertheless put considerable faith in deterrence, routinely expecting it to prevent challenges and revolts...Reason leads analysts, strategists and academics to increasingly complex and abstruse calculations of the military balance and tactic for demonstrating resolve on the assumption that signals of this kind significantly affect the cost-calculus of those whom deterrence and compellence are practiced against.[4]

Of course, Pericles had no computerized decision-making tools and Lacedaemonius did not sail with the *Aegis* fire control system—computers were more than 23 centuries in the future. Nonetheless, this brief introduction by way of events over two millennia past reminds us of three crucial points.

---

2. *Ibid.*
3. Thucydides, *The Peloponnesian War*, 1:49.7, cited in Kagan, *Peloponnesian War*, p. 47.
4. Richard Ned Lebow, "Thucydides and Deterrence" in *Security Studies* 16(2), April-June 2007, pp. 163-188.

2002, he was President of Global Horizons, Inc. consulting on defense, international security issues and overseas business development. He previously served as Chief of Staff for Arizona Congressman Jon Kyl, Assistant for Strategic Policy and Arms Control to Senate Republican Leader Bob Dole, as professional staff for the Senate Committee on Foreign Relations and on the staff of the Joint Chiefs of Staff. He holds degrees from the University of Arizona, London School of Economics and Harvard University and is a Ph.D. candidate at Ilia State University in Tbilisi, Georgia.

First, the concept of deterrence is far more ancient than the Cold War. Second, it is much broader than Cold War deterrence, or at least than the popular perception of Cold War deterrence. Third, deterrence, despite the best laid plans of the best and the brightest—Pericles!—often fails.

However, deterrence can also succeed, as one more account from the ancients illustrates. According to Livy, in 168 BC, the Roman Senate sent Gaius Popillius Laenas to intercept Antiochus IV, king of Seleucid Syria, bound to invade Ptolemaic Egypt, a Roman ally. The Roman stood at the outskirts of Alexandria with a single servant.

> Popillius, stern as ever, drew a circle around the king with a stick he was carrying and said, 'Before you step out of that circle give me a reply to lay before the Senate.' For a few minutes [Antiochus] hesitated, astounded by the peremptory order, and at last replied, 'I will do what the Senate thinks right.'[5]

As sure as the Corinthian commander misunderstood the refined Athenian signals two-and-a-half centuries earlier, Antiochus understood the meaning of the Roman Senate—if you cross this line in the Nile Delta sand, then you are at war with the world's only superpower. The Roman message was delivered face-to-face, elegantly but unequivocally, just a generation after Publius Cornelius Scipio earned the *agnomen* Africanus by demonstrating what happens to those who attack Roman allies and dare to challenge Rome.[6]

Cold War Deterrence and Cyber Deterrence

The objective of these introductory remarks is not to wallow in the classics, but to use history to liberate our 21st century challenge of deterring cyber attacks from that unique, narrow and often misperceived four decade bit of 20th century history known as the Cold War.

Could Cold War-style Mutual Assured Destruction—MAD—work against cyber weapons? In a word, no. As Lebow writes in his analysis of Thucydides, "Deterrence and compellence only take on meaning in context. Abstract universal modes have little applicability to individual cases where idiosyncratic factors can,

---

5. Titus Livius (Livy), *Ad Urbe Condita (History of Rome)*, George Baker, trans., (New York: Peter A. Mesier, 1823), 6: xlv (12).

6. The Second Punic War was, after all, provoked by Hannibal's 219 BC attack on Saguntum, a Roman ally. Rome was the world's only superpower in 168 BC quite simply because Scipio Africanus had destroyed Carthage in 202 BC.

and often do, prove decisive."[7] However, that does not mean that any kind of deterrence is impossible or that there are no valuable lessons from the Cold War.

If there is any enduring lesson in the Cold War experience, it is that we had better pay attention to idiosyncrasies, as Lebow puts it. As Keith Payne, one of our country's leading deterrence theorists carefully explains, "Only recently, courtesy of greater access to past Soviet decision-making practices, has it become virtually unarguable that the Soviet leadership never accepted the west's definition of rationality with regard to nuclear weapons." Rather than trying to understand the Kremlin, we employed a sort-of mirror-imaging technique developed by Thomas Schelling, "With," Payne writes, "little or no reference to the specific thought, goals and values of the Soviet leadership."[8]

Given this, we should not want to transplant MAD onto the 21st century cyber challenge, even if we could. Moreover, Cold War deterrence was much more complicated than just MAD, or at least more complicated than popular perceptions of MAD. It was never, "You nuke me and I'll nuke you."

From at least the period that began with the Czech coup in February 1948 and ended with the US hydrogen fusion bomb test at Enewetak in November 1952—Berlin blockade, Soviet nuclear test, NSC-68, NATO, invasion of South Korea, German rearmament—forward, deterrence was a broad and complicated concept.

It is neither possible nor desirable here to trace the evolution of Cold War nuclear strategy and deterrence.[9] There were many twists, turns, variants and adaptations. It is, however, reasonable to generalize that throughout the Cold War, the objective of deterrence was, of course, to deter a nuclear attack, but, more importantly, it was to deter a Soviet move against core American interests, primarily, although not exclusively, understood to mean an attack against Western Europe.

We did not deter nuclear war or conventional war; we deterred the Soviet Union. Neither did we deter the Soviet Union with nuclear weapons; we deterred it with a panoply of capabilities that included nuclear weapons. By 1953, writes Lawrence Freedman, "the United States now had a range of

---

7. Lebow, "Thucydides and Deterrence," p. 187.
8. Keith Payne, *The Fallacies of Cold War Deterrence and a New Direction*, (Lexington: University of Kentucky Press, 2001), pp. 19-20, 25. The entire volume is an excellent treatment on Cold War deterrence and how to build more effective deterrence in the post-Cold War era. See also Keith Payne's *Deterrence in the Second Nuclear Age*, (Lexington: University of Kentucky Press, 1996).
9. The best full treatment on nuclear policy remains Lawrence Freedman, *The Evolution of Nuclear Strategy*, (New York: St. Martin's, 1983). For this particular period see pp. 63-75. For a good overview of Cold War deterrence see Payne, *Fallacies*, pp. 17-37.

nuclear capabilities from hydrogen bombs large enough to take out a city of any size, to small weapons for battlefield use."[10] Moreover, the nuclear arsenal was complemented by conventional forces, a system of alliances, particularly NATO, German rearmament and American sea control. And these were backed by traditional diplomacy, public diplomacy—USIA offices were regular targets for communist agitators—economic development, particularly the Marshall Plan, and democratic development. Finally, declaratory policy and demonstrated will to resist communist aggression—Berlin, Korea, to name a few—also played crucial roles.

In sum, although we may use MAD as shorthand for Cold War deterrence, deterrence during that era was never one-dimensional and never simple. So, if we see the Cold War as an era simpler than our own—which it probably was—we should not now be lured by the siren song of some easy deterrent formula. Notions of a breezy acronym backed by some tit-for-tat cyber weapon should be swept off the table.

The Post Cold War Cyber Deterrence Challenge

In the post-Cold War period—inability to coin a descriptive phrase indicates its complexity—we are challenged by a variety of nation-states, mostly unconnected by any common ideology. Add to them sub-national groups of various capabilities right up to the capability to kill thousands of people inside the United States, and things look even more complex. And when we turn specifically to cyber challenges, things become even murkier because the price of admission is much lower than it would be for most weapons of mass destruction or even coordinated airplane hijackings. Consequently, we must also consider criminal syndicates and loosely knit groups of cyber-anarchists.

As we shall see, one of the key questions is, whom are we trying to deter? And it would be rash to think of smaller states and sub-national groups as lesser-included cases of a deterrent posture designed against, say, China or Russia.

However, before turning to this and related questions, let us consider what we mean by deterrence. The US Department of Defense defines deterrence as "The prevention of action by the existence of a credible threat of unacceptable

---

10.   Freedman, *Evolution*, p. 77.

counteraction and/or belief that the cost of action outweighs the perceived benefits."[11]

One could hardly argue with this definition, although Martin Libicki in his *Cyberdeterrence and Cyberwar* offers a variant, borrowed from William Kaufman that may be a bit more graspable in concrete terms.

> Deterrence consists of essentially two basic components: first, the expressed intention to defend a certain interest; secondly, the demonstrated capability actually to achieve the defense of the interest in question, or to inflict such a cost on the attacker that, even if he should be able to gain his end, it would not seem worth the effort to him.[12]

He goes on to say, "If deterrence is anything that dissuades an attack, it is usually said to have two components: deterrence by denial (the ability to frustrate the attacks) and deterrence by punishment (the threat of retaliation)." Note that while the DoD definition does not exclude the former, it leans toward the latter. For the purpose of his discussion of cyber deterrence, Libicki excludes deterrence by denial. While acknowledging that denial is important and that denial and punishments work synergistically, he points out that denial is tantamount to defense, which we should be doing anyway, regardless of its contribution to deterrence.

Without evaluating the efficacy of the computer network defense measures undertaken, one can observe that the US Government is well aware of the dual nature of deterrence and the role that defense—that is, denial—plays. Consider, for example, the Department of Defense's response in the November 2011 so-called Section 934 Report to a direct question posed by the Senate.

> Deterrence in cyberspace, as with other domains, relies on two principal mechanisms: denying an adversary's objectives and, if necessary, imposing costs on an adversary for aggression. Accordingly, DoD will continue to strengthen its defenses and support efforts to improve the cyber security of our government, critical infrastructure, and Nation. By denying or minimizing the benefit of malicious activity in cyberspace, the United States will discourage adversaries from attacking

---

11. *DoD Dictionary of Military Terms. http://www.dtic.mil/doctrine/dod_dictionary/data/d/3763.html,* accessed April 12, 2012.

12. Martin C. Libicki, *Cyberdeterrence and Cyberwar,* (Santa Monica, RAND, 2009), pp. 6-7.

or exploiting our networks. DoD supports these efforts by enhancing our defenses, increasing our resiliency, and conducting military-to-military bilateral and multilateral discussions.[13]

For now, what is clearly missing from the denial side of the deterrence formula is an effective, coordinated effort to defend the computer networks of US critical infrastructure, most of which are privately owned. At the time of this writing, the Congress is locked in a debate over how to approach this matter.[14]

With that said, the really interesting questions surround deterrence by punishment. So, agreeing with Libicki, "From this point on, deterrence refers to deterrence by punishment."[15]

Parenthetically, anyone inclined to repose Cold War-style faith in deterrence alone should recall that Athenian miscalculations in the Battle of Corcyra hastened the Peloponnesian War, "A terrible war," writes Kagan, "that changed the Greek World and its civilization forever."[16]

No matter how hard we try to get it right, Payne writes, "Deterrence is unreliable; prepare for its failure."[17]

> Despite near-constant claims by US civilian officials, military leaders, and prominent academics, no particular nuclear balance, no weapon system, no declaratory policy, no technological advance, no presidential statement, no intelligence breakthrough, and no organizational gimmick can predictably 'ensure' deterrence. Doing so would require omniscience and omnipotence, qualities even Washington lacks.[18]

To think otherwise, about cyber or anything else, would be sheer hubris.

---

13. United States of America, Department of Defense, *Department of Defense Cyberspace Policy Report,* November 2011, p. 2, *http://www.defense.gov/home/features/2011/0411_cyberstrategy/docs/NDAA%20Section%20934%20Report_For%20webpage.pdf,* accessed April 11, 2012.

14. Compare the approaches represented by the *Secure IT Act of 2012,* introduced by Senator John McCain (R-AZ) and the *Secure IT Act of 2012* introduced by Senator Joe Lieberman (I-CT). Cybersecurity Act of 2012 (S. 2105), *www.hsgac.senate.gov,* accessed April 10, 2012; Secure IT Act of 2012 (S. 2151), *http://www.govtrack.us/congress/bills/112/s2151/text,* accessed April 14, 2012.

15. *Ibid.,* p. 7.

16. Kagan, *Peloponnesian War,* p. xxiii.

17. Payne, *Fallacies,* 193-196.

18. *Ibid.,* p. 98.

Returning to the definitional matters raised by Libicki, there is one in which this chapter differs with *Cyberdeterrence and Cyberwar*. Libicki confines his definition of cyber deterrence to deterrence in kind, that is, a cyber attack for a cyber attack. This is because his objective is to explore whether the United States should develop an offensive cyber capability for the purpose of deterrence.[19]

In contrast, this chapter addresses the broader matter of whether deterrence against cyber attacks is feasible. In this context, it is better to leave the definition open to any form of retaliation available to the United States, understanding, of course, that in some cases, there may be no feasible measures. Seen in this way, cyber responses comprise one layer in a hierarchy of potential responses, tougher than legal, diplomatic or economic measures, but not as tough as a military response.[20]

Four Questions

So, what are the prospects for deterring cyber attacks by mounting a credible threat—or threats—of unacceptable counteraction(s) by a variety of means at our disposal? The answer hinges upon the answers to four antecedent questions:

- What do we want to deter?
- Whom do we want to deter?
- How shall we deter?
- Will we know against whom to react?

What Do We Want to Deter?

What do we want to deter? During the Cold War, the answer to this question was perhaps daunting but reasonably simple. It was fuzzy around the edges—local wars and communist subversion—but in the main, it involved nuclear weapons, tanks and seizure of large swathes of territory.

---

19. Libicki, *Cyberdeterrence*, pp. 7, 11, 26. Libicki addresses a statement made by General James Cartwright, former JCS Vice Chairman: "History teaches us that a purely defensive posture poses significant risks…When we apply the principle of warfare to the cyber domain, as we do to sea, air and land, we realize the defense of the nation is better served by capabilities enabling us to take the fight to our adversaries, when necessary, to deter actions detrimental to our interests."
20. See Libicki's useful chart. *Ibid.*, p. 29.

Cyber presents a much murkier set of challenges, exacerbated by our—we all do it—propensity to call every non-cooperative cyber event an attack. Secretary of Defense Leon Panetta, for example, recently told a Louisville audience, "We are literally getting hundreds of thousands of attacks every day that try to exploit information in various agencies and departments and frankly throughout this country."[21]

A deterrent posture aimed at hundreds of thousands of attacks daily boggles the mind, so, if there is a prospect for 21st century cyber deterrence, its object must be paired down. Let us begin with an overview of the kinds of cyber "attacks" that we face.

At the top of the computer network attack hierarchy is unauthorized access that alters algorithms or data to disrupt a computer's intended function to the extent of causing physical damage. It is difficult to do and, therefore, rare, but potentially catastrophic.

A recent example was the Stuxnet worm, discovered in 2010, which reportedly destroyed 1,000 centrifuges at Iran's Natanz uranium enrichment facility. Apparently, Stuxnet was designed to attack a Siemens-made programmable logic controller that operated the centrifuges. Soon after the revelation of Stuxnet, an Institute for Science and International Security study suggested that Stuxnet had induced a modest increase in the centrifuge motor speed, which caused vibrations sufficiently strong to break the motor.[22]

Retired General Michael Hayden, a former director of both the National Security Agency and the Central Intelligence Agency, believes that Stuxnet is a harbinger of things to come. "We have entered into a new phase of conflict," he told the *60 Minutes* television program, "in which we use a cyber weapon to create physical destruction, and in this case, physical destruction in someone else's critical infrastructure."[23]

Stuxnet may have brought the matter to our television screens, but the idea has concerned cyber security officials for some time. For example, in a 2007 experiment called Aurora, the Department of Homeland Security, in

21. United States of America, Department of Defense, *Remarks by Secretary Panetta at the McConnell Center, University of Louisville, KY*, March 1, 2012, *http://www.defense.gov/transcripts/transcript.aspx?transcriptid=4988*, accessed April 12, 2012.

22. Yaakov Katz, "Stuxnet may have destroyed 1,000 centrifuges at Natanz," *Jerusalem Post*, December 24, 2010, *http://www.jpost.com/Defense/Article.aspx?id=200843*, accessed April 10, 2012.

23. Steven Musil, "'60 Minutes' Profiles Threat Posed by Stuxnet," *CNET News*, March 4, 2012, *http://news.cnet.com/8301-1009_3-57390326-83/60-minutes-profiles-threat-posed-by-stuxnet/*, accessed April 10, 2012.

conjunction with the Department of Energy's Idaho National Laboratory, accessed the controls of a diesel-powered electrical generator. "In a previously classified video of the test," a CNN story says, "the generator shakes and smokes, and then stops."

In a CNN interview, Joe Weiss of Applied Control Solutions said, "What people had assumed in the past is the worst thing you can do is shut things down. And that's not necessarily the case. A lot of times the worst thing you can do, for example, is open a valve—have bad things spew out of a valve... The point is, it allows you to take control of these very large, very critical pieces of equipment and you can have them do what you want them to do."[24]

With some debate over legal definitions, reasonable people would probably agree that a cyber attack directed from outside the United States intended to cause physical damage, death or injury would be an act of war, a worthy object of deterrence and, should deterrence fail, justification for retaliation.

The video of the Idaho generator shaking, steaming, smoking and dying takes just over a minute. However, conceptual challenges for deterrence arise if one considers less clear possibilities. For example, what if the attacked computer network is only disrupted such that damage is gradual and subtle? Or, what if it is just corrupted to cause errors, confusion or slowdown? What if it even shuts down a network's intended function, but does no physical damage? For example, is a distributed denial of service (DDoS) attack on the New York Stock Exchange the kind of attack that we should consider in the context of deterrence?[25]

Despite the challenges, we can devise a definition of threats worth at least trying to deter—any disruption to government or privately-owned computer networks that threatens life-sustaining services that could result in mass casualties or mass evacuation; catastrophic economic damage to the United States; or severe degradation of national security. Anything less, even if a true computer network attack, is a nuisance, maybe even a threat, but an object of defense, not deterrence.

---

24. Jeanne Meserve, "Sources: Staged Cyber Attack Reveals Vulnerability in Power Grid," CNN US, September 26, 2007, *http://articles.cnn.com/2007-09-26/us/power.at.risk_1_generator-cyber-attack-electric-infrastructure?_s=PM:US*, accessed April 12, 2012. Watch the video on YouTube at *http://www.youtube.com/watch?v=fJyWngDco3g*, accessed April 12, 2010.

25. DDoS attacks come from hundreds, maybe thousands of infected computers herded without their owners' knowledge into a botnet. Upon command of the so-called botherder, each computer in the botnet blasts requests at the target website until it is overwhelmed and unable to perform its intended function.

Note that the language in the preceding paragraph is borrowed from an early version of the Lieberman Cybersecurity Act of 2012. It was justly criticized as being too vague as a matter of law and has since been modified.[26] Nonetheless, it is useful at the conceptual level of this chapter in which we are not defining what is and is not covered as a matter of law but roughly describing what we might want to deter, which is, of course, subjective, event-specific and a bit fuzzy around the edges.

This point must not be taken lightly—circumstances will matter. While we cannot rule out that some virtual group of cyber-hooligans or *jihadis* may conduct a serious attack against the United States simply to prove their point or flex their muscle, it is more likely that such a serious attack would come in the context of some developing geopolitical situation. Such attacks could be precursors to a kinetic attack on the United States, its forces or allies, or they could be diversionary measures aimed at drawing our attention away from some world situation. It must be an essential element of deterrence that the United States make clear that it will not tolerate such attacks, that it will punish perpetrators and that it will not allow the associated situation to play out.

Let us now jump from the top of the cyber attack hierarchy to the bottom—cyber crime and cyber hooliganism. We could probably agree that, "My father was until recently Governor of the Kogi State Bank..." is not the opening line of a national security threat. Of course, there are many more serious economic crimes being perpetrated online, but most of them are not serious threats to national security. This is not to diminish the law enforcement task at hand, but to remove common crimes from the list of serious disruptions that might be deterred—unless, of course, they meet the criteria stated above.

Likewise, we must stop the shrieking every time someone defaces the CIA's unclassified home page or steals the names and credit card numbers from an online analytical service, even one that caters to security professionals. Again, this is not to suggest that these matters are unimportant or not to be pursued, but they are not serious national security concerns to be deterred.

That leads us back to the middle of the cyber attack hierarchy, below computer network attacks and above ordinary crime and hooliganism. Panetta misspeaks when he refers to "attacks"—in most of these incidents, nothing is destroyed or damaged, nor does the computer owner lose its functionality.

---

26. Cybersecurity Act of 2012. For a review of that early version see Stephen M. Spina, and J. Daniel Kees, "Cybersecurity Act of 2012 Introduced," *National Review*, February 21, 2012, *http://www.natlawreview.com/article/cybersecurity-act-2012-introduced*, accessed April 12, 2012.

Most of what the Secretary is describing is computer network exploitation, usually for the purpose of stealing information—espionage. Panetta is correct, however, in describing the dimensions of the problem as "hundreds of thousands every day." Of course, not every attempt is successful and some successful exploits are more serious than others. Nonetheless, the problem is huge.

Libicki excludes computer network exploitation—espionage—from his discussion of cyber deterrence for four reasons: 1) the computer owner suffers no harm (apart from lost secrets), 2) it is difficult to detect, 3) the laws of war rarely recognize espionage as *casus belli,* and 4) everyone does it.[27] In the end, this may emerge as the only practical approach; however, the problem is so vexing that it deserves a bit more discussion.

So long as espionage meant Ian Fleming or John LeCarré characters snapping photographs of secret documents with their cigarette lighters, dodging the matter may have been acceptable. However, Stalin is supposed to have said, "Quantity has a quality all its own." Today, in the cyber realm, we may be at the point at which espionage against the United States has assumed a quality all its own. General Keith Alexander, National Security Agency Director and Cyber Command Commander told a Senate committee that the Chinese theft of US intellectual property is the "greatest transfer of wealth in history."[28]

The real concern in this goes beyond a bit of money and a patent or two. Right now, while some are expecting a cyber Pearl Harbor to jolt us into action, as recently retired FBI Executive Assistant Director Shawn Henry put it, "We're not winning".[29] That means that the United States is, and has been for some time, funding research and development for the People's Liberation Army modernization. We could wake up one day to a *fait accompli*—no Pearl Harbor, cyber or kinetic—the PLA may be able, for example, to deny US access to the western Pacific.

Nonetheless, Center for Strategic and International Studies Senior Fellow James A. Lewis said, following up on Henry's remarks, "There's a kind of willful desire not to admit how bad things are, both in government and certainly in the private sector."[30]

---

27. Libicki, *Cyberdeterrence,* p. 23.

28. Lisa Daniel, "DOD Needs Industry's Help to Catch Cyber Attacks, Commander Says," US Department of Defense, *American Forces Press Service,* March 27, 2012, *http://www.defense.gov/news/newsarticle.aspx?id=67713,* accessed April 14, 2012.

29. Devlin Barrett, "US Outgunned in Hacker War," *Wall Street Journal,* March 28, 2012, *http://online.wsj.com/article/SB10001424052702304177104577307773326180032.html,* accessed, April 14, 2012.

30. *Ibid.*

Closely related to computer network exploitation—in the strategic sense if not the technical—is the problem of supply chain contamination. Buying so many components from abroad, particularly but not exclusively from China, the United States risks relying upon equipment that contains hard to detect malicious firmware. Scott Borg of the Internet Security Alliance sums up the challenge.

> There is a serious danger that the supply chain for electronic components, including microchips, could be infiltrated at some stage by hostile agents. These hostile agents could alter the circuitry of the electronic components or substitute counterfeit components with altered circuitry. The altered circuitry could contain "malicious firmware" that would function in much the same way as malicious software. If the electronic components were connected to any network that enemy attackers could access, the malicious firmware could give them control of the information systems. Even if the malicious firmware was not connected to any network accessible to the attackers, it could still contain logic bombs that could cause terrible harm. A logic bomb in a weapons system, for example, could lie dormant until the system engaged in certain activities indicating a high degree of mobilization. These symptoms of mobilization could then trigger the logic bomb. The logic bomb could shut down the larger information system or, worse, turn the equipment controlled by the information system against those operating it.[31]

All this is rather daunting and so complex that it may indeed be undeterrable. If we consider each case singularly, we would agree with Libicki

---

31. Scott Borg, *Securing the Supply Chain for Electronic Equipment: A Strategy and Framework*, Internet Security Alliance, undated, *http://www.whitehouse.gov/files/documents/cyber/ISA%20 -%20Securing%20the%20Supply%20Chain%20for%20Electronic%20Equipment.pdf*, accessed April 14, 2012. Generally, on Chinese cyber activities see The US-China Economic Security Review Commission, *Occupying the Information High Ground: Chinese Capabilities for Computer Network Operations and Cyber Espionage*, March 7, 2012. *http://www.uscc.gov/RFP/2012/USCC%20 Report_Chinese_CapabilitiesforComputer_NetworkOperationsandCyberEspionage.pdf*, accessed April 14, 2012. For a good summary and commentary on the report see Mike Lennon, "US Official on Cyber Attacks: 'It's Getting Harder for Chinese Officials to Claim Ignorance,'" *Security Week*, March 9, 2012. *http://www.securityweek.com/uscc-commissioner-cyberattacks-getting-harder-chinas-leaders-claim-ignorance*, accessed April 14, 2012. See also William T. Hagestad II, *21st Century Chinese Cyberwarfare* (Ely, England: IT Governance Publishing, 2012); Richard A. Clarke "How China Steals our Secrets," *New York Times*, April 2, 2012, *http://www.nytimes.com/2012/04/03/ opinion/how-china-steals-our-secrets.html?scp=1&sq=richard%20clarke&st=cse*, accessed April 15, 2012; and generally Richard Clarke, *Cyber War* (New York: Harper Collins, 2010).

that because computer network exploitation—and, added here, supply chain contamination—"is so difficult to detect, a deterrence policy could only be activated by exception. Harsh punishments for crimes that are rarely detected lose credibility."[32]

However, with mounting evidence of particularly, though not exclusively, Chinese actions, perhaps we need to depart from tit-for-tat deterrence and focus on deterring a policy or a way of doing things. US officials frequently complain and demand redress, but thus far have been unwilling to impose any costs. This is likely because we perceive that doing this would result in an immediate cost to us that we are unwilling to bear or to risk. However, if the medium term consequences are as gruesome as some say, perhaps we should reconsider.

Regrettably, this chapter will not resolve this matter; however, it offers the following suggestion. The effect of particularly but not exclusively Chinese computer network exploitation and supply chain corruption should be thoroughly examined and debated, in classified and unclassified forums. If we determine that it is doing serious damage to US national security, then we should consider whether some new approach to deterrence, or, to return to Cold War terminology, compellence, is in order.[33]

In sum, we should carefully consider whether it is possible to deter computer network attacks on government or privately-owned networks that threaten life-sustaining services that could result in mass casualties or mass evacuation; catastrophic economic damage to the United States; or severe degradation of national security. Additionally, we should examine the effects of computer network exploitation and devise a course of action, which may include some form of deterrence or compellence. In other words, the United States must seriously consider whether deterring actions that could result in catastrophic harm in the medium term is worth some near term pain or sacrifice.

Whom do we want to deter?

We should at least consider whether we can deter anyone who could and would carry out an attack that meets the criteria set forth above. This would certainly include nation-states, with China at the forefront, but with Russia not far behind. Richard Clarke, former Special Advisor to the President for

---

32. Libicki, *Cyberdeterrence*, p. 23.
33. Thomas Schelling *Arms and Influence* (New Haven: Yale University Press, 2008).

Cybersecurity, writes, "US Intelligence officials do not, however, rate China as the biggest threat to the United States in cyberspace. 'The Russians are definitely better, almost as good as we are,' said one."[34] Clarke goes on to quote Admiral Mike McConnell, former Director of National Intelligence, "The vast majority of the industrialized countries in the world today have cyber attack capabilities."[35]

That makes things vastly more complicated than the Cold War, but there is more. Concern about terrorist groups mastering computer network attack skills dates back to 2000 when Japanese police discovered that *Aum Shinrikyo*, the group that delivered a deadly sarin nerve gas attack in the Tokyo subway in 1995, had been developing software for Japanese companies and government agencies.[36]

Since 9/11, of course, the greatest fear is that al Qaeda and its offshoots—no strangers to the Internet—will develop an affinity for offensive cyber operations. Cofer Black, former chief of the CIA's Counter Terrorism Center, told the 2011 Black Hat Conference that facing "strategic defeat," al Qaeda "will enter the cyber world because it's comparatively remote, comparatively safer than strapping on a bomb."[37]

The same news report continues, "In a speech on July 14 [2011], [former] Deputy Secretary of Defense William Lynn III said it was 'clear' terror groups were 'intent on acquiring, refining, and expanding their cyber capabilities…If a terrorist group gains disruptive or destructive cyber tools, we have to assume they will strike with little hesitation,'" he said.[38]

Finally, some officials apparently believe that the loosely knit hacker group Anonymous could soon acquire capabilities to conduct major operations such as affecting the US power supply.[39]

---

34. Clarke, *Cyber War*, p. 63. See also Jeffrey Carr, *Inside Cyber Warfare*, 2nd. ed., (Mountain View, California: O'Reilly Media, 2011).

35. Clarke, *Cyber War*, p. 64.

36. Sims, Calvin, "Japan Sect's Companies Developed Software," *SunSentinel.com*, March 2, 2000, *http://articles.sun-sentinel.com/2000-03-02/news/0003020007_1_nippon-telegraph-computer-companies-sect*, accessed April 12, 2012.

37. Lee Ferran, "Former CIA Counter-Terror Chief: al Qaeda Will Go Cyber," *ABC News*, August 4, 2011, *http://abcnews.go.com/Blotter/cia-counter-terror-chief-al-qaeda-cyber/story?id=14224256#.T4xBfNkwDPg*, accessed April 14, 2012.

38. *Ibid.*

39. The remarks are attributed to General Alexander in a closed White House meeting, however, there has been no public statement from the General, nor any further corroborating information.

Deterring—if it is possible—groups like al Qaeda and Anonymous could involve aspects of domestic law enforcement, which should be treated in a manner more thorough than this chapter permits. Consequently, the remainder of the chapter will focus on possible external aspects of deterrence that the United States would execute as a nation-state. However, this is not to diminish the considerable deterrent effect that effective law enforcement can have on certain domestic perpetrators, whether affinity terrorists or hacktivists and hooligans.

There can be no doubt that as a matter of policy, nation-states, terrorist groups and seriously threatening hacker groups should be deterred—the question is whether we know how to do that, a matter addressed in the next section.

How Shall We Deter?

Based on what we have learned about Cold War deterrence and extensive analysis of the post-Cold War situation, Payne has devised "an initial effort to define a methodology supportive of a new, more empirical approach to deterrence."[40] He explains:

> If discussions of deterrence are to have a chance of being more insightful than misleading, the Cold War assumption of a rational cum reasonable and predictable opponent must be discarded in favor of as much information as possible concerning the specific opponent and the specific context. In this manner, the opponent's cost-benefit calculus may be more accurately modeled and the likely effectiveness of US deterrence threats in practice may be more accurately anticipated. As part of the policy-formulation process, a challenger's particular thought, beliefs, and values must be examined to reduce the prospect for wholly surprising responses to US deterrence threats.[41]

Payne's analysis is not directed at cyber attacks, but the steps in his proposed methodology would be a good beginning in any case. A summary adapted to our discussion thus far follows:

Siobhan Gorman, "Alert on Hacker Power Play," *Wall Street Journal*, February 21, 2011, *http://online.wsj.com/article/SB10001424052970204059804577229390105521090.html*, accessed April 12, 2012.

40. Payne, *Fallacies*, p. 104.

41. *Ibid.*, p. 99.

- Identify challenging or potentially challenging nation-states or groups and their leaderships.

- Identify those country or group characteristics that could be significant.

- Construct a strategic profile of the challenger, if possible, pertinent to a specific matter.

- Assess whether the nation-state or group under consideration is likely to be deterrable. This point is crucial: "If not, then alternatives to deterrence policies obviously would take on greater priority."

- Identify the policy options realistically available to the United States

- Identify any gaps between what is needed and what is available.[42]

To these should be added two more points. First, we must devise a policy in which the country or group being deterred perceives a benefit to desisting. If it believes that the United States will seek to destroy it no matter what it does, it is unlikely to be deterred from this or that action, including a cyber attack. Second, we must assess capabilities needed to assure that the United States prevails if the challenger is undeterrable or is not deterred.

These points are remarkably similar to the "Key requirements and priorities for achieving an effective capability to carry out a cyber deterrent strategy" presented by Richard L. Kugler in his book chapter *Deterrence of Cyber Attacks*. The objective, writes Kugler, is "tailored deterrence."[43]

- "A clear and firm declaratory policy spelling out the US intention to deter cyber attacks."

- High global situational awareness.

- Good command and control systems.

- Effective cyber defenses.

- "A wide spectrum of counter-cyber offensive capabilities, including cyber attack and other instruments for asserting US power in order to enforce deterrence before, during, and after crises."

---

42. *Ibid.* pp. 104-114.

43. Richard L Kugler, "Deterrence of Cyber Attacks," *Cyberpower and National Security*, Franklin D. Kramer, Stuart H. Starr and Larry K. Wentz, eds. (Washington: Nation Defense University Press, 2009), pp. 325, 331-336.

- Good US inter-agency coordination and allied cooperation.
- Cyber deterrence methodologies and metrics.[44]

Readings of Payne and Kugler can be summed up fairly simply: 1) realistically assess the values of the challenger or potential challenger and hold them at risk—at all costs, do not mirror image; 2) be prepared; and 3) be prepared for failure. Even if we avoid the now obvious shortcomings of US Cold War deterrence policies, this will not be easy, even for relatively familiar nation-states like Russia, and even less easy for more difficult to understand—for us, at least—countries and groups. However, as Kugler observes, "Even terrorist groups are motivated not just by ideology and hatred, but also by strategic goals and self-preservation."[45]

Of course, no matter how hard we try, we must always prepare for failure. In the case of cyber, defense and resilience are essential.

Then there is the possibility that, try as we might, we may not be able to figure out what the challenger or potential challenger under scrutiny really holds valuable. Or, having figured it out, we realize that holding that value or values at risk is impossible or impractical for the United States. As Payne says, in that case, other measures assume a greater priority.

There are two requisites to considering any kind of cyber deterrent strategy. First, we must have first-rate intelligence and information about every challenger or potential challenger. Second, we must have a full range of capabilities to consider in order to maximize the chances of success at the lowest level possible:

- Diplomatic, economic and legal
- Retaliation in kind, that is, cyber measures
- Military, culminating in nuclear capabilities

Restricting ourselves to retaliation in kind would deprive us of possible avenues to success, possibly at a lower level of conflict. And, though there are other good and sufficient reasons for the United States to develop offensive cyber capabilities, in the deterrence realm, offensive cyber capabilities would provide another option, possibly controlling escalation to military measures.

---

44. *Ibid.*, p. 332.
45. *Ibid.*, p. 326.

Cyber deterrence will not work in every instance in which we would like to work; however, since most of its requirements are analytical and declaratory, it is worth the effort.

As a declaratory matter, the United States is already half way there. Our current deterrent posture is declared in the May 2011 *International Strategy for Cyberspace:*

> When warranted, the United States will respond to hostile acts in cyberspace as we would to any other threat to our country. All states possess an inherent right to self-defense, and we recognize that certain hostile acts conducted through cyberspace could compel actions under the commitments we have with our military treaty partners. We reserve the right to use all necessary means—diplomatic, informational, military, and economic—as appropriate and consistent with applicable international law, in order to defend our Nation, our allies, our partners, and our interests. In so doing, we will exhaust all options before military force whenever we can; will carefully weigh the costs and risks of action against the costs of inaction; and will act in a way that reflects our values and strengthens our legitimacy, seeking broad international support whenever possible.[46]

As a matter of policy, we appear to have arrived at a deterrence policy. As a matter of posture, we have not done the hard analytical work described above, determined exactly what "all necessary means" are and tailored declaratory policies for specific challengers and potential challengers.

Moreover, we cannot hide behind the cloak of classification—for the most part, deterrence is an open affair. By the way, there is a lesson here to be drawn from the Cold War. Of course, we never publicly discussed weapon designs or specific operational details. However, a quick perusal of the bibliographies in the works by Freedman and Payne cited herein reveals an incredible wealth of information and discussion about nuclear and deterrent strategy. Our Cold War debate was remarkably open.

One final question remains and that is whether we will know who the perpetrators of a cyber attack are.

---

46. White House, *International Strategy for Cyberspace: Prosperity, Security, and Openness in a Networked World*, May 2011, *http://www.whitehouse.gov/sites/default/files/rss_viewer/international_strategy_for_cyberspace.pdf*, accessed April 11, 2012.

Will we know against whom to react?

Knowing who did it—attribution—is a major issue in cyber policy. However, it is often overstated to the degree that, in Kugler's words, it "wholly paralyzes any attempt to think fruitfully about a cyber deterrence strategy."[47]

At the outset, let us state that no one suggests that the United States act rashly or blindly. On the other hand, as Kugler points out, "Deterrence depends on the capacity of the United States to project an image of resolve, willpower, and capability in sufficient strength to convince a potential adversary to refrain from activities that threaten US and allied interests." Dithering over attribution detracts from such a posture. In some instances, attribution may be a showstopper, but not in all.

Cyber forensics is not perfect, but it is much better than some think. Moreover, it need only provide some pieces of the puzzle. Coupled with country or group knowledge derived from the process suggested above and understanding that "Major cyber attacks should not be seen in isolation, but in the context of larger global security affairs,"[48] in many cases, a fairly clear picture will emerge.

For example, during and after Russia's 2008 attack on Georgia, many analysts were paralyzed by their inability to prove on their screens who was responsible for the cyber attacks upon Georgia. However, one-dimensional proof is unrealistic and unnecessary. Coupled with an in depth knowledge of Russia's unique nexus of government, business and crime, and put in the context of a long string of belligerent Russian moves, culminating in war, it emerged quite clearly that Russia was responsible. Whether the person behind the keyboard was a soldier, a criminal or a member of the *Nashi* youth group was not as important as who was ultimately responsible.[49]

Of course, in the 2008 case, apart from seizing the moral high ground, Georgia had little to gain. The US has more flexibility.

For one thing, the United States disposes of a full range of capabilities with which to implement a cyber deterrence policy. It need not fire off a cyber-salvo, as some analysts imply. An array of capabilities allows it to gain time

---

47. Kugler, "Deterrence of Cyber Attacks," p. 309.

48. *Ibid.*, p. 310.

49. The best analyses of the 2008 Russia-Georgia war are *Russia/Georgia Cyber War—Findings and Analysis*, Project Gray Goose: Phase I Report, October 17, 2008. *http://www.scribd.com/doc/6967393/Project-Grey-Goose-Phase-I-Report*, accessed, April 12, 2012; and Tom Young, "US Report Links Russian Hackers and Military," *ITNews*, August 18, 2009, *http://www.itnews.com.au/News/153255,us-report-links-russian-hackers-and-military.aspx*, accessed April 12, 2012.

in case of any uncertainty, while still beginning to act. Diplomatic, economic and legal pressures could be options, as could the mobilization, although not necessarily the use, of military forces.

There is one more option that makes deterrence policy in the face of an attribution challenge palatable. The Atlantic Council's Jason Healey has pioneered the concept of national responsibility to circumvent the "attribution fixation." Healey writes, "For national security policymakers, knowing 'who is to blame?' can be more important than 'who did it?'"

Healey argues that, "As a policy (not legal) matter, nations can and should hold one another responsible to stop [cyber] attacks and clean the cyber environment." He argues that this is consistent with current US policy as articulated in the *International Strategy for Cyberspace* and that the United States came close to implicit recognition of such a policy in its handling of the fallout from Chinese intrusions into Google networks in 2010.[50]

Of course, it would be better if a critical mass of nations agreed to such a policy, however, for the United States, this is not necessary. Only fairly strong international backing could have helped Georgia to challenge Russia on such grounds in 2008. However, the United States is sufficiently powerful that it could easily incorporate such a policy into its cyber deterrent declaratory policy. Moreover, if Washington were to take the lead on this, it would likely be followed by a critical mass of like-minded countries.

With that said, a note of caution is appropriate. The principle of national responsibility is a way of moving, as Healey's title suggests, beyond attribution. However, it should only be inserted into US national policy if we intend to insist upon it and have the will to impose sanctions against states that fail to cooperate. Essentially, we would be deterring non-cooperation in cyber attack investigations.

These considerations do not completely overcome the attribution problem, but if carefully considered, they can help forge a path toward an effective US cyber deterrence policy.

Conclusion

Deterrence has been succeeding and failing for 25 centuries, and probably longer. There is now no reason to expect more or less from it in the

---

50. Jason Healey, "Beyond Attribution: Seeking National Responsibility for Cyber Attacks," *Atlantic Council Issue Brief*, February 22, 2012, *http://www.acus.org/publication/beyond-attribution-seeking-national-responsibility-cyberspace*, accessed April 11, 2012.

cyber realm. Understanding that deterrence could fail, and preparing for that contingency, we should not deprive ourselves of what could be a useful tool for cyber security. Nor should we confine ourselves to narrow misperceptions of what Cold War deterrence was or to artificial formulations such as only deterrence in kind.

Deterrence—the prevention of action by the existence of a credible threat of unacceptable counteraction and/or belief that the cost of action outweighs the perceived benefits—requires careful preparation, which, in turn, requires a full range of potential retaliatory measures:

- Diplomatic, economic and legal
- Retaliation in kind, that is, cyber measures
- Military, culminating in nuclear capabilities

The United States should seek to deter nation-states, terrorist groups and seriously threatening hacker groups from perpetrating any disruption to government or privately-owned computer networks that threatens life-sustaining services that could result in mass casualties or mass evacuation; catastrophic economic damage to the United States; or severe degradation of national security. Moreover, there is at least a strong argument that we should seek to deter cyber espionage and supply chain contamination.

With regard to deterring cyber espionage and supply chain contamination, critics are likely to argue that this is impossible because the costs of retaliation to the United States would be too high. This is to mistake pain for impossibility. Careful analysis may determine that the costs of such deterrence are indeed too high; however, we must take care to analyze the right things. The question is not whether paying more for washing machines and televisions will be painful—it will be. The correct question is whether the cost in the medium term of inaction today is greater or less than the cost of action today.

The United States must overcome what Lewis calls the "willful desire not to admit how bad things are."

The United States must also dodge the paralyzing effect of what Healey calls "attribution fixation." Attribution of cyber incidents is indeed a formidable challenge; however, it can often be overcome with cyber forensics and common-sense consideration of surrounding circumstances, augmented by the principle of national responsibility. Hostile or irresponsible states should not be allowed to hide behind attribution.

In this regard, a strong deterrent posture, backed by a full array of possible retaliatory measures, actually buys time and makes room for further analysis and requests for cooperation in the investigation of cyber incidents. Moreover, national responsibility and deterrence are mutually reinforcing because a demand for the former helps inform decisions about the latter. Non-cooperation would be another factor to consider along with the results of forensic analysis and consideration of all the surrounding circumstances.

In sum, cyber deterrence, well applied, is worth a try. However, we must be ever mindful that deterrence may fail. Despite the best laid plans of Pericles, Athens and Sparta went to war, and Athens was defeated. The United States must be prepared for every cyber eventuality.

CHAPTER 7

US Shaping and Use of International Norms for Cyberspace

Barry Pavel

Introduction

The United States' use of cyberspace as an effective instrument for advancing US interests in the world today is less akin to the United States' use of nuclear weapons in the 1950s than it is to early caveman's use of primitive tools carved out of stone. For a nation that prides itself on innovation, creativity, and, in a word, power, we are dreadfully impotent and unskilled in seeking to take advantage of cyberspace to strengthen US influence in the world. Luckily, the entrepreneurial spirit that continues to animate our country in the private sector is thriving in cyberspace, and it will ultimately save the day for the United States's effective pursuit of national interests.

Yet, in order for that to happen, the way our government seeks to shape norms and behavior in cyberspace, and the way we talk about it and operate in it ourselves, need to change significantly.

Barry Pavel is Director of the Brent Scowcroft Center on International Security at the Atlantic Council, focusing on emerging security challenges, defense strategies and capabilities, and key European and global defense issues. Prior to joining the Atlantic Council, he was a career member of the Senior Executive Service in the Office of the Under Secretary of Defense for Policy for almost eighteen years. From October 2008 through July 2010, he served as the Special Assistant to the President and Senior Director for Defense Policy and Strategy on the National Security Council staff, serving President George W. Bush and President Barack Obama. Mr. Pavel led the development of five of the first eight Obama Administration Presidential Study Directives. He was the initiator and architect of the NSC's first-ever National Security Priorities Review and a key contributor to the President's 2010 National Security Strategy; led the NSC's oversight of the four Defense Department strategic reviews (the Quadrennial Defense Review, Nuclear Posture Review, Ballistic Missile Defense Review, and space posture review), including the President's September 2009 decision on European missile defense and all Presidential decisions on nuclear policy and posture; co-led the development of the President's June 2010 National Space Policy; and contributed to the

This chapter outlines the current status of norms in cyberspace and how the US Government seeks to use those norms to advance its interests in cyberspace. It then posits the desired end-state, or at the very least a way-station, for a much better set of cyber circumstances for the country. Finally, it outlines some minimum steps for how we might move toward that desired end-state.

The Baseline Cyber Situation

The United States is in its infancy in wielding cyberspace to achieve important national aims. There is so much more that could be done, if only we had a nimble government structure that was designed for the 21st century (or even the late 20th century), instead of being borne out of World War II. If only we had a culture of innovation, entrepreneurship, and collaboration that drove our government organizations to work seamlessly together to both wield cyberspace tools effectively and to advance our national interests in cyberspace.

After all, the United States reaps the greatest rewards from the existence of the cyberspace domain. Cyberspace is a national advantage for the United States. It is an advantage for our economic power, for our military power, for diplomacy, and for all other national instruments. Cyberspace "fits" the United States' culture, geography, private sector orientation, and many other traits of this country. It is a source of substantial innovation for the United States in the new digital economy, as well as an increasingly powerful tool for democratization, for economic prosperity, for connecting the United States and our culture with those of all other nations in the world, and for many other US national goals in the international arena. It also is, critically, the foundation of our military strength and our very ability to project military power in the world.

Yet, despite pockets of enormous cyber skill throughout the private sector and in key places in our government, we are far from realizing the benefits and potential of cyberspace at a basic level. Moreover, we remain extraordinarily

President's policies on Europe and NATO, Korea, cyberspace, DoD operational plans and activities, military family policy, and other matters. Mr. Pavel also served as the Chief of Staff and Principal Deputy Assistant Secretary of Defense for Special Operations/Low-Intensity Conflict & Interdependent Capabilities from 2006 through 2008. He helped Assistant Secretary of Defense Michael Vickers develop policy on the capabilities and operational employment of special operations forces, strategic forces, and conventional forces. His main areas of work covered strategic capabilities policy, including development of the first Department of Defense cyber deterrence strategy and better aligning the Department's approach to cyberspace activities and capabilities with defense strategy and policy.

vulnerable to a variety of malicious uses of cyberspace against us, some of which are ongoing on a daily basis and damaging our core national security interests. As a nation, we must steel ourselves to develop a strategy for better protecting ourselves against damaging cyber activities, and for better wielding cyber tools to advance our national interests.

Before discussing four key elements of the current state of play in cyberspace as they relate to behavior and to expectations of behavior (i.e., norms), it is important to briefly discuss cyber terminology. Even the most seasoned national security statesmen and experts continually use inaccurate terminology for cyberspace activities, particularly malicious cyberspace actions. To them, and to many of the journalists who write about these matters, cyber "attacks" occur all the time and encompass essentially all negative cyber activities ranging from cyber bullying all the way up to major cyber disruptions of physical facilities and activities. The proliferation of the phrase "cyber attack" may be the single most unproductive aspect of analytic discussions of cyberspace. This phrase is used far too often and far too imprecisely. So, rule number one on cyber terminology is: Not everything is an "attack."

Below are six key terms offered for use regarding a range of commonly discussed malicious cyber activities. These terms undoubtedly can be improved upon, and should be, but they are offered as a starting point for wading through the current morass of undisciplined use of cyber terminology.

- Intelligence, Surveillance, and Reconnaissance. This common military term should work well when applied to cyberspace; it essentially describes collection of information and monitoring of activities. In cyberspace, this is becoming more commonplace. It should not be considered an "attack."

- Infiltration. This term should be used to describe when an actor has penetrated your network or computer and established a position there, at times in order to conduct intelligence, surveillance, and reconnaissance.

- Exfiltration/espionage. Once someone has access to your network or computer, they might be able then to extract data, files, etc. Currently, China is conducting such activities on an unprecedented scale, mobilizing armies of people to steal data across a wide range of private and public sector organizations not just from the United States, but from dozens of advanced countries around the world. Other countries also routinely conduct espionage and exfiltration in cyberspace, but China's efforts dwarf those of the others, and must be stopped (more on that later).

- Manipulation. Instead of taking your data, sometimes actors have an interest in manipulating or corrupting your data, preferably without your knowing it. If unknown to the targeted organization, this could preclude a military operation or collapse a business (e.g., a financial institution).

- Disruption. Perhaps most important for operational military purposes, some actors acquire and retain access in military networks in order to prevent or disrupt your use of the networks when you most need them, for example, in a crisis or conflict. These actions should be considered "attacks."

- Industrial control system attacks. Finally, perhaps the most sophisticated type of malicious cyber activities are attacks that target *industrial control systems* that monitor and control industrial, infrastructure, or facility-based processes[1] (in other words, dams, rail traffic, etc.). The Stuxnet virus that was widely reported to be used to damage Iranian uranium enrichment infrastructure in 2010 should be considered as such an attack, the purpose of which is to cause actual damaging, physical effects.

In order for cyberspace to be used by the United States, and by the rest of the world, in a more effective fashion, and to move cyberspace away from the "Wild West" that it currently appears to be, this discussion focuses on four key deleterious aspects of current behavior in cyberspace.

Currently, sovereign nations are not held responsible for cyber activities emanating from their territory. Part of this is due to lack of capability, but a good deal of it is a matter of lack of will. Sometimes, it appears that governments are sponsoring, directly or indirectly, malicious cyber activities against another government, but when confronted about such activities, the government in question will claim lack of knowledge or lack of ability to stem or halt the offending activity. In no other areas of international behavior is such a response tolerated or accepted. Since the birth of the Westphalian system in 1648, nation-states have been held accountable for activities originating from their territory; the Westphalian concept of sovereignty holds (including in international law) that states are responsible for governing their territories and that other states should not interfere in such governance. And while various states today reign less effectively over their territory than others (e.g., Somalia), creating what are often called "ungoverned areas," the behavior of states in the international area remains based on this core concept.

---

1.   Wikipedia.

Yet, for a range of damaging cyber activities, otherwise strong and established nation-states claim deniability and inability.

Cyber "traffic" is completely unregulated. Bad data packets, good data packets, all cyber traffic currently moves through cyberspace unrestricted and unregulated. This is not the case in other domains (except for outer space). On our highways, vehicles in every country on earth are required to be registered as safe, and this also is used to identify them when they are involved in something that goes wrong on the roads. (Most countries also require insurance for operating a vehicle.) In our airways, aircraft too must be certified as safe, and are re-certified routinely. So too on the sea lanes of the world, boats, ships, and other seaborne vessels require registration to ensure they are safe and will not endanger other vessels. Thus, in all other domains that are heavily trafficked by people, registrations are required to ensure safe use and to incentivize responsible behavior. When it is determined that the standards of behavior have been violated in all other domains, such registrations are revoked by governing authorities. No such standards or registrations exist regarding behavior in cyberspace.

China and Chinese-inspired and -affiliated groups and individuals are in the midst of conducting a multi-year, multi-petabyte (or, potentially, multi-exabyte) industrial and military exfiltration and espionage effort across a wide range of key commercial and military sectors in a number of developed countries. The campaign began a long time ago, but has intensified and broadened exponentially in recent years. This broad, well-resourced campaign constitutes a major perturbation of the existing international order, specifically its economic and private enterprise elements, as well as international security.

Many countries have moderate offensive cyberspace capabilities; a few have very advanced offensive capabilities. Like conventional militaries, there are a few cyber military great powers, while several have moderate cyber capabilities. The "order of battle" for cyberspace is hard to discern, but it is reasonably clear that Russia, China, and the United States are the premier cyber military actors in the world. Between Russia and China, it also is generally acknowledged that China has the largest and "noisiest" offensive cyber efforts; China is operating on a massive scale and does not always do so with elegance and precision. Russia, on the other hand, is known for being extremely skillful, precise, and "quiet." These characterizations also apply to criminal and other groups linked with these governments.

Other countries are reported or assumed to have serious cyberspace capabilities; these include friendly countries and allies of the United States, such as the United Kingdom, France, Australia, Israel, India, South Korea, and Japan. Also among the cyber players are less friendly regimes, including Iran and North Korea.

Desired End-State (and Why)

It is in the interests of the United States, and indeed of all cyber-faring nations, to establish a greater degree of order and predictability of behavior in cyberspace, and to strengthen other norms that have been seen to contribute to security and stability in other domains of human behavior. This discussion focuses on four aspects of a desired end-state, or way-station, in cyberspace that would contribute to achieving such ends.

First, countries should be held responsible for cyberspace activities emanating from their territory. In this regard, cyberspace should be normalized—it should be treated no differently than other domains. In other areas of human activity, sovereign states are held responsible, and for the most part, accountable, for activities that originate from their territory. This practice, codified in international law, has been upheld (albeit not perfectly) for over 350 years, and has contributed to predictability, stability, and security. And while states may claim that they cannot live up to this standard—which actually may be the case in some instances—the rule and the norm should be that they can, and they will. When international terrorists operate from a country, other countries who may be the victims of terrorist activity work with the host country to find, root out, and cease the activities of the terrorists. In cases where the country is unable to do so, other countries partner with it to seek to achieve their common goals. In such cases when that does not work either, or when the country is unwilling to work jointly, and the threat proves to be sufficiently grave, the outside countries then try to address the activities of concern more directly. Malicious cyberspace activities should be held to analogous standards, with analogous international activity by the states concerned.

Second, "licenses" for responsible use of cyberspace should be considered and, if deemed feasible and desirable, implemented. The international community needs to get a better handle on cyberspace as a domain. The tension here is between privacy and free speech on the one hand, and security/stability on the other. Judgments on this tension will not be weighed in detail here, but if there is agreement that too much malicious cyber activity is ongoing on a daily basis, and that it is getting worse, and that it is affecting core elements of the international economic and security order, then it is time to weigh the costs and benefits of moving to a different regime with greater focus and alacrity. Such a regime could call for Internet Service Providers or others to certify computers.[2] As stated previously, in no other domain of international human activity are potentially dangerous moving vehicles unregulated. This exception should be challenged in a comprehensive fashion.

Third, and similarly, intellectual property rights in cyberspace need to be more strictly adhered to and enforced, and international law enforcement authorities need to address economic espionage in cyberspace with greater attention, coordination, and resources. The global economy cannot be sustained in the physical world while it is undermined continuously and comprehensively in the increasingly important virtual world. The rules of the economic game in cyberspace need to be more closely monitored and more strictly enforced, especially as the cyberspace-driven economy continues to grow to constitute an increasing proportion of the overall economy. If current trends continue, we will witness our global economic order descending into a global economic disorder, as well-organized international criminal groups, and China and a handful of other states, steal increasing proportions of legitimate and lawful private sector enterprises' core business data. This must change; if it does not, the primary actors in international business will resemble the Mafia more than the multinational corporation.

Fourth, a deterrence regime should continue to be established to address cyberspace challenges that affect national security interests. Great progress has been made over the last two years, particularly in the wake of the Defense Department's development, publication, and initial implementation of the *Department of Defense Strategy for Operating in Cyberspace* in July 2011 and the White House's publication of *International Strategy for Cyberspace* in May 2011. For the first time, these strategies began discussing key elements of cyber deterrence in public; in essence, they began erecting a regime for deterring major cyberspace challenges to the United States. For example, the White House strategy stated, "When warranted, the United States will respond to hostile acts in cyberspace as we would to any other threat to our country.... We reserve the right to use all necessary means—diplomatic, informational, military, and economic—as appropriate and consistent with

---

2.   I am indebted to Jayson Healey for this specific suggestion.

applicable international law, in order to defend our Nation, our allies, our partners, and our interests."

Yet, much more needs to be done to fully establish a cyberspace deterrence regime that helps to diminish dangerous and damaging international behavior by states, strengthen predictability and order in cyberspace, and dissuade catastrophic cyberspace activities that could threaten US security in a crisis or conflict. Key steps toward these ends are outlined in the next section. But what would the key characteristics of such a regime look like?

First, cyberspace deterrence should be raised to the top of official bilateral and multilateral security agendas. If it is not discussed in senior-level meetings of officials, then it is not happening (and it currently is not). Without such high-level, official, government attention in appropriate fora, a deterrence regime will be deficient. Just as nuclear weapons rose to the top of the agendas of important international meetings in the 1950s and 1960s, so too must cyberspace weapons and actions (even more so because they damage the global economy on a daily basis). Second, attribution standards for the purposes of national security cyberspace policy should be clarified. Most importantly for this purpose, it should be made clear that the United States does not require "court of law" level evidence in order to act on major cyberspace security attacks or other malicious cyber actions against it. If there is a major cyberspace attack, especially in the context of a real-world military crisis, then such context should constitute at least a portion of the judgment regarding the origins of the cyberspace attack and who sponsored or directed it.[3]

This is an argument for "the duck theory:" if it walks like a duck, quacks like a duck, and looks like a duck, it's a duck. If a major Strait of Hormuz crisis is in full swing, and there is a catastrophic cyberspace attack on US Central Command's information and command and control networks, and if the post-attack attribution effort reinforces the case, then Iran should rise to the fore as the likeliest source of the attack. This is not an argument for a preemptive strategy nor for using blind assumptions as the primary basis for major national security policy decisions; this is an argument for bringing international context into deliberations on major international cyberspace crises and conflicts, and for avoiding legal arguments that are not brought to bear for other national security decisions informed by imperfect intelligence.

---

3.   See Jason Healey, "Beyond Attribution: Seeking National Responsibility for Cyber Attacks," Atlantic Council Issue Brief, 2011, *http://www.acus.org/publication/beyond-attribution-seeking-national-responsibility-cyberspace*, for a very detailed treatment of the different levels of national responsibility for cyber attacks.

Third, responses to catastrophic military cyberspace challenges should never be considered to be limited to cyberspace; rather, as the White House strategy suggested, if the United States suffers a major cyberspace attack on its military or on its civilian population, then the US response should be based on classic deterrence principles and, where appropriate, the laws of war (e.g., proportionality). The multifaceted US response should be driven by the damage to national security interests suffered and further anticipated, the need for escalation dominance as the crisis continues to unfold, the need to avoid civilian casualties, and other traditional considerations associated with the use of force. There may be circumstances in various scenarios that do call for responses in cyberspace; but this should not be the rule for high-consequence cyberspace attacks.

How to Get There

In order to make progress toward the desired economic and security end-state outlined above, five critical steps must be taken with purpose and a sense of urgency.

First, public/private partnerships for cyberspace security must be broadened, strengthened, and clarified. This is so for a number of reasons, not least because a lot of US and other countries' critical infrastructure (e.g., power, water, etc.) is owned and operated by private sector entities. For example, a cyber attack that threatens electricity not only affects our society and economy, but also our military operations, which cannot be conducted without power.

The US Government convenes certain fora for discussing relevant private/public cyber issues with selected private-sector parties, but this nascent network must be broadened greatly, exercised intensively, and significantly strengthened overall for more effective and rapid joint national efforts in cyber crises. Such exercises also would help clarify the division of labor in cyber crises; "who does what" across the Federal Government and relevant private-sector entities is not yet clear for likely scenarios.[4] Once major functions and roles are clarified, there then needs to be an intensive effort to increase awareness of the division of cyber labor among the relevant public and private actors. This is an urgent set of tasks.

---

4. This year's annual US Government "National Level Exercise" run by the Federal Emergency Management Agency was focused on this very question. See *www.fema.gov/plan/nle/*.

Second, the United States must begin to discuss and assign state responsibility for malicious cyberspace activities more frequently and at greater volume. Nations need to be held responsible for major cyber attacks and other significant malicious cyber actions emanating from their territory. Jayson Healey of the Atlantic Council has developed a ten-point scale for determining state responsibility based on whether a nation ignores, abets, or conducts a cyber attack.[5] At one end of the scale, states prohibit such attacks, and at the other end, the government executes the attack in coordination with integrated third-party proxies. This scale is instructive for informing government deliberations regarding appropriate policy and operational responses to cyber attacks. Such an approach helps to couch the response in broad strategic terms and is less reliant on particular technical forensic data.

In order to support these efforts, the United States also should begin discussing attribution more in public. This is so for two reasons: First, the reality is that the capabilities for attributing major cyberspace attacks and other significant malicious cyber actions are growing.[6] Just a few years ago, this was not the case, and attribution was cited as effectively precluding the establishment of a deterrence regime regarding cyberspace threats. Now, however, increasingly, experts are noting improvements in attribution capabilities and highlighting how attribution is not a binary question, but one of degree. As indicated above, attribution of cyber attacks, just like other types of intelligence that are used to inform national security decision-making, is never perfect in the real world. The context of the crisis will add information to any direct technical data and be used, in combination with other intelligence information, to inform decisions on appropriate and effective responses.

In addition, as a declaratory policy, the United States should trumpet advances in attribution capabilities in order to erect a more robust and sustainable cyber deterrence regime. At the height of the Cold War, the United States military did not know where every Soviet nuclear weapon was located at any particular time. Yet this fact was never announced; instead, US declaratory statements focused on the confidence of US decision-makers in being able to respond to any Soviet nuclear attack with a devastating retaliatory blow against a range of Soviet targets. Similarly, US Government spokesmen

---

5. Healey, "Beyond Attribution".
6. See, for example, "Few Elite Chinese Hackers are to Blame for Stealing US Defence Secrets," *Defence Report*, March 17, 2012, *http://defencereport.com/few-elite-chinese-hackers-are-to-blame-for-stealing-us-defence-secrets/.*

need to focus their cyberspace declaratory statements on their confidence that any catastrophic cyberspace attack would be attributed quickly and dealt with severely.

Thus, assigning appropriate state responsibility for cyber attacks coming from their territory (a top-down policy approach), combined with highlighting effective attribution capabilities (bottom-up), should go a long way to helping to establish, over time, patterns of behaviors and the extent to which such norms are violated.

Third, the United States needs to launch and sustain a cyber counter-intelligence effort on a massive scale. The breadth, depth, duration, and damage caused by China's current cyber theft campaign mandates a national-scale effort to protect US industry, national security, prosperity, and indeed the structure and functioning of the current global economic order. We should mobilize our nation and our allies and partners to combat this large-scale affront. Despite declining federal budgets, the nation must pay the public costs for this critical public good, or risk a massive illegitimate transfer of wealth and national power to China. The costs also should be borne more structurally and systematically by private companies; investing in cyber defenses should be considered akin to hiring armed security for brick-and-mortar institutions in areas where such security is a cost of doing business. Currently, cyberspace is a bad neighborhood.

In addition, the United States needs to more forcefully "out" China and any other countries that are conducting such aggressive cyber intelligence/exfiltration efforts. During the Cold War, overzealous communist spies were publically and dramatically expelled from the country when it was deemed appropriate to do so. We need to do the same in the ongoing Cyber Cold War that we are waging. US officials need to talk about this much more in public venues, not just after they retire.[7]

Further, strong consideration should be given not just to erecting much more effective cyber defenses, but also to going on cyber offense in a much more transparent and public fashion against the ongoing perpetrators of the espionage campaign. Today, it is still considered very sensitive for any US Government official to discuss cyber offense in public.[8] This restriction has

---

7. See Mike McConnell, Michael Chertoff, and William Lynn, "China's Cyber Thievery is National Policy—and Must be Challenged," *Wall Street Journal*, January 27, 2012.

8. A major and very recent exception can be found at David E. Sanger, "Obama Order Sped Up Wave of Cyberattacks Against Iran," *New York Times*, June 1, 2012.

its roots in the recent past when the Intelligence Community dominated cyberspace activities for the United States Government. But that can no longer be the case if we are to establish and sustain a functioning deterrence regime. Cyberspace is an offense-dominant domain, and the ability to retaliate in cyberspace with true and clear effects must be part and parcel of a broader cyberspace deterrence toolkit for the United States. Thus, US declaratory policy has not caught up with the real world. The days when offensive cyber activities were rare are over; it is time to come out of the cyber closet, at least a little bit, in light of the large-scale cyber espionage that is being conducted against the United States and our allies and partners every day.

Again, this is not to suggest that we limit responses to major cyber attacks to the cyberspace domain alone; however, we do not want the use of cyberspace to retaliate to be taken off the table.

Fourth, the United States Government needs to begin to treat cyberspace tools like true national instruments of power. During the Cold War, nuclear weapons were integrated over time into the country's national security toolkit effectively, and thus were wielded in crises and, in some cases, conflicts, as extraordinarily effective coercive military instruments undergirding diplomacy. In peacetime, nuclear weapons were credited with playing a structural stabilizing role in preventing the Cold War from becoming a hot war.

National security theorists and planners for a long time considered four main types of national instruments of power, using the acronym "DIME" for:

- Diplomatic power
- Informational power
- Military power
- Economic power.

US Government defense and national security planners have sought to integrate "DIME" tools into their daily planning and strategy efforts. However, after the 9/11 attacks, many planners became aware of a broader range of critical tools that should be incorporated into their planning; those planners also happened to have been in or approaching middle age, so the new acronym "MIDLIFE" came into use to cover the following tool set:

- Military
- Informational
- Diplomatic
- Law enforcement
- Intelligence
- Financial
- Economic

Before the next 9/11, which could be a cyber 9/11, the United States needs to raise cyberspace tools to the level of another major national instrument ("MIDLIFE-Crisis?"). Like some of the other national instruments, however, cyberspace has its soft and hard sides. Soft power aspects of cyberspace tools include the approach taken by Secretary of State Hillary Clinton to champion Internet freedoms and provide related aid to various democratization movements.[9] In addition, some US embassies abroad conduct diplomacy via cyberspace—they use Twitter, Facebook, and other social media tools to great advantage.

However, in order to fully realize the soft-power aspects of cyberspace, the State Department should establish an Assistant Secretary of State for the Internet to work across other US Government agencies and to work with foreign counterparts to more effectively advance US interests in and for cyberspace.[10] The United States needs to be as adept at "cyber statecraft"[11] in the 21st century as it was at traditional statecraft during the Cold War.

As for hard power, even though it is clear that the United States has offensive cyber capabilities, the United States does not do as good a job as it should of integrating cyber tools into other hard power strategies, plans, security cooperation, and military operations. Much more needs to be done until it can be said that cyberspace is living up to its potential as a major coercive tool underwriting the diplomacy of the United States in the 21st century.

---

9. "Gloria Goodale, "Hillary Clinton Champions Internet Freedom, but Cautions on Wikileaks,"" *Christian Science Monitor*, February 15, 2011.

10. I am indebted to Nao Matsukata for this idea.

11. The term "Cyber Statecraft" has been coined by Jason Healey at the Atlantic Council. The Atlantic Council's Cyber Statecraft Initiative helps foster international cooperation and understanding of new forms of competition and conflict in cyberspace through global engagement and thought leadership.

Fifth, and last, the United States must become more cyber resilient. Because cyberspace remains an offense-dominant domain, where cyber intruders and disrupters appear to still have the upper hand, the resilience of both private and public sector organizations needs to be greatly strengthened. We will fail in our defensive efforts, so we need to be able to work through those failures and continue our work and our operations. This means that we need a much more focused program (which would greatly reinforce the counter-intelligence campaign discussed above) to improve our cyber defenses as well as our cyber recovery abilities. The theory and literature on resilience is robust and should continue to be applied to cyberspace.[12] An important side benefit of strengthening our cyber resilience will be to strengthen cyber deterrence. Potential attackers should be increasingly deterred as our cyber resilience grows, as they will be less and less able to achieve their damaging effects.

Conclusion

The preamble of the United States Constitution states: "We hold these truths to be self-evident, that all men are created equal, that they are endowed by their Creator with certain unalienable rights that among these are Life, Liberty, and the Pursuit of Happiness."

The benefits of a more ordered Internet for the purposes of "Life" (security), "Liberty" (democratization), and "the Pursuit of Happiness" (prosperity) could not be clearer.

This chapter has outlined the current, nascent, unsatisfactory state of cyberspace, essentially, how it resembles the Wild West in terms of norms and patterns of behavior. It also has outlined where we should be seeking to take cyberspace to improve this situation for the good of all. Finally, it described key elements of the steps to get us toward that desired end-state, with a particular focus on increasing predictability of behavior and increasing enforcement and punishment of dangerous behavior. We will not reach a docile, ordered cyberspace domain anytime soon, but we need to make progress, and we need to start now.

---

12. For example, see Yossi Sheffi, *The Resilient Enterprise: Overcoming Vulnerability for Competitive Advantage* (Cambridge, MA: MIT Press, 2005).

CHAPTER 8

Facts and Fictions of Cyber Diplomacy

Alfred Rolington

Framing the Challenge

The interconnectivity of cyberspace, the reach of its structure and the sophistication of its technology are about to significantly change national security, geopolitics and global trade. The cyber threat level is now putting many elements of a country's defense and commercial life at risk of failure and shut down. These attacks can be driven from anywhere and are difficult to identify, predict and protect against. This new breed of attack puts the need for an agreed global, as well as national, cyber strategy much higher up the security threat agenda than was the case even a few years ago.[1]

There is a new recognition, by most government ministers, of the changing aspects of globalization, its networked electronics, the rise of new users of social media and the extensive leakage of information and even intelligence with the likes of Wikileaks. This increase of social media, and the staggering amounts of available information on the web, is known to have enormous advantages over traditional information collection and communications methods.

---

1. The FBI's former top cyber law enforcer Shawn Henry said that there were lots of cyber attacks and that he was working on two thousand before he left the FBI in March 2012. Andrea Shalal-Esa, "Scores of US firms keep quiet about cyber attacks," *Reuters* online, June 13th 2012, *http://www.reuters.com/article/2012/06/13/net-us-media-tech-summit-cyber-disclosur-idUSB-RE85C1E320120613.*

Alfred Rolington has a wealth of experience in the intelligence industry having formerly been the Chief Executive Officer for Jane's Information Group, Oxford Analytica and Lloyd's Business and Transport Press. He is currently authoring a book entitled *Strategic Intelligence for the 21st Century* by Oxford University Press due in 2013.

Mobile communication and the web are extensively used by negotiators in their collection of information from outside the established government intelligence cycle and are being added to their use of email, in a variety of secure and unsecure connections and communications technologies. This networked world changes the time frames in which you work and governments and corporations negotiate. We can give, as well as send, information and intelligence that historically would have taken certainly days, sometimes weeks, to achieve, but this immediacy brings new challenges, new opportunities, as well as new threats.[2]

And there have already been numerous cyber attacks on the US telecommunications, power grids and air traffic control systems. A number of governments have attempted to discover their capability of bringing systems down by cyber attacks. As is well known, the Russians made attacks on Georgia and Estonia, and China has attacked Taiwan, among others.

The goal the United States set for itself is laid out in the Obama Administration's *International Strategy for Cyberspace*. "The United States will work internationally to promote an open, interoperable, secure, and reliable information and communications infrastructure that supports international trade and commerce, strengthens international security, and fosters free expression and innovation. To achieve that goal, we will build and sustain an environment in which norms of responsible behavior guide states' actions, sustain partnerships, and support the rule of law in cyberspace."[3]

In the United States, President Obama and Secretary of State Clinton have identified cyberspace as a major aspect of foreign relations and policy going forward. General Petraeus, at the Central Intelligence Agency, and Robert Gates, then Secretary of Defense, raised the issue of cyberspace to the highest levels and discussed the implications, for security and defense, in the United States going forward. In the past five years, the FBI has increased the awareness of the cyber issues and, along with Fordham University, held three cyber focused conferences. The most recent FBI cyber conference held January 2012, in New York, was where General Keith B. Alexander, Commander of

---

2. *Titan Rain* is the name given by the US Federal Government to computer system attacks since 2003. And they have named cyber attacks on specific government systems as Moonlight Maze—gov. sytems1.

3. White House, *International Strategy for Cyberspace: Prosperity, Security, and Openness in a Networked World*, May 2011, *http://www.whitehouse.gov/sites/default/files/rss_viewer/international_strategy_for_cyberspace.pdf*, p. 8.

US Cyber Command of the National Security Agency, spoke about the reality of cyber threats.[4]

The Threats We Face

More recently, on March 20, 2012, General Alexander spoke before the House Committee on Armed Services about the United States military's improving cyber abilities and that, since the creation of a new cyber strategy in 2010, they had been progressing on a number of fronts to secure networks and improve response capabilities. He said that the risks, threats and attacks were becoming more dangerous and that governments were using cyber attacks on other governments and that they were also using cyber techniques against critics within their own nations.

As Alexander further explained, with over seven million computers and tens of thousands of servers potentially accessible via the web, in the Department of Defense, let alone all the other aspects of the United States Government, which have a multitude of systems, the sheer size of the problem is exceptional. And this, of course, is only the beginning.[5]

Western governments and their diplomats understand that national threats are often created or changed by the macro-economic landscape, the geopolitical perspective and by some of the prominent individuals involved. Cyberspace, although obviously affected by these changes, has stayed out of the diplomatic daylight until recently when cyber threats and attacks that occurred made the broad national dependency on interconnected electronic infrastructure far more obvious. This is altering the diplomatic dynamics.

Consequently, governments have been persuaded to create specific cyber departments, bringing senior members of their infrastructures, together with commercial cyber organizations, to discuss new threat levels and fully understand what can be done to reduce, and hopefully eradicate, some of these threat levels. The process has also prompted negotiations with other nations and international corporations. All of this, it is hoped, will begin to build a clear picture of the risks, threats and opportunities from which a clearer cyber strategy might emerge.

---

4. International Conference on Cyber Security January 9th-12th 2012 in NYC in association with Fordham University at Lincoln Centre.

5. Statement of General Keith B. Alexander Commander United States Cyber Command before the House on Armed Services Subcommittee on Emerging Threat and Capabilities—20th March 2012.

And yet currently, even though this is now a perceived dynamic threat, there are few agreed commercial, government and diplomatic definitions of cyberspace, and even fewer agreements about how to curb and stop the threats. These difficulties have grown as the technology, perceived threats and real attacks have altered our understanding, and perception of the cyber arena.

Currently, cyberspace represents to most senior government officials, policymakers and corporate security directors, a combination of global networks that are dependent upon each other. These networks range from civil aviation flight systems to electric power networks, the Internet and computer-based linked processes used by the public, government and corporations.

From a theoretical and practical perspective, cyberspace has three interconnected layers. First, there is the layer of electric transmitters and receivers for the entire national and international communications networks. Second, the software and programming that engages and enhances the connectivity and processing of data and information. And third, there is the data, messaging and verbal connectivity using mobiles, social networks and the web. These three layers change, merge and overlap as the technology, and the amounts invested in the infrastructure alter. All are at potential risk of attack.

As is well known, often when a country's economics change, so does the amounts spent and invested in defense, security and the intelligence process. This is currently playing out with America, China, Russia, the Middle East and Europe. Over the next decade, these issues will become a significant aspect of a country's defense budget. China will grow significantly over the next few decades and be spending much larger amounts than previously on defense and military expansion. It will, to a degree, follow the western, and particularly the American, tradition of defense spending as it sees America as a military, economic, social and commercial model that can, and should, be to a large extent followed.

However, during the same period, the United States and Europe will be reducing their defense and intelligence budgets in line with their fiscal and budgetary re-modeling. Nevertheless, the United States will undoubtedly, and for the foreseeable future, remain the largest defense spender in the world. The United States will be spending as much as most of the others put together, on traditional security and defense. However, the major issue of cyber threat, and its potential warfare threat, will continue to grow during this period and become something all developing and developed countries will need to take into account. This significant increasing problem of cyber security will become even more prominent as other national economies grow and become more reliant on the interconnectivity of their global reach.

Already most of the larger world economies, nations and corporations have been subject to cyber threats and attacks. Partial and sometimes complete shut-downs of parts of their foundational power and electronic systems have occurred. One relatively small, but significant aspect, has been highlighted is China's capability to shut down electricity systems. Similar capabilities within the United States have also grown over the last decade. Confrontation of these issues will radically increase worldwide tensions over the next decade as its influence affects all developing and developed nations.

A recent example is in Australia, where the Gillard Government blocked Huawei, the Chinese technology company, from being part of the tendering process for a multi-billion dollar national broadband network. This follows advice that the Australian government took from ASIO, the Australian Security Intelligence Organization. However, the government openly offered no evidence that Huawei was a cyber attack threat or working on behalf of the Chinese government. This policy will test trade relationship between Australia and China and create political and commercial friction.[6]

In order to understand and engage with the process, a number of governments have created new departments to coordinate processes and engage with the problem. The United States was first in creating its own focused department within the State Department to analyze and engage with the problem. Now this issue is rising higher on the agenda of many governments and organizations. Cyber discussions and diplomacy engagement with other countries and organizations will play an active, and what is thought, a positive part in the cyberspace reality going forward.

The Thinking of American Leaders

From an American viewpoint, Secretary Hillary Clinton appointed Christopher Painter as the Coordinator of Cyber Issues for the United States in February 2011. Painter has been involved in cyber discussions from a government, commercial and legal perspective for over twenty years. He sees the issue in a broad, as well as, specific threat. Like General Alexander, Painter realizes the new levels of risk and opportunity that all governments and commercial

---

6.   Maggie Lu-YueYang/Reuters, "Australia Bars Huawei From Broadband Project," *New York Times*, March 26, 2012, *http://www.nytimes.com/2012/03/27/technology/australia-bars-huawei-from-broadband-project.html.*

organizations face are growing significantly as the technology and the cyber understanding changes. It is in his opinion, 'unlike any previous technological change'. When interviewed for this chapter and asked about previous technological global changes and threats, Painter was asked to compare the cyber threat with previous global networks such as the telephone system (which has been used as a similar example of new challenges and threats) and he said that it had been seen as partially similar but that in his opinion it does not carry anything like the depths and global spread of the threats and opportunities posed by cyberspace. The telephone system required international discussions and negotiations for its cross-border connections to be made, but in comparison to cyberspace was more one-dimensional. Painter has seen the difficulties and coordination issues that the cyber threat poses and he actively brought together 18 different government agencies into a meeting room to discuss the various views on cyberspace—focusing on the potential threats and opportunities. And, again quoting Painter, there was initially "Nothing joined-up. There was no overarching framework and that is now what we are setting out to create."

There is, in Painter's view, a new level of risk ranging across the whole geopolitical spectrum down to the local crime level. Detailed discussions need, in his opinion, to take place internally within government, within and engaging with commercial organizations and then with all countries, or as many as will engage in the process. The G8 world leaders and the Organisation for Economic Co-Operation and Development (OECD) have already agreed to discuss and coordinate policy and frameworks surrounding cyberspace and this will, as the current head of the FBI has stated, "bring cyber threats to the top of the threat list in years to come."[7]

And so, a broader view of the globalizing electronic networks and challenges must include the real dependency of nations and international organizations on their electronic and electric infrastructures. These systems often drive and control aspects of everything from electric grids, to rail and air networks, to satellite control. Added to this are the massive volumes of electronic database information now available to the policymakers and their analysts which can also be threatened, and occasionally brought down. This potentially affects the immediacy of the timeframes in which everyone is expected to work and react and what back-up exists, if the system fail or are attacked.

---

7.   Robert Mueller. Director of the FBI testified before the Senate Select Committee on Intelligence in January 2012 that cyber threats would become the major concern above terrorism.

These issues have substantially added to the opportunities and problems of trade, geo-politics, security and the need for international relationships. This has added to the need for agreement and diplomacy at government, military and corporate levels of intervention. The need to link these elements, that are often difficult to define and monitor, has been recognized and is in part taking place. As discussed at G7 and G20 meetings, the United States now has an *International Strategy for Cyberspace* and has allocated the month of October every year when it will focus the media on the issues surrounding cyber networks. As the President said in his opening remarks of the strategy for cyberspace and security, "Cyber security is not an end unto itself; it is an obligation that our governments and societies must take on willingly, to ensure innovation continues to flourish, drive markets, and improve lives."[8]

What all of this suggests is that the methods and cyber security discussions should aim at being a more open diplomatic process allowing all to see the ways forward, and for America to make its position very clear to all. Its stated aim is to conduct and discuss implementations of secure networks and agreements with overseas partners giving cyber electronic networks security and clarity of purpose.

The Past is Prologue

In peacetime, these open debates and engaging ambitions are perfectly reasonable and like other security and trade agreements, they form the basis of much diplomatic activity during periods of non-aggression. However, deception and secrecy during war is totally understandable and acceptable to most voters. In wartime it becomes clear to outsiders and different nations that America, as with many other nations, will discuss and determine its networks, which link internationally with the global electronic networks, normally in an open and secure way unless threats and attacks take place and then it will shut down and counter the attacks. Some governments, however, even at times of non-threat and peace, have in the past had many alternative actions that they wish to secretly pursue and so have kept their diplomacy closed and were difficult to judge and often kept much of the process secret.

The problems associated with closed diplomacy as a driving principle have been seen over the years as being not as effective when one is trying to integrate global secure policy. Historically, going back before electronic connectivity and telecommunications networks, there was an argument that suggested

8.   White House, *International Strategy for Cyberspace.*

143

that secrecy and deception could be maintained and operated without the opposition's knowledge. Examples of this range from opening and reading people's mail, to ship information derived from different ports. As merchant trading and shipping became a broader and international activity, so did the idea of having one's own nationals in foreign ports to oversee the actions of your own nation's shipping and trade routes. Lloyd's of London undertook this initiative initially for information concerning merchant ships that come into different ports that might be brought into the Lloyd's insurance process. Lloyd's posted their representatives into the hundreds, and later thousands, of ports all around the world. These agents collected information about the comings and goings of merchant shipping and the cargos and crews that were used. They also collected information about the vessel's ownership and the ownership of some of the different types of cargo. All of this information was very useful commercially and helped create one of the oldest and still commercially current newspapers, which was launched in the early eighteenth century, known as *Lloyd's List*.[9] However, the Lloyd's insurance information process began earlier as part of the Lloyd's coffee house in the seventeenth century and became more sophisticated as the decades and centuries moved on. Much of it was originally based on insuring the Atlantic slave trading ships.

During the Napoleonic War of 1803-1815, this information could be used to focus on French naval activity. The British Government used this information, which became intelligence used by the British Navy. Instead of just collecting data about commercial shipping, the Lloyd's agents also collected data about the movement and docking of the French Navy and were actively collecting and passing information to the British Government, who used it to track the French Navy. And so what had begun as an open, but commercially secure, information collection process soon became something that the United Kingdom's military and later their and other western intelligence services would actively use.

Deception of diplomatic intent and the clear and unbiased use of information recently became a problem with the Iraq War, and even before with aspects of the Vietnam War. The misrepresentation and falsification of information and intelligence became known after the issues surrounding Iraq's apparent nuclear program was shown to be false. With Vietnam, this later

---

9. *Lloyd's List* the shipping newspaper began publishing in 1734, *Wikipedia*.

became clear with the changes to information and intelligence over the Gulf of Tonkin issue.[10]

The apparent and deliberate misuse of information in a national sense really began with the Crimea War in the 1850s. This was the first time in conflict that electric telegraph communications could be used to deliver news reports to the public about a current conflict and it took place within hours rather than days or weeks of an action or conflicts. *The Times* of London reported, within hours of particular aspects of the Crimea War, and changed the public's views of the conflict, which the British Government had tried to put across. Diplomacy was made more difficult as *The Times* used aspects of news and propaganda without any government oversight. This significantly changed the role and position of the press, government and the military in times of conflict, and soon after this changed the reporting process of the American Civil War.

Secrecy during war is understandable, but misrepresentation and counter-intelligence used to politically achieve an end that fits with a corporate or the current government's, and in particular individual political leaders, bias and view undermines the very process of clear verifiable intelligence. This of course negatively affects the intelligence cycle itself. During peacetime, discussions and negotiations with these deceptions are potentially a serious problem to clearer and purposeful negotiations. So where possible, the intentions of diplomatic discussions should be actively kept open and promoted as such. The more the discussions are kept in the open and the better informed the voting public is, the more the process can be driven faster and more effectively. Virtual discussions or a "Virtual Embassy" could be created which would encourage understanding and the exchange of data and information. This should also take place on the web, both from a government and independent standpoint, and to this subject we shall return towards the end of this chapter. This is very important in these days of information deluge, social networks and blogs. However, the actual negotiation would, of course, be closed while they take place, even though society expects more openness from its negotiators and so more open explanation of the process from government is required.

---

10. The Gulf of Tonkin or the USS *Maddox* incident, are the names given to two separate incidents. The first a sea battle between the *Maddox* and North Vietnamese torpedo boats and the second where false radar imagery gave the impression of another torpedo attack which in reality did not happen. However analysis of the second false attack did not get passed to President Johnson and he ordered retaliatory airstrikes.

The Arab Spring and the use of social networks brought this more clearly to the attention of the global public, and of course, to the attention of other governments. It is no longer easy to contain the broader elements of social issues when blogs and mobile communications are as widespread as they are today. The shutting of networks and interference of government has become far harder to contain. Although, of course, many governments continue to counter and try to contain the effects, some of the potential outcomes of these electronic networks, and their methods change the views and potentially initiate new actions on the ground.

America has been at the forefront of open information flows and this is, of course, cited by the founding fathers in the original American Constitution. Far more recently, the State Department has explained the government's position on more open government with the active open publishing of key documents. This takes place within twenty-five or thirty years of their creation. President Clinton's Executive Order of April 2000 drove the opening of more documents to public scrutiny, unless it can be shown that continued secrecy was in the national interest. Nevertheless, this process, given the changes with the web and social networking, is in need of review once again.

Now given the need for negotiation concerning cyberspace the focus on open discussions would prove to be beneficial and would set an example to other nations, not only of America's intent, but also its understanding of the needs of the current electronic global reality for a broader public debate. Trying to negotiate secure cyber networks in a secure vacuum would not help to solve the underlying issues and would darken America's position in the global economy.

Open diplomacy has press and public relations benefits, but is difficult to achieve when aspects of the potential opposition will actively try to use America's (potential) open discussions as a way of understanding and using this knowledge and information to their advantage. And so aspects of how the networks would be policed and secured, of course, will remain secret. A clear open discussion with other governments and corporations involved in the process would enable America to set the timeline and the potential advantageous outcomes. This process once set in motion should not be too restrictive or contained. The current administration began this by outlining its views with its International Cybersecurity Strategy, which the President introduced with four of his cabinet secretaries at a White House briefing in May 2011.

146

The aim of the strategy is to work with other nations to create a more open and secure information and communications network and infrastructure that ensures security, broadens the concept of free expression, and supports free trade. The aim is to build an environment where discussion, agreements and cooperation can openly take place in an environment where the players feel freer to discuss different aspects of the global electronic environment. As Secretary of State Hillary Clinton has said, the strategy is not aimed at being, 'One size fits all,' and as she has made clear the aim is to build a consensus around a shared vision of the future cyberspace with the purpose to ensure that it serves, rather than impedes social, political and economic growth. The government brought together a range of different parts of government with the intention of showing that this is a structured and integrated approach that the Obama Administration wishes to build.

Giving depth and clarity to the broad strategic vision is the next task of government. And here diplomacy has serious risks as it requires honest input by all concerned. The problem is that open discussion suggests, and often implies that negotiations might be let out of the bag and into the Wikileaks space. This is of course something which all policymakers are too aware might happen. There are also other issues that arise if open negotiations take place so that the public can view the process. There is the real risk that policy makers will pander to public opinion and not clearly negotiate in a tough process the way they might if the negotiations were fully closed.

The Way Forward

Cyberspace as an opportunity and threat potential is not going to reduce. It will certainly increase over the next decades and so the negotiations and diplomatic process must be seen as ongoing. The opportunities to use the cyber threat to negotiate with many national and corporate bodies are vast, as they all understand or are beginning to appreciate the real far reaching significance of these issues. This requires a clear strategic policy with independent reports about the purpose and tasks that should be created.

The more sensible solution is for the intentions, and some of the specific aims of the process, to be made open and apparent to the public and the potential opponents while the negotiations remain closed until agreement is reached or not reached. To make this a clear diplomatic process, one aspect that should be regularly considered is a tiered approach to the cyber negotiations. And as an example I will conclude with a four-tiered approach.

First, a principle of open discussion and understanding of America's position, and that it intends where it can, to negotiate a secure framework with other friendly nations as to how the cyberspace might be secured.

Second, limits would be explained and discussed. And one limit would be the Monroe Doctrine which should be explained as a fall back position. Monroe's Doctrine, which was brought into effect in December 1823, expresses where America draws the line and considers outside action against the United States as threatening, and requiring assertive action on the part of the United States.[11] If outside governments attempt to interfere or attack US cyberspace, then this will be seen as cyber warfare and action against the aggressor will take place.

And third, the government's policy should to be clearly put in place. It should set out the boundaries, areas for negotiation and limits that will be applied to the whole threat level. Negotiations of law that can be agreed and enacted should be considered and put in place; however, there are issues if not done in a clear negotiated way.

For instance, in the international copyright arena there are two pieces of law with apparently similar objectives for acting against alleged copyright infringement that are enacted by blocking elements of the web. These are the ACTA—Anti-Counterfeiting Trade Agreement—and SOPA—Stop Online Piracy Act—however, although their intentions can be said to be comparable, legally they have very different bases. The ACTA is a trade agreement set up by an international diplomatic discussion and agreement. While SOPA is about the theft of American property and focuses on websites and services outside of the United States borders which can get US electronic visitors. SOPA has been criticized for seeming to offer the American legal authorities an open door to challenge copyright globally. SOPA was seen to be overriding European Union and other countries laws and has, therefore, been temporarily put on hold. This type of law making by one country without broader more global discussion should be avoided.

And fourth, there could be another aspect of negotiation that might be tried, as it was with the issue of Iran, and that is Virtual Embassies created on the web where discussion of the particular subject can be openly encouraged and information offered. A Virtual Embassy, governmentally conceived and

---

11. The Monroe Doctrine was introduced December 2nd, 1823 and stated that further European colonization or interference would be viewed as acts of aggression requiring US intervention.

enacted, can be seen as important for raising an issue in a global way. This should happen alongside traditional direct diplomatic negotiations. There should be a reporting system as part of the Virtual Embassy that explains to society where policy and its limits are set and allows for discussion and input from the public and organizations.

In a western society, where conspiracy theories remain popular and create belief systems, it is important that an independent Virtual Cyber Discussion site is established so that opinions can be expressed and discussed without direct government intervention. This should be created along the lines of Wikipedia and should be internationally constructed as part of the G7 and going forward the G20 process.

The facts and fictions within the cyberspace discussion will increase as they always do, when a national threat becomes more real to the general public. However, to grasp the cyber opportunities and nettles early would give the United States credibility and respect within the world in general. It would also offer the United States and its allies more protection from what will undoubtedly be an on-going threat and potentially significant attacks in the future.

CHAPTER 9

Location-Based Laws in a World without Boundaries
Can the Territorial Waters of Cyberspace Be Defined?

Gus P. Coldebella

It is a familiar notion in the law that the place something happens determines what legal regime applies.[1] In the physical world, national borders are generally well defined, making questions of applicable law, jurisdiction, and enforcement relatively easy to answer.[2] Not so in the cyber domain. Once someone crosses the cyber "border"—using "the screens and passwords that separate the tangible from the virtual world"[3]—the relevance of physical location is, for many purposes, diminished. Information can be communicated—transactions completed, currency exchanged, games played, news read, tweets posted, tax returns filed, e-mails sent, texts received, products advertised, links clicked—from any corner of the world, instantaneously, generally without regard to the parties' physical location. The Internet also facilitates scores of nefarious activities, from criminal conduct (identity theft, stealing money from bank accounts, phishing), to espionage (extracting sensitive information from government or private sector networks), to remote attacks on infrastructure or through insider access to computers. These activities—legitimate and illegiti-

---

1. The US Supreme Court has said that "[t]he general and almost universal rule is that the character of an act as lawful or unlawful must be determined wholly by the law of the country where the act is done." *American Banana Co. v. United Fruit Co.*, 213 US 347, 356 (1909).

2. See Kristin M. Finklea, *The Interplay of Borders, Turf, Cyberspace, and Jurisdiction: Issues Confronting US Law Enforcement*, at 4 (Cong. Res. Serv., Feb. 15, 2012).

3. David R. Johnson and David Post, "Law and Borders: The Rise of Law in Cyberspace", *Stan. L. Rev* 48, (1996): 1367, 1378, *http://ssrn.com/abstract=535.*

Mr. Coldebella is a partner in the Washington, DC office of Goodwin Procter LLP. He served as the principal deputy general counsel and the acting general counsel of the US Department of Homeland Security from 2005 to 2009, and is a senior fellow at George Washington University's Homeland Security Policy Institute.

mate alike—can be conducted across international borders in the blink of an eye, all while obscuring or masking the actor's identity and location.

In their 1996 article *Law and Borders: The Rise of Law in Cyberspace*, Professors Johnson and Post observed that:

> Cyberspace radically undermines the relationship between legally significant (online) phenomena and physical location. The rise of the global computer network is destroying the link between geographical location and: (1) the *power* of local governments to assert control over online behavior; (2) the *effects* of online behavior on individuals or things; (3) the *legitimacy* of a local sovereign's efforts to regulate global phenomena; and (4) the ability of physical location to give *notice* of which sets of rules apply. The Net thus radically subverts the system of rule-making based on borders between physical spaces, at least with respect to the claim that Cyberspace should naturally be governed by territorially defined rules.[4]

They go on to argue that this new online paradigm requires new bodies of law, designed to transcend traditional, territory-based lawmaking. After all, if a sovereign asserts "a right to regulate whatever its citizens may access on the Net, these local authorities are laying the predicate for an argument that. … [a]ll such Web-based activity … must be subject simultaneously to the laws of all territorial sovereigns."[5] This could lead to a parade of evils: similarly-situated parties being treated dissimilarly based on their physical location, multiple sovereigns claiming jurisdiction over particular transactions, and each sovereign applying its own—likely different—legal norms to that transaction. To solve these jurisdictional woes, Johnson and Post argue that cyberspace should be considered a separate "place" for purposes of legal analysis, and a new, mutually agreed-upon body of law applied to the cyber domain, regardless of where an actor happens to be.[6]

To be sure, the complications that arise in web-based commercial transactions and interpersonal interactions are suffused with thorny issues, not least of which is determining applicable law. Whether this location-transcendent approach is a useful alternative for regulating the cyber interactions of private

---

4. *Id.* at 1370.
5. *Id.* at 1378-87.
6. *Id.*

parties in certain areas (e.g., trademark, copyright, defamation, fraud, antitrust) is a compelling question. However, devising new, international, cyber-based rules of the road *for nation-states*—governing criminal law enforcement, security, intelligence, and military engagement—does not seem to be readily susceptible to this paradigm, nor is it necessarily desirable. This is so for a number of reasons.

First, it is clear that different legal frameworks have different societal purposes, and purposes of these types of laws—the laws that determine civil and criminal liability—are not the same as those governing a nation-state's intelligence, military, security, and law enforcement functions. For laws governing liability, certainty is a priority. Certainty about applicable law allows private parties to, among other things, order their affairs to avoid potentially costly legal risk. Uncertainty, on the other hand, may cause parties to determine that legal risk is impossible to calculate and therefore that participation in the relevant marketplace is not worthwhile. In the United States, the laws applicable to our military, security and law enforcement services are not laws governing liability, but are generally laws of *authorization* and *limitation*.[7] The main purpose of these legal frameworks is maintaining and enhancing national security and enforcing the laws of the United States; they do so by specifying what the American people will authorize their intelligence, military and law enforcement services to do (and where they may do it, and to whom), consistent with important national priorities such as privacy and civil liberties principles. Since it is not the central purpose of the authorization/limitation category of laws to provide a clear definition of private parties' civil and criminal liability,[8] there is not as high a priority on creating cross-jurisdictional consistency and certainty about what law applies.

There is another important difference between these two broad categories of laws. The legal frameworks that nation-states rely upon, such as laws governing armed conflict, intelligence collection and covert activity, concern activities of those nation-states *against* international actors, including other

---

7.   This distinction holds even though some limitations on security activities of the United States are crafted as criminal laws. See, e.g., 18 USC § 1385 ("Whoever, except in cases and under circumstances expressly authorized by the Constitution or Act of Congress, willfully uses any part of the Army or the Air Force as a posse comitatus or otherwise to execute the laws shall be fined under this title or imprisoned not more than two years, or both.").

8.   While criminal statutes certainly allow citizens to order their affairs to avoid legal liability, the laws regarding the *conduct* of law enforcement agencies are materially similar to those regarding the intelligence and military services in that they authorize what such agencies may do, and establish limits on how, where, and to whom they may do it.

nation-states. Broad-based international consensus on these legal frameworks is therefore not only unlikely, but may be undesirable. For example, US law authorizes activities such as espionage and use of military force. Espionage, however, is likely to be considered unlawful under the domestic laws of whatever country is targeted, and other nations are likely to have an interest in curtailing the actions that the US military is authorized to take.[9] An international discussion to limit nation-states' military or intelligence-based cyber options is not likely to be productive, because binding agreements may be perceived as "efforts to restrict and limit cyber espionage and other nation-state cyber activities. … [and] the advantages of having a cyber warfare capacity are simply too great for many international actors to abjure."[10] It is unlikely that self-interested nations vying for cyber parity or superiority would agree to restrictive rules in this quickly-evolving space.

This is not to say that there is no utility in international conventions on cyber security. Just the opposite: Given the transnational character of cyber crime—i.e., that online activity initiated in one country can cause harm in another—it is important for nations to agree on criminalization and joint enforcement, to allow international investigations of such crimes, and extradition and prosecution of the criminals who commit them. Thus far, the process of international agreement on what constitutes cyber crime has been slow.[11]

For all of their differences, there is a material similarity between the two categories of law discussed above. Liability-defining laws and authorization/limitation laws both have tethers to locations. Very generally, certain laws, executive orders, and other directives authorizing military, intelligence and law enforcement activities often contain geographic limits; the power of US agencies that operate in the cyber domain is, by law, frequently limited by *where* something happens (as well as who caused it to happen).[12] And these limits are, at least theoretically, in tension with certain unique characteristics of the cyber threat: (i) that Internet allows actors in one country, or several countries, to commit cyber crimes, espionage, or attacks remotely in another country or countries, and (ii) that the perpetrators of this online activity—the "who"—and the location from which they are initiating the activity—the

---

9.   See Paul Rosenzweig, *National Security Threats in Cyberspace: A Workshop*, at 17 (Sept. 2009).

10. *Id.* at 26.

11. *Id.* at 13 (discussing the ongoing ratification process of the Convention on Cybercrime developed by the Council of Europe, in which only 26 countries have ratified the treaty in eight years.)

12. See *supra* n.8.

"where"—are relatively easy to mask. These common hallmarks of cyber activity—that it is *transnational*, and that it can be accomplished largely *anonymously*, making attribution difficult—are potentially troublesome for those applying traditional location-based legal regimes. When cyber activity takes place internationally or transnationally—or, worse yet, when there are doubts about where the activity is taking place or who is conducting it—agencies may have real concerns that their legal authorities do not allow them to engage the perpetrator. These concerns might stymie their ability to, for example, pursue criminals, conduct counter intelligence, or wage offensive cyber attacks. The question for policymakers in the Executive Branch and Congress, therefore, is whether location-based limits affect the United States' cyber response, and whether various legal regimes—particularly the statutes, executive orders and other laws that authorize federal law enforcement, intelligence, and military action—require updating to keep up with the transnational nature of our most worrisome cyber threats.

In the realm of law enforcement, for example, "[p]hysical and virtual boundaries play significant roles in both criminal activity and police work."[13] This is so because the power to legislate what is criminal and what is not, as well as the power to enforce criminal statutes once passed, are incidents of sovereignty. Criminal statutes, therefore, generally apply within a sovereign's territorial borders—causing a tension with the almost exclusively transnational nature of illicit cyber activity. And even though Congress may demonstrate an intent to have US federal criminal laws apply outside of the territorial jurisdiction of the United States,[14] and even though various crimes related to cyber security *do* apply extraterritorially,[15] there remain significant barriers to investigation and prosecution of crimes that take place internationally.[16]

13. See Finklea, *Interplay of Borders*, at 2.
14. See *Morrison v. National Australia Bank Ltd.*, 130 S.Ct. 2869, 2877 (2010) ("It is a longstanding principle of American law that legislation of Congress, unless a contrary intent appears, is meant to apply only within the territorial jurisdiction of the United States. This principle represents a canon of construction, or a presumption about a statute's meaning, rather than a limit upon Congress's power to legislate."); see also *EEOC v. Arabian American Oil Co.*, 499 US 244, 248 (1991) ("Both parties concede, as they must that Congress has the authority to enforce its laws beyond the territorial boundaries of the United States. Whether Congress has in fact exercised that authority in this case is a matter of statutory construction.").
15. See, e.g., *United States v. Ivanov*, 175 F. Supp. 2d 367, 370 (D. Conn. 2001) (holding that the Hobbs Act, 18 USC § 1951, the Computer Fraud and Abuse Act, 18 USC § 100, and the access device statute, 18 USC § 1029, were intended by Congress to apply exterritorially).
16. For a comprehensive review of this area, see Charles Doyle, *Extraterritorial Application of American Criminal Law*, at 22-39 (Cong. Res. Serv., February 15, 2012).

Moreover, the anonymity with which malicious actors are able to conduct computer crime—giving rise to the nearly insurmountable difficulties regarding attribution—leads to the "vexing situation" in which:

> high-profit criminality can occur with low risk of capture. This turns our deterrence model of law enforcement on its head. Deterrence only works when there is a credible threat of response and punishment (the degree of punishment mattering less than the degree of certainty of being caught). But deterrence cannot work without attribution and the nature of cyberspace makes attribution viciously difficult.[17]

Add to this the fact that computer crime is committed remotely—eliminating the need of the criminal to come anywhere close to his intended victim—and both investigation and capture become much more difficult.[18]

Similar concerns arise in a military response or in clandestine action against those who would do us harm (through espionage or attack) via cyberspace. Leaving aside the questions of when a cyber event is an "armed attack" and therefore warrants a military response under the laws of war—an issue discussed elsewhere in this volume[19]—the ability of cyber actors to obscure their physical location has serious ramifications for the United States's ability to direct military or intelligence resources, because of geography-based limitations in the authorizing law.

Uncertainty, then, may be more a function of the location—and identity-obscured nature of cyber attacks, rather than the United States's current legal authorities. In fact, US Army General Keith Alexander, Commander of US Cyber Command, recently testified that he believed no new legal authorities were necessary for Cyber Command to conduct its overseas mission. The Obama Administration's *Cyberspace Policy Review* recommended that technological efforts be redoubled to enhance our ability to attribute cyber activity to allow us to respond to it appropriately—a recommendation with which we wholeheartedly agree.

---

17. See Rosenzweig, *National Security Threats*, at 17.
18. *Id.*
19. See Chapter 6, this volume, "Cold War Paradigms: Does MAD Work with Cyber Weapons?".

CHAPTER 10

Preemptive Strike and First Use

Richard Weitz, Ph.D.

In the wake of the information revolution of the late 20th century, the new battlefield of cyberspace has forced the world powers to alter their grand strategies to include the new interests they must protect and the new capabilities that they must develop. Each national actor must decide what assets they will defend and how they will do so. Cyber threats seem especially menacing because of the general dependence of both private and public systems on the Internet, networks, and electronics. They are also disconcerting to policymakers because it is unclear how to respond effectively, in part because of the uncertain impact and novel nature of these threats. Unlike most conventional weapons, cyber attacks are cheap, rapid, and potentially catastrophic. Cyber war is by nature offensive, while defensive measures seem difficult.

With the development of any new technology with military applications, various doctrines and systems are needed to organize the application of these technologies. For example, the creation of nuclear weapons necessitated developing new strategies regarding their potential military uses—including under what conditions they might be employed, how they might be used, and how their application could be controlled so that they would contribute to the pursuit of rational military goals and national interests rather than taking on their

Richard Weitz is Senior Fellow and Director of the Center for Political-Military Analysis at Hudson Institute. His current research includes regional security developments relating to Europe, Eurasia, and East Asia as well as US foreign, defense, and homeland security policies. Dr. Weitz is also a non-resident Senior Fellow at the Center for a New American Security (CNAS), where he contributes to various defense projects. Before joining Hudson in 2003, Dr. Weitz worked for the Institute for Foreign Policy Analysis, Center for Strategic and International Studies, Defense Science Board, DFI International, Inc., Center for Strategic Studies, Harvard University's Kennedy School of Government, and the US Department of Defense.

own logic. Henry Kissinger, Herman Kahn and other great thinkers grappled with these questions at the dawn of the era of nuclear war. This process is occurring today in the novel realm of cyber conflict.

Since cyberspace is a relatively new war fighting domain, the doctrine and strategies that define how cyber weapons could be used in the future are in an early stage of development. Cyber attacks pose their own unique challenges, not least of which are issues relating to attribution, the speed of attacks, difficulty in detection, and credibility of deterrence. Yet, longstanding military concepts such as a preemptive war and first use need to be considered by cyber policies, doctrines, and strategies. What level of cyber response is appropriate for what level of cyber attack? Should the United States respond to a serious cyber attack only in the cyber domain or by using other forms of military force? Although it is difficult to define what retaliatory equivalency should look like with cyber attacks, in part because of the constantly evolving nature of the threat, a versatile framework for understanding cyber attacks and the retaliation to cyber attacks is mandatory. Without a suitable retaliatory doctrine, the United States will be, at the very least, less well-prepared if a significant cyber attack is launched against it.

Fortunately, despite its novelty, analysts of these issues can profitably consider previous military writings and experience in the non-cyber realm in developing an effective cyber retaliatory equivalency doctrine. It is unsurprising that cyber war has drawn comparisons to both nuclear weapons and terrorism. All three means of attack present the defender with the need to defend against difficult to locate, fast-moving, asymmetrical threats that may strike with little to no warning and inflict potentially catastrophic losses. The United States has relied on strategies of preemption and prevention over the preceding decade to counter WMD and terrorism threats. So it is reasonable to question whether strategies based on anticipatory self-defense may be well suited to the threat of cyber attack.

Attributes of Cyber Attacks

In the "Securing Cyberspace for the 44th Presidency" report, which has had great influence on the Obama Administration's cyber security policies, cyber attacks were recognized as having joined "terrorism and weapons of mass destruction (WMD) as one of the new, asymmetric threats that put the

United States and its allies at risk."[1] The Bush and Obama approaches to contemporary transnational threats were formed in response to hostile forces that offered the possibility of killing thousands and imperiling US strategic centers in a single, potentially unpredictable blow. Both administrations acknowledged that this situation warranted exceptional actions on the part of the United States. It is important to examine exactly which elements of cyber conflict so readily invite this frequent comparison.

Cyber attacks—whether terrorist, "hacktivist," or military in nature—are a form of asymmetrical conflict that profoundly favors the offensive due to a combination of attribution, geography, associated costs, and timing. In the cyber domain, the attacker is afforded the luxury of being able to strike at targets worldwide without regard for geography. The attackers may be located in various countries or situated in a single room.[2] Time also favors the cyber attacker. The difficulty of attribution and means to consistently predict the source of unforeseen assault ensures that attackers may methodically and effective conduct network reconnaissance "without fear of retaliation, until a suitable vulnerability is found."[3] When implementing certain tactics, such as distributed denial of service (DDoS) attacks, organizers often have the capacity to enlist the assistance of thousands of (often politically) motivated supporters.[4] Attackers need not even be constrained by the need to recruit willing participants; botnets may readily be created without the knowledge of the infected computers' users. Faced with an adversary afforded such significant advantages, defenders must not only work to harden networks against such threats, but create a larger strategy that discourages or prevents such attacks from occurring in the first place.

Both nuclear and cyber theorists worry about incentives to strike first in a confrontation due to the offence-dominant nature of both domains.[5] As with nuclear weapons, cyber security is often seen as offense-dominant due to the rapidity of cyber strikes, the difficulty of quickly identifying the attacker, and

1. James A. Lewis, et al. "Securing Cyberspace for the 44th Presidency," Center for Strategic and International Studies, December 2008. *http://csis.org/files/media/csis/pubs/081208_securingcyberspace_44.pdf.*

2. Rain Ottis, "Theoretical Offensive Cyber Militia Models," Cooperative Cyber Defence Centre of Excellence, 2011, pp. 307-308. *http://www.ccdcoe.org/articles/2011/Ottis_TheoreticalOffensiveCyberMilitiaModels.pdf.*

3. Kenneth Geers, *Strategic Cyber Security* (NATO Cooperative Cyber Defence Centre of Excellence, June 2011), *http://www.ccdcoe.org/publications/books/Strategic_Cyber_Security_K_Geers.pdf,* p. 102.

4. Ottis, , "Theoretical Offensive Cyber Militia Models," pp 308-309.

5. Thomas Schelling, *Strategy and Arms Control* (New York: Twentieth Century Fund, 1961), p. 9.

the possibility that a successful preemptive attack will degrade any retaliatory response, perhaps decisively. States possessing nuclear weapons devote considerable effort to developing and sustaining highly tailored offensive arsenals that could preempt or credibly deter external threats regardless of the defenses that the target might deploy. A similar process is occurring in the cyber domain. Military and intelligence services are investing heavily in developing highly classified offensive cyber tools designed to deter and disable potential threats, including those in the information domain.[6] The new US Cyber Command is continuing this tradition by developing additional offensive information capabilities. In 2009, then Deputy Secretary of Defense Bill Lynn insisted that the US Department of Defense (DoD) would "resist the temptation and the false comfort of trying to retreat behind a fortress of firewalls." Rather than trying to create "a digital version of the Maginot Line", Lynn argued that the military should "remember the lessons of maneuver warfare" and pursue "new tactics and technologies" that would allow US forces to use agility "to out-maneuver their adversary".[7]

Previous Forms of Preemptive War

The United States and other countries have long employed preemptive strikes against adversaries, including most recently against individual terrorists or terrorist organizations. For the United States, the 1837 Caroline Incident has most clearly defined the conditions under which force could be used preemptively since it led to articulation of the concept anticipatory self-defense—the position that a serious threat of armed attack may justify military defense action.[8] Daniel Webster, then US Secretary of State, argued that the United States could employ force even without itself being attacked when "the necessity of that self-defense is instant, overwhelming, and leaving no choice of means and no moment of deliberation [and that] such an attack

---

6. David E. Sanger, John Markoff, and Thom Shanker, "US Steps Up Effort on Digital Defenses," *New York Times*, April 28, 2009, at *http://www.nytimes.com/2009/04/28/us/28cyber.html*.

7. William J. Lynn, "Speech on Cyber Security at the Center for Strategic and International Studies," as delivered by Deputy Secretary of Defense William J. Lynn , Center for Strategic and International Studies, Washington, D.C., June 15, 2009, at*http://www.defenselink.mil/speeches/speech.aspx?speechid=1365*.

8. Jackson Nyamuya Maogoto, *Battling Terrorism: Legal Perspectives on the Use of Force and the War on Terror* (Hampshire: Ashgate Publishing Limited, 2005), p. 17.

be proportional to the threat."[9] When Israel attacked an Iraqi nuclear reactor in 1981, it also claimed anticipatory self-defense.[10]

The argument for the initiation and legitimacy of preemptive war, whether limited in scope to a single strike or as a full scale invasion is grounded in Article 51 of the UN Charter, which, depending on how it is interpreted, allows preemptive actions for self-defense. It states that: "Nothing in the present Charter shall impair the inherent right of individual or collective self-defense if an armed attack occurs against a Member of the United Nations, until the Security Council has taken measures necessary to maintain international peace and security."[11] This leads to a debate between those who interpret Article 51 with a restrictive view and those who interpret it with an expansionist view. The former tend to believe that states may exercise the right of self-defense only if an armed attack occurs, while the latter believe that the "inherent right to self-defence" means that no country should be forced to endure a first strike before defending itself, especially if the threatening state might possess weapons of mass destruction.[12]

Although largely successful as policy during the Cold War, the United States has viewed deterrence somewhat skeptically in its response to the 21st century challenges of transnational terrorism and weapons proliferation among rogue states. Setting the tone for post-9/11 policy, President George W. Bush's 2002 address at the United States Military Academy at West Point highlighted the limitations of deterrence, stating "the promise of massive retaliation against nations, means nothing against shadowy terrorist networks with no nation or citizens to defend. Containment is not possible when unbalanced dictators with weapons of mass destruction can deliver those weapons on missiles or secretly provide them to terrorist allies."[13] The 2002 National Security

9.   Joanne M. Fish, Samuel J. McCraw, and Christopher J. Reddish, "Fighting In The Gray Zone: A Strategy To Close The Preemption Gap," Strategic Studies Institute, September 2004, p. 2, http://www.strategicstudiesinstitute.army.mil/pdffiles/pub412.pdf.

10. Hans Kochler, ed., *The Use of Force in International Relations: Challenges to Collective Security* (Wilfersdorf: International Progress Organization, 2006), p. 134.

11. "Chapter Vii: Action With Respect To Threats To The Peace, Breaches Of The Peace, And Acts Of Aggression: Article 51," United Nations Charter, http://www.un.org/en/documents/charter/chapter7.shtml.

12. C. S. Owens, "Unlikely Partners: Preemption and The "American Way of War." (2003) p.4.

13. George W. Bush, "Text of Bush's Speech at West Point," *New York Times*, June 1, 2002, http://www.nytimes.com/2002/06/01/international/02PTEX-WEB.html?pagewanted=all.

Strategy justified the preemptive use of force against terrorists.[14] The Bush Administration's position with regard to such threats asserts that since deterrence is not a credible option, the right of self-defense affords countries the prerogative to act preemptively in order to neutralize such threats before they may materialize. The 2002 US National Security Strategy further clarified this assessment by emphasizing that the potentially devastating impact of terrorist attacks and WMD, as well as the covertness of such tactics, fuel the need for preemptive action.[15]

President Bush argued that Article 51 permitted the United States to launch a preemptive war on Iraq for purposes of self-defense.[16] Although many did not share Bush's interpretation of Article 51, other countries have periodically resorted to unconventional methods beyond their territory to neutralize external threats. Furthermore, in 2009, a joint counterterrorism doctrine prepared by the US Chairman of the Joint Chiefs of Staff includes a section on "conducting preemptive attacks on terrorist targets."[17]

The principal logic of this argument has been adopted by the Obama Administration in its prosecution of counterterrorist operations in Central Asia, the Middle East, and Africa. As US Department of State Legal Advisor Harold Koh explained in an influential 2010 speech to the American Society of International Law, the legal justification for deadly force applied abroad in the name of self-defense consists of, *inter alia,* three elements: 1) "the sovereignty of the other states involved," 2) "the willingness and ability of those states to suppress the threat the target poses," and 3) "the imminence of the threat."[18] Koh went on to explain "the United States has the authority under international law, and the responsibility to its citizens, to use force, including lethal force, to defend itself, including by targeting persons such as

14. The White House (Under George W. Bush), "III. Strengthen Alliances to Defeat Global Terrorism and Work to Prevent Attacks Against Us and Our Friends," The National Security Strategy, September 2002, *http://georgewbush-whitehouse.archives.gov/nsc/nss/2002/nss3.html.*

15. George W. Bush, "2002 National Security Strategy," The White House, September, 2002. *http://georgewbush-whitehouse.archives.gov/nsc/nss/2002/.*

16. David M. Ackerman, "International Law and the Preemptive Use of Force Against Iraq," Congressional Research Service, April 11, 2003, p. 1, *http://www.au.af.mil/au/awc/awcgate/crs/rs21314.pdf.*

17. "Joint Publication 3-26: Counterterrorism," prepared under the direction of the Chairman of the Joint Chiefs of Staff, November 13, 2009, p. III-12, *http://www.fas.org/irp/doddir/dod/jp3_26.pdf.*

18. Harold Hongju Koh, "The Obama Administration and International Law," United States Department of State, March 25, 2010, *http://www.state.gov/s/l/releases/remarks/139119.htm.*

high-level al-Qaeda leaders who are planning attacks."[19] Koh added, "Some have argued that our targeting practices violate domestic law, in particular, the long-standing domestic ban on assassinations. But under domestic law, the use of lawful weapons systems—consistent with the applicable laws of war—for precision targeting of specific high-level belligerent leaders when acting in self-defense or during an armed conflict is not unlawful, and hence does not constitute 'assassination'."[20]

This discussion is especially relevant because of the recent discussion about assassinations by US Attorney General Eric Holder. On March 5, 2012, Holder broadly repeated these conditions, stressing that the principle of sovereignty is no longer applicable if "the nation [from which a threat emanates] is unable or unwilling to deal effectively with a threat to the United States."[21] Holder added that, "The US Government's use of lethal force in self-defense against a leader of al Qaeda or an associated force who presents an imminent threat of violent attack would not be unlawful—and therefore would not violate the Executive Order banning assassination or criminal statutes."[22]

More recently, the Obama administration's Presidential Policy Directive (PPD-14) affirms the continued validity of Section 1021 of the National Defense Authorization Act for FY 2012 (Public Law 112 81)(NDAA), which states "That the President is authorized to use all necessary and appropriate force against those nations, organizations, or persons he determines planned, authorized, committed, or aided the terrorist attacks that occurred on September 11, 2001, or harbored such organizations or persons, in order to prevent any future acts of international terrorism against the United States by such nations, organizations or persons."[23]

---

19. Koh, "Speech".

20. *Ibid.*

21. Eric Holder, "Attorney General Eric Holder Speaks at Northwestern University School of Law," US Department of Justice, March 5, 2012. *http://www.justice.gov/iso/opa/ag/speeches/2012/ag-speech-1203051.html.*

22. Jason Ryan, "Holder: When War on Terror Targets Americans," ABC News, March 5, 2012, *http://abcnews.go.com/Blotter/holder-speak-targeted-killings-americans/story?id=15851232.*

23. US Government Printing Office, "Joint resolution to authorize the use of United States Armed Forces against those responsible for the recent attacks launched against the United States," Public Law 107-40, September 18, 2001, Bill Number S.J. Res. 23, Statutes at Large Citations 115 Stat. 224 and 225, *http://www.gpo.gov/fdsys/pkg/PLAW-107publ40* and *http://www.gpo.gov/fdsys/pkg/PLAW-107publ40/pdf/PLAW-107publ40.pdf.*

International Law and Sentiment

Complicating matters further, the unsettled legal status of cyber conflict renders the applicability of customary international law and the Law of Armed Conflict uncertain. Debates persist over such issues as:

- What constitutes an act of aggression (must an attack have kinetic effects, target a government network, or exceed a certain threshold)?

- What degree of certainty is required regarding the identity of the aggressor to permit legitimate retaliatory action?

- How do traditional legal concepts apply (discrimination, proportionality) when networked interoperability shatters the distinction between military and civilian targets and when the risk of unintended collateral damage is potentially high but unknown?

What appears evident, however, is that a great deal of cyber conflict can occur within the boundaries of accepted international norms, including actions that may be labeled as preemptive. The standard apparently accepted by the Obama Administration is that anticipatory self-defense may be acceptable if it corresponds to the *Caroline* doctrine—when the threat is "instant, overwhelming, and leaves no choice of means."[24]

Still, the question of whether to implement a policy of first use in cyber warfare has been a difficult decision for both military and civilian leaders due to the negative international response that it brings about. A distinction must be made between two types of first strikes; (1) a preemptive strike and (2) a preventive strike. The difference between these two terms lies in the justification of the military action. A preemptive strike implies that the threat is instant, overwhelming, and leaves no choice.[25] If the preemptive strike does not meet these criteria, it may be deemed illegitimate by the international community, which would deprive the actor of support. A preventive strike is carried out by a state when a threat is not imminent but is growing to the point where a state could become vulnerable to attack or is in a position of strategic weakness.[26] Preventive military action is often viewed as illegitimate

---

24. Stephen Murdoch, "Preemptive War: Is It Legal?," *DC BAR*, January 2003. *http://www.dcbar.org/for_lawyers/resources/publications/washington_lawyer/january_2003/war.cfm*.

25. *Washington Post*. "Six Degrees of Preemption." *Washington Post* September 29, 2002.

26. Dan Reiter, "Exploding the Powder Keg Myth: Preemptive Wars Almost NeverHappen," International Security, Vol. 20, No. 2 (Fall 1995) p.6.

because it is impossible for the aggressor to have incontrovertible evidence of his victim's long-term hostile strategic goals.

The use of Stuxnet was clearly a preventive cyber attack on Iran's nuclear program. While Iran's nuclear program may be used for military purposes, this is presently difficult for foreign governments to prove. The only reason this attack went without major criticism was the multilateral support for curbing Iran's nuclear wapons potential, which gave the attack de facto legitimacy. Stuxnet can be compared to the Israeli air strike on Iraq's Osirak nuclear complex in 1981. Although evidence pointed to a possible long-term threat, there was no immediate threat of Iraq launching a nuclear attack against Israel. Thus many believed this attack to be illegitimate and it even received condemnation from the Reagan Administration.[27]

The potentially nonlethal nature of cyber weapons may cloud the assessment of an attack's legality, leading to more frequent violations of the principle of distinction in this new form of warfare. In essence, an attacker may believe that his actions do not constitute an act of war due to the means in which the facility was taken offline. If this is the case, both state actors and non-state actors alike will embrace preemptive cyber warfare strategies, which could potentially escalate to conventional warfare. Most countries hold a restrictive view of preemption to avoid setting a precedent that would allow other states to start wars by claiming their own right to preempt.[28]

The Risk of Being Second

Although the relative novelty of cyber conflict leaves much room for debate, the distinct advantages enjoyed by the attacker have encouraged the view that it is necessary to erect a credible defense that not only protects against attacks, but one that effectively deters such attacks from ever taking place. It is due in no small part to such considerations that the Obama Administration's cyber-defense policy is based on the dual notions of dissuasion and deterrence.

One factor driving interest in cyber preemption is fear of experiencing a devastating first strike by an adversary. The Obama Administration's May 2010 National Security Strategy states that "[o]ur digital infrastructure, therefore, is a strategic national asset, and protecting it…is a national security priority." To

27. C. S. Owens,. "Unlikely Partners: Preemption and The "American Way of War" (2003) p. 13.
28. Owens, "Unlikely Partners," p.11.

this end, the administration argues that the United States "will deter, prevent, detect, defend against, and quickly recover from cyber intrusions and attacks."[29]

Unfortunately for policy makers, the exact nature of the threat posed by cyber attacks remains uncertain, leaving in doubt whether it is possible to "quickly recover" from a surprise first strike. Analysts, pundits, and policy experts remain at odds as to the dangers and potential effects of a weaponized cyberspace. Former DoD official Michael Nacht, an architect of US Cyber Command's national security strategy, has indicated that cyber technology has the capacity to revolutionize strategic thought, likening its effect on defense planners to the advent of nuclear weaponry.[30] Conversely, a 2009 report by the Cyber Consequences Unit examining cyber warfare against Georgia during its 2008 war with Russia observed that cyber attacks could achieve the same tactical impact as missiles and bombs in neutralizing Georgian communications facilities, but little more. In this instance, cyber attacks represented a tactical improvement by reducing civilian casualties, but did not significantly alter the fundamental military strategy in the conflict.[31]

The Bush Administration's 2002 National Security Strategy specifically emphasized that a key justification for preemption was the notion that the "greater the threat, the greater is the risk of inaction."[32] Cyber attacks are typically disruptive and have the capacity to cause significant damage to infrastructure. Nevertheless, as of yet, it does not appear that cyber attacks have caused fatalities or destruction comparable to terrorist, let alone physical, attacks. For the Obama Administration, a key-limiting factor is the notion of the imminence of threat. Here it is also uncertain that most cyber attacks rise to the same threat level posed by terrorism or WMDs in the hands of rogue states.

To this end, certain observers have suggested that cyber attacks pose challenges, but manageable ones. Bruce Schneier, the chief security officer for BT Group, has stated that the actual threat may be exaggerated, noting that

---

29. Obama, Barack, "National Security Strategy ", The White House, May, 2010. *http://www.whitehouse. gov/sites/default/files/rss_viewer/national_security_strategy.pdf.*

30. Kate Jastram and Anne Quintin, "The Internet *in Bello*: Cyber War Law, Ethics & Policy," Berkeley School of Law, November 18, 2011. *http://www.law.berkeley.edu/files/cyberwarfare_seminar—summary.pdf.*

31. John Bumgarner and Scott Borg, "Overview by the US-CCU of the Cyber Campaign against Georgia in August of 2008," United States Cyber Consequences Unit (August 2009), *http://www. registan.net/wp-content/uploads/2009/08/US-CCU-Georgia-Cyber-Campaign-Overview.pdf.*

32. Bush, "2002 National Security Strategy".

"Stuxnet and the Google infiltration are not cyber war—who died?"[33] Professor of International Affairs Stephen Walt has similarly opined that a fixation on cyber conflict risks "spend[ing] tens of billions of dollars protecting ourselves against a set of threats that are not as dangerous as we are currently being told they are."[34]

Nuclear Nuances

The strategy of nuclear deterrence formed the cornerstone of US nuclear policy for the second half of the 20th century, effectively preventing nuclear war during the Cold War. This perceived success has led numerous cyber observers and strategists to argue for its adoption as a model for cyber strategy.[35] The essence of this position is to apply denial and deterrence to potential cyber conflicts. First, governments work together to develop norms regarding the use of cyber weapons. Second, governments develop some degree of retaliatory capacity (whether cyber-based, diplomatic, kinetic, or all of the above) in order to ensure compliance with these norms.[36]

A common comparison, which many writers have made, has been to the doctrine of Mutually Assured Destruction (MAD), the most notable use of deterrence in American strategy. From the development of Soviet nuclear weapons until today, the US defense against these weapons rested on the premise that a first strike could not destroy the US offensive nuclear capabilities and that a second strike would inflict an unacceptable amount of damage on the Soviets, Chinese and now Russians. The fear of a second strike was expected to deter even a nuclear-armed adversary from ever launching a preemptive strike. This type of deterrence involved an equivalence of means—a "tit for tat"—in which the means of deterrent was the same as that which would be used in an attack.

The United States had a different strategy of deterrence in regard to the Soviets' conventional capability. Dubbed "Massive Retaliation," this doctrine held that a Soviet attack on Western Europe would trigger a nuclear response

---

33. Maggie Shields, "Cyber war threat exaggerated claims security expert," *BBC News*, February 16, 2011. *http://www.bbc.co.uk/news/technology-12473809*.

34. Stephen M. Walt, "Is the cyber threat overblown?," *Foreign Policy*, March 30, 2010, *http://walt.foreignpolicy.com/posts/2010/03/30/is_the_cyber_threat_overblown*.

35. Lewis, et al. "Securing Cyberspace," p. 19.

36. "Defcon 19: Kenneth Geers—Strategic Cyber Security: An Evaluation of Nation-State Cyber Attack," video presentation at *http://www.youtube.com/watch?v=0r_2GvYdVas*.

from the United States.[37] The deterrent here was disproportional to the attack, and was not equivalent. The United States also reserved the right to use nuclear weapons first—both to preempt their use by the other side and to affect the outcome of a conventional war confrontation.

But cyber deterrence only vaguely resembles nuclear deterrence. A nuclear attack is so devastating that there is little question as to the type of retribution. Furthermore, only a few states possess nuclear weapons and their delivery systems are easy to trace, meaning that nuclear attacks can be attributable to nation-states. These countries have fixed locations, governments, responsibilities, and vulnerabilities. In contrast, cyber capabilities are cheaper, more anonymous, and probably less lethal than nuclear attacks.

Cyber attacks present the possibility of unpredictable assaults being launched by many possible actors, who can conceal their attacks through various techniques, against both US strategic objects and unhardened civilian targets. Such attacks may be extremely difficult to attribute to a particular adversary (whether another state or organization). They may occur with little or no warning and their preparation may be impossible to detect. Thus, there exist few credible ways of deterring them.

Preparing the Cyber Battlefield

The United States has at a minimum accepted the principle of "active defense"—the capacity to respond to cyber attacks with offensive cyber capabilities. US Cyber Command Head General Keith Alexander has repeatedly emphasized the necessity of having "offensive capabilities, to, in real time, shut down somebody trying to attack us."[38] Similarly, the National Defense Authorization Act for Fiscal Year 2012 for the first time explicitly permits the Department of Defense to "conduct offensive operations in cyberspace to defend our Nation, Allies and interests."[39]

A critical element of active defense is the concept of cyber exploitation, which involves "intelligence collection capabilities conducted through the use of computer networks to gather data from target or adversary automated

---

37. Herman S. Wolk "The 'New Look'," *Air Force Magazine*, August 2003. *http://www.airforce-magazine.com/MagazineArchive/Pages/2003/August%202003/0803look.aspx.*

38. Ellen Nakashima, "US eyes preemptive cyber-defense strategy," *Washington Post*, August 29, 2010, *http://www.washingtonpost.com/wp-dyn/content/article/2010/08/28/AR2010082803312.html.*

39. H.R. 1540, United States Congress. *http://www.gpo.gov/fdsys/pkg/BILLS-112hr1540enr/pdf/BILLS-112hr1540enr.pdf.*

information systems or networks."[40] This form of intelligence gathering is essential as a means of fulfilling the goals of active defense, as it enables the defender to have the information necessary to respond in an effective manner. Responsive cyber attacks, as advocated by Gen. Alexander, cannot be conducted in a timely manner without previous intelligence regarding the structure of an adversary's system. As James Lewis of the Center for Strategic and International Studies observed, effectively penetrating a hostile network is "the cyber equivalent of fumbling around in the dark until you find the doorknob."[41] To continue the analogy, knowing where that doorknob is in advance significant improves the defender's position.

From a legal point of view, cyber exploitation (and more specifically, cyber espionage) appears to have the same legal status as non-cyber espionage. The more essential documents of international law (*inter alia*, the Hague Convention, the UN Charter and the Geneva Conventions) are largely silent on such covert activities. It has been argued that peacetime espionage (the category under which preparations for active defense would seem to fall) cannot be entirely legal, as it constitutes a breach of a state's obligation to respect the sovereignty and territorial integrity of other states.[42] While it is certainly possible that acts such as covert intelligence collection can be correctly labeled as violations of sovereignty, it is equally true that there is a long history among states of at least passively tolerating espionage as an expected element in international relations. As Christopher Baker argues, "international law neither endorses nor prohibits espionage, but rather preserves the practice as a tool by which to facilitate international cooperation."[43]

Preparation of the battlefield through the use of dormant code must always be analyzed in its larger context of both adversaries' capabilities and doctrine as well the current state of affairs. A hostile intent must be established in order to warrant a military response for the use of such a cyber weapon.

---

40. Joint Publication 1-02, "Department of Defense Dictionary of Military and Associated Terms," April 12, 2001, (As Amended through October 31, 2009), p. 111.

41. Eric Schmitt and Thom Shanker, "US Debated Cyberwarfare in Attack Plan on Libya," *New York Times*, October 17, 2011, *http://www.nytimes.com/2011/10/18/world/africa/cyber-warfare-against-libya-was-debated-by-us.html?_r=1&pagewanted=print*.

42. A. John Radsan, "The Unresolved Equation of Espionage and International Law", *Michigan Journal of International Law* vol. 28, no. 597, (July 2007). *http://ssrn.com/abstract=1003225*.

43. Christopher D. Baker, "Tolerance of International Espionage: A Functional Approach", *American University International Law Review* vol. 19, no. 5 (2003), pp. 1091-1113.

A complicating factor in assessing the legality of active defense is the uncertainty surrounding exactly what elements are present in such a strategy. Although unlikely to be considered a friendly act, there appears to be a general passive acceptance of cyber espionage. Yet mapping vulnerabilities in adversarial networks and collecting intelligence by infiltrating computer systems is certainly not the limit of active cyber defense. The famed Stuxnet worm provides an excellent example of the capacity of a highly aggressive active cyber defense. One of the most noteworthy characteristics of Stuxnet was that the worm was programmed to enter a system and remain dormant, activating only if certain conditions were met and thereby only attacking its designated target.[44]

In an active defense hypothesis, such a worm may be created and implanted in an adversary's system in anticipation of a future attack. Should one occur, the worm (the presence of which would remain unknown to the adversary due to its dormancy) would be activated with the goal of damaging the hostile network's ability to continue its attack. It is widely presumed in the United States that foreign countries have placed "hacked hardware in key US defense systems.[45]

In such a case, "the distinction between cyber attack and cyber exploitation may be very hard to draw from a technical standpoint, and may lie primarily in the intent of the user."[46] Oona Hathaway et al. further clarify by noting that "[m]ere cyber-espionage, or cyber-exploitation, does not constitute a cyber attack, because neither or these concepts involves altering computer networks in a way that affects their current or future ability to function."[47] Utilizing this dual definition, it is possible to assert that, as a non-activated worm does not alter or otherwise affect the targeted system, it cannot be classified as a cyber attack and falls under the less malignant and hitherto largely accepted category of non-destructive cyber exploitation.

44. "Stuxnet Virus: A Guide," *The Telegraph (London)*, November 25, 2010, *http://www.telegraph.co.uk/technology/internet/8159665/Stuxnet-virus-A-guide.html.*

45. Adam Rawnsley, "Fishy Chips: Spies Want to Hack-Proof Circuits," *Wired*, June 24, 2011, *http://www.wired.com/dangerroom/2011/06/chips-oy-spies-want-to-hack-proof-circuits/#more-49990.*

46. William A. Owens, Kenneth W. Dam, and Herbert S. Lin, *Technology, Policy, Law, and Ethics Regarding US Acquisition and Use of Cyberattack Capabilities* (Washington D.C.: National Academy Press, October 28, 2009), p. 22.

47. Oona A. Hathaway, Rebecca Crootof, Philip Levitz, Haley Nix, Aileen Nowlan, Willian Perdue and Julia Spiegel, "The Law of Cyber-Attack," Yale Law School, *http://www.law.yale.edu/documents/pdf/cglc/LawOfCyberAttack.pdf.*

In recent years, the United States has accepted a philosophy that if "a cyber attack produces the death, damage, destruction or high-level disruption that a traditional military attack would cause, then it would be a candidate for a 'use of force'."[48] However, US officials have not conclusively indicated whether the presence of an inactive worm in US defense systems could produce the same result. On the one hand, it seems questionable to violently retaliate for the presence of a computer virus that is, at the moment, causing no harm (an action made all the more difficult by the previously discussed challenges in attribution). On the other hand, it is quite plausible that a state would react with force (if it could determine the perpetrator) to the discovery of explosives placed (again, preemptively) beneath one of its critical radar stations.

Logic bombs are strategic assets that come in the form of malicious code designed to execute if specific events occur or at a predetermined time. When triggered, this code may disable computer systems, delete data, or activate a DoS attack. Logic bombs could be considered an act of aggression should their ultimate purpose be discovered. In practice, the vast amount of uses for logic bombs complicates any classification of this type of cyber weapons. A logic bomb's conventional equivalent would seem to be deep cover agents or sleeper cells. As in the conventional battle space, these agents could lay dormant for decades until being activated and can perform many duties ranging from the gathering of intelligence to direct action missions. Cyberspace is no different; a logic bomb can be activated to release malware which gives intelligence agencies a back door in an enemy's intelligence networks or it could be used to disrupt vital logistical networks or both private and public infrastructure. For a legal decision to be made, intent must be conclusively discovered.

The discovery of a Russian clandestine network in 2010 is an excellent comparison to the use of logic bombs. In this case, the discovery of clandestine agents who had been dormant for years did not prove to be an act of war and thus required no military response. Had the agents been found to be sabotaging air traffic control centers or disabling safety features on nuclear power plants, there could have been a conventional military response due to the threat and intent to cause physical damage.

A comparison can also be made with "insider" threats—those people whose position allows them to circumvent many of the institution's external

---

48.   Siobhan Gorman and Julian E. Barnes, "Cyber Combat: Act of War," *Wall Street Journal*, May 30, 2011, *http://online.wsj.com/article/SB10001424052702304563104576355623135782718.html#ixzz1NwErjZtY.*

defenses, which are typically directed outward. Steven Chabinsky believes that "the primary cyber-risk to our critical infrastructure is from disgruntled employees who have insider knowledge and access."[49] One reason why Google might have reacted so strongly to China's Internet attacks in January 2010 was that, according to the media, Google suspected that one or more of its Chinese-based employees had abetted the December 2009 penetration of the company's internal networks.[50] According to these reports, Google experienced the nightmare of a double Trojan Horse attack, with at least one of its local Chinese employees opening the company's firewalls to allow virtual Trojan Horses to penetrate its internal network. What was unusual was that the particular malware program involved in the penetration, Hydraq, knew precisely what data to attack and where to find it. Local Chinese media have reported that after January 13, when Google went public with its information about the alleged Chinese cyber attacks, the company denied some of its Chinese employee's access to Google's internal networks while transferring or putting on leave personnel in the company's China office.[51]

Military action based solely on the discovery of a logic bomb would be akin to a preventive strike against a threat that was not immediate. However, the deployment of a strategic asset such as a logic bomb during a time when two countries are approaching conflict could be deemed as a first strike. For example, Chinese information warfare doctrine stresses seizing control of an adversary's information flow.[52] In the event of an escalation of conflict between China and the United States over Taiwan, Chinese infiltration of US networks, both civilian and military, could be considered a first strike due to the potential for risk to both forward deployed military assets and civilians at home. In this instance, the PRC would be showing a hostile intent of disrupting C4ISR capabilities of their adversaries, which in the case of a conflict in the Taiwan Straits could allow the PLA to launch military operations such as a cross-strait landing before the United States could effectively intervene.[53]

---

49. Cited in Don Tennant, "The Fog of (Cyber) War," *Computerworld* (April 2009), p. 30, *http://www.abanet.org/natsecurity/cybersecurity_readings/the_fogof%20_cyberwar.pdf.*

50. "Google Probing Possible Inside Help on Attack," *Reuters,* January 18, 2010, *http://www.reuters.com/article/idUSTOE60H07V20100118.*

51. *Ibid.*

52. Bryan A. Krekel, U. S.-China Economic, Commission Security Review, and Sector Northrop Grumman Corporation. Information Systems. "Capability of the People's Republic of China to conduct cyber warfare and computer network exploitation" (Northrop Grumman Corp., Information Systems Sector 2009), p.11.

53. *Ibid.,* p.12.

Placing malicious software on another country's computer systems and waiting to activate it until it is necessary is dangerous. What if the malicious software is accidently activated or found? Could the software be shut down immediately if it accidently activated or if an error occurred? Could it be guaranteed that there would never be a lapse in control over the software by the government that put it there? If, in the future, the country no longer poses a threat or even becomes an ally how do you delete the software off their systems? How is it decided what level of threat from another country warrants such an action? Some might consider it a good idea to put such software on a country's networks just in case hostilities occur. But if a state found that software on its networks it could, for instance, increase tensions between two countries and could actually make war more likely.

Concluding Observations

Given the more threatening characteristics of a cyber attack—the difficulty of attribution, tracking, shielding, predicting, and ensuring proportionality in any response—the preemptive strategies applied in recent years towards both rogue states and individual terrorists seem to present a compelling option in dealing with threats emanating from cyberspace. The United States has resorted to preemption specifically because of the inability to effectively deter certain threats, the difficulty of predicting them, and the high potential risks assumed by inaction. In such cases, the use of force can be justified as essential to neutralize (or at least make manageable) certain potential threats.

While cyber attacks share many of the inherent challenges associated with terrorism and WMDs, their danger is also a matter of scale. Cyber attacks have been successfully used to create short-term havoc and neutralize soft targets such as media and government websites. Their capacity to cause widespread fatalities and devastation on par with car bombs and sarin gas is, at this juncture, entirely hypothetical. As the risk calculus in cyber conflict is far less ominous than with other threats, the preemptive use of force is less readily justifiable.

A second issue further calls into question the propriety of armed preemption in response to the threat of cyber attacks. If a state seeks to neutralize the threat of a rogue adversary possessing nuclear weapons, there are few actions short of the use of force that may accomplish this goal. Without killing or capturing an al-Qaeda tactician, it is difficult to prevent him from implementing his plans. With cyber conflict, however, there exist an entire array of options that may inhibit a cyber opponent from attacking or quickly halt his attack once underway. Although some of these (such as Stuxnet-like worms) may create physical damage, any number of tactics short of violence is available, in both the real and cyber domains.[54]

The 21st century incarnation of preemption came to existence as a result of a careful (if controversial) weighing of the risks posed by non-traditional threats and the costs of undertaking preemptive action. This fundamental calculation is still applicable to cyberspace. Only the potential weight assigned to these risks and costs has changed. How policy makers view these elements will be the ultimate determinant of the appropriateness of preemptive action.

---

54. It is for this reason that the CSIS Commission on Cybersecurity for the 44th Presidency advocated that the United States develop a credible offensive cyber capability, even while arguing against the first use of such a capacity. "[T]he absence" their report argued "of an offensive capability make deterrence a hollow threat"; see Lewis et al, p. 23.

CHAPTER 11

What Is Cyber Equivalence?
The Problem of Equivalent Response

Richard Weitz, Ph.D.

A cyber war "equivalence doctrine" posits that a cyber attack could in some extreme cases be considered comparable to a conventional attack and would thereby represent an act of war, subject to proportional military retaliation. The defender could respond to a cyber attack with non-cyber means, including conventional military operations and perhaps even unconventional ones. One unnamed US military official tersely said that, "If you shut down our power grid, maybe we will put a missile down one of your smokestacks."[1]

As part of its cyber deterrence strategy, the United States reserves the right to use armed force against hostile cyber attacks. In the *International Strategy for Cyberspace*, the Obama administration maintains that: "When warranted, the United States will respond to hostile acts in cyberspace as we would to any other threat to our country. All states possess an inherent right to self-defense, and we recognize that certain hostile acts conducted through cyberspace could compel actions under the commitments we have with our military treaty partners. We reserve the right to use all necessary means—diplomatic, informational, military, and economic—as appropriate

---

1. Siobhan Gorman and Julian E. Barnes, "Cyber Combat: Act of War," *Wall Street Journal*, May 30, 2011, *http://online.wsj.com/article/SB10001424052702304563104576355623135782718.html*.

Richard Weitz is Senior Fellow and Director of the Center for Political-Military Analysis at Hudson Institute. His current research includes regional security developments relating to Europe, Eurasia, and East Asia as well as US foreign, defense, and homeland security policies. Dr. Weitz is also a non-resident Senior Fellow at the Center for a New American Security (CNAS), where he contributes to various defense projects. Before joining Hudson in 2003, Dr. Weitz worked for the Institute for Foreign Policy Analysis, Center for Strategic and International Studies, Defense Science Board, DFI International, Inc., Center for Strategic Studies, Harvard University's Kennedy School of Government, and the US Department of Defense.

and consistent with applicable international law, in order to defend our Nation, our allies, our partners, and our interests."[2] The US Department of Defense (DoD) Cyberspace Policy Report of November 2011 contains the same text and further states that "we will exhaust all options prior to using force whenever we can; we will carefully weigh the costs and risks of action against the costs of inaction; and we will act in a way that reflects our values and strengthens our legitimacy, seeking broad international support wherever possible."[3] Moreover, it recognizes that "Deterrence in cyberspace, as with other domains, relies on two principal mechanisms: denying an adversary's objectives and, if necessary, imposing costs on an adversary for aggression."[4]

Pentagon spokesperson Col. David Lipan said that, if a cyber attack was sufficiently serious, "a response to a cyber incident or attack on the United States would not necessarily be a cyber response, so as I said all appropriate options would be on the table."[5] This statement implies that DoD, when responding to a cyber attack, can use whatever measures deemed necessary to retaliate effectively—including retaliating through cyberspace or through more traditional means.

In this declaratory posture, the Obama Administration maintains that it could use lethal force to punish cyber attackers. This doctrine broadens the meaning of equivalent retribution. Equivalence does not refer to the mode of attack—cyber, conventional, economic, etc.—but to the effect. An equivalent response is one that inflicts a proportionate amount of damage on the aggressor. As Austin Bay put it: "If a cyberspace based attack inflicts damage comparable (equivalent) to a conventional attack using bombs, gunfire or beam weapons, then the cyber attacker can expect the United States to retaliate with a range of weaponry, not just anti-viral software or a cyberspace-only counterattack."[6]

---

2. White House, *International Strategy for Cyberspace: Prosperity, Security, and Openness in a Networked World*, May 2011, 14, *http://www.whitehouse.gov/sites/default/files/rss_viewer/international_strategy_for_cyberspace.pdf*.

3. Department of Defense, "Department of Defense Cyberspace Policy Report," November 2011, p. 2, *http://www.defense.gov/home/features/2011/0411_cyberstrategy/docs/NDAA%20Section%20934%20Report_For%20webpage.pdf*.

4. *Ibid.*

5. Larry Shaughnessy, "Pentagon doesn't rule out military force against cyber attacks," CNN, May 31, 2011, *http://articles.cnn.com/2011-05-31/us/military.cyberattack_1_cyberattacks-military-force-military-computers?_s=PM:US*.

6. Austin Bay, "Cyber Warfare—The Doctrine of Equivalence", *Washington Examiner*, May 31st 2011, *http://washingtonexaminer.com/2011/05/cyberwarfare-doctrine-equivalence/40033?page=0%2C0%2C0%2C3&quicktabs_1=0*.

In this view, large segments of the US economy, military, infrastructure, and basic government functions rely extensively on information networks. From infrastructure destruction to simple viruses, the effects of cyber attacks are felt in the physical world. This approach can also justify an asymmetric response, one that goes beyond cyber retaliation or even preemptive cyber attacks.

For some though, the new doctrine of cyber equivalence raises alarm. Critics claim that lethal force used in response to non-lethal force is inappropriate, especially in cases where it is difficult to attribute the attack to a particular actor. Retaliating disproportionally also tends to promote the horizontal and vertical escalation of the conflict, resulting in higher mutual damage. In their article entitled, "A Military Response to Cyber Attacks is Preposterous," Cato scholars Christopher Preble and Benjamin Friedman claim that, "The trouble is that some acts of war, like naval blockades, damage only commerce. The same goes for all reported cyber attacks. Launching a war to retaliate for a non-lethal attack seems disproportionate, especially where it is unclear whether the attacker served the government. Taken literally, the new policy might have us risking nuclear exchange with Russia because it failed to stop teenagers in Moscow Internet cafés from attacking *Citibank.com*."[7]

Defining Aggression

A cyber attack's impact must be evaluated as to whether it constitutes an unlawful use of force. For instance the use of malware or IP spoofing to gain access to intelligence on a state's servers would not be considered an unlawful use of force under most circumstances. Cyber espionage is technically not an illegal use of force under international law due to its comparison with the downing of a US U-2 spy plane over Russia. In this case, the UN Security Council determined that although Soviet airspace had been violated, the use of the U-2 did not constitute an unlawful use of force in regards to Article 2(4) of the UN Charter.[8] The 2007 denial-of-service attack that targeted Estonian financial institutions, media, ministries and parliament were deemed by NATO not to constitute clear military action.[9]

---

7.   Benjamin H. Friedman and Christopher Preble, "A Military Response to Cyber Atacks is Preposterous," *Reuters*, June 2, 2011. *http://blogs.reuters.com/great-debate/2011/06/02/a-military-response-to-cyberattacks-is-preposterous/*.

8.   Thomas C. Wingfield, *The Law Of Information Conflict: National Security Law In Cyberspace* (Aegis Research Corp. 2000), pp. 352-53.

9.   "Russia accused of unleashing cyber war to disable Estonia," *The Guardian*, May 17, 2012, *http://www.guardian.co.uk/world/2007/may/17/topstories3.russia*.

A key element in the threshold for conventional retaliatory action exists when a country's civilian population or infrastructure is put at risk. Industrial processes and public and private infrastructure are controlled by supervisory control and data acquisition (SCADA) systems. These industrial control systems are vulnerable to cyber attacks. As was proved with the Aurora Project, a government initiative to test the vulnerability of turbines to cyber attacks, systems controlling vital infrastructure can be shut down causing catastrophic damage.[10] Similar vulnerabilities can be found in the SCADA systems controlling air traffic and nuclear power plant safety systems.[11] The potential risk this type of cyber attack poses to civilian populations compares to the devastating terrorist attacks of September 2001, which garnered a conventional military response.

From this perspective, a cyber attack that causes physical damage could constitute an armed attack under Article 51 of the UN Charter.[12] A country's response to an attack on its SCADA systems might not be limited strictly to cyberspace. As previously stated, the UN Charter specifically states that each country has the inherent right to self-defense; thus a state's response would be limited only by its capabilities, will, and calculations regarding best how to achieve its interests. In the case of the United States, retaliatory options range from precision strikes on an aggressor's cyber warfare facilities to an invasion of the aggressor's territory, as with Afghanistan following 9/11.

The Attribution Problem

Analysts have long highlighted the difficulties of identifying those responsible for cyber acts as one of the most significant impediments to devising and implementing an effective strategy for deterring or punishing cyber attacks. Identifying a specific entity as the source of a cyber security incident is typically difficult, time-consuming, and often inconclusive. It is extremely difficult to trace a particular attack to a particular actor. Even if it can be proved that the attack came from a certain country, if the attacker has done a thorough job of manipulating other computers, it can be impossible to pinpoint the blame.

Moreover, intelligence and security experts find it difficult when examining cyber acts to infer threat intent since alternative explanations—such as

---

10. "Sources: Staged Cyber Attack Revales Vulnerability in power grid," CNN, *http://articles.cnn. com/2007-09-26/us/power.at.risk_1_generator*-cyber-attack-electric-infrastructure?_s=PM:US.

11. Ariel, J, Schaap. "Cyber Warfare Operations: Development and Use Under International Law," *Air Force Law Review*, 2009, p. 146.

12. Schaap, "Cyber Warfare Operations," p. 147.

actions due to accidents or negligence or software "bugs"—may be impossible to exclude. Given these conditions, potential perpetrators of cyber attacks can plausibly believe that they can conceal their acts sufficiently to avert detection and especially retaliation. Deterrence strategies based on threats of retaliation require the capacity to plausibly attribute the source of any attack, but this is considerably more difficult to accomplish in the diffuse cyber realm.

One solution is to hold the entity with the best-presumed motive responsible. In the wake of Stuxnet, everyone immediately assumed Israel was behind the attack. Unfortunately, this method leaves the retaliator vulnerable to provocations, false flags, or the simple fact that the actor with the best motive is not the only actor with a motive. Neither is it sufficient to blame the entities that refuse to cooperate since there may be other reasons for their reluctance. In either case, there may not even be a villain at all. Many system errors and malfunctions are wrongly attributed to hackers.

Some analysts believe deterrence is a viable strategy in the cyber context as well, based on a combination of imperfect attribution augmented by credible capabilities for retaliation, defense, and dissuasion.[13] In this view, although attribution poses a challenge, it is a surmountable one, particularly as technological advancements allow for better cyber forensics.[14] But until then, the anonymity of cyber attacks undermines a central tenant of deterrence, namely the assuredness of an effective and appropriate retaliatory strike. Differences related to attribution and disproportionality explain why a "tit for tat" strategy is harder to follow in cyberspace.

Tracing an attack back through cyberspace though is not the only way to discover the attacker's identity. Human intelligence may discover the culprit, although this evidence may not be accepted as credible by third parties, especially if the sources and methods employed to make the attribution are not disclosed. In certain other cases, an attacker could, through carelessness or pride, reveal that they were behind an attack.[15] Nevertheless, these methods for identifying an attacker will not always be consistent or available.

---

13. "Statement of Franklin D. Kramer," House Armed Services Committee Subcommittee on Terrorism and Unconventional Threats, April 1, 2008, *http://www.carlisle.army.mil/DIME/documents/Kramer_Testimony040108.pdf.*

14. Richard L. Kugler, "Deterrence of Cyber attacks", in *Cyber power and National Security* (Washington DC: National Defense University Press and Potomac Books, 2009), p. 326.

15. Martin Libicki, *Cyber deterrence and Cyberwar* (Santa Monica: RAND Corporation, December 19, 2011), p. 49, *http://www.rand.org/pubs/monographs/2009/RAND_MG877.pdf.*

Martin Liwicki points out three ways in which the possibility of inaccurate attribution can weaken cyber deterrence: "Hitting the wrong person back not only weakens the logic of deterrence (if innocence does not matter, why be innocent?) but makes a new enemy." In addition, "The defender must not only convince itself but should also convince third parties that the attribution is correct (unless retaliation is kept quiet, and only the victim of retaliation can tell that is has taken place)." And most significantly," the attacker has to be convinced that the attribution is correct. If the attacker believes the retaliator is just guessing or that the retaliator has ulterior motives for retaliating, it may conclude that carrying out further attacks will have no effect on whether or not it will face further punishment."[16]

The difficulty of attributing the source or sources of a cyber attack makes the possibility of a catalytic war higher in the cyber realm than in the nuclear field. A catalytic war is a situation in which one actor will attack another in the hope of starting a war between that target and a third party. Nuclear analysts have speculated that a country or, more recently, a terrorist group might detonate a nuclear weapon in the hopes that an innocent government would be blamed for the incident and suffer retaliation. Now the same fears are arising in the case of potential cyber attacks. For example, Michael Vatis raises the possibility "that one nation (or a non-state actor) could launch a cyber attack against the United States while making it appear as though the attack were coming from another country (or non-state actor), thereby causing the United States to take retaliatory steps against the wrong entity."[17] Obama Administration officials have stated that the fear of what are also known as "false flag" attacks led them not to blame the Chinese Government for the intrusions of Google. Opponents of the Beijing Government or even criminals might have been seeking to obscure their involvement to mislead Americans to blame the PRC leadership.[18]

The attribution problems inherent in the Internet have led Michael McConnell, former Director of National Intelligence, to argue that "we need to re-engineer the Internet to make attribution, geolocation, intelligence

16. *Ibid.*, p. 42.
17. Michael A. Vatis, "Cyber Attacks During the War on Terrorism: A Predictive Analysis," Institute for Security Technology Studies at Dartmouth College, September 22, 2001, p. 99-113, *http://www.dtic.mil/cgi-bin/GetTRDoc*, AD=ADA395300&Location=U2&doc=GetTRDoc.pdf.
18. John Markoff, David E. Sanger, and Thom Shanker, "In Digital Combat, US Finds No Easy Deterrent," *New York Times*, January 26, 2010, *http://www.nytimes.com/2010/01/26/world/26cyber.html.*

analysis and impact assessment—who did it, from where, why and what was the result—more manageable."[19] But such a restructuring will take considerable time even if it were possible.

Lack of Equivalent Assets

There are three main types of attackers in cyberspace. National governments can plausibly launch a range of attacks, from simple intrusions to infrastructure disruptions to denial of service attacks. The massive capabilities of Russia and China pose serious potential threats to US cyber defense. A 2009 report prepared for the US-China Economic and Security Review Commission, concludes that China's offensive cyber weapons "will be widely employed in the earliest phases of a conflict, and possibly preemptively against an enemy's information systems and C4ISR systems."[20] While Russia and China appear to present the most cyber threats, North Korea has demonstrated its cyber attack capabilities against South Korea.[21] Defectors say that the Pyongyang regime now culls the brightest students from North Korea universities and funnels them into special "secret" schools that concentrate on hacking and developing cyber warfare programs."[22]

Organized non-state actors such as international crime syndicates and terrorist organizations can also launch cyber attacks. According to the Federal Bureau of Investigation (FBI), cyber terrorists have not engaged in direct attacks over the Internet seeking to inflict physical damage on their target, but they have launched numerous denial-of-service attacks and defaced websites. They also use the Internet to recruit members, radicalize followers and incite viewers to commit terrorist acts. "Thousands of extremist websites promote violence to a ready and a willing audience," FBI Director Robert Mueller said in a recent speech. "They are posting videos on how to build backpack bombs

---

19. Mike McConnell, "Mike McConnell on How to Win the Cyber-War We're Losing," *Washington Post*, February 28, 2010, *http://www.washingtonpost.com/wp-dyn/content/article/2010/02/25/AR2010022502493.html*.

20. Bryan Krekel (principal author), "Capability of the People's Republic of China to Conduct Cyber Warfare and Computer Network Exploitation," Prepared for the US-China Economic and Security Review Commission, October 9, 2009, p. 6-7, *http://www.uscc.gov/researchpapers/2009/NorthropGrumman_PRC_Cyber_Paper_FINAL_Approved%20Report_16Oct2009.pdf*.

21. Chico Harlan and Ellen Nakashima, "Suspected North Korean Cyber Attack on a Bank Raises Fears for S. Korea Allies," *Washington Post*, August 29, 2011, *http://www.washingtonpost.com/world/national-security/suspected-north-korean-cyber-attack-on-a-bank-raises-fears-for-s-korea-allies/2011/08/07/gIQAvWwIoJ_story.html*.

22. Ed Barnes, "North Korea's Cyber Army Gets Increasingly Sophisticated," Fox News, May 17, 2011, *http://www.foxnews.com/world/2011/05/17/north-koreas-cyber-army-gets-increasingly-sophisticated/*.

and bio-weapons. They are using social networking to link terrorist plotters and plans." Analysts have also documented a steady increase in terrorists' use of the Internet. In addition, transnational criminal organizations routinely conduct cyber operations including identity theft and fraud.

The Internet offers terrorists certain advantages over more traditional means of communication and operation. These include easy access, low cost, little government control, potentially enormous domestic and foreign audiences, anonymous communications, rapid information exchanges, multimedia platforms, and the ability to influence other mass media entities that rely on the Internet for stories. The Internet also gives terrorists tremendous operational flexibility. When extremist websites have been identified, hacked, or shut down by Internet Service Providers (ISPs), the terrorists have turned to chat rooms and message boards for communication. Their websites commonly disappear from and return to the web. Al-Qaeda operatives post their messages and videos on Islamist forums. They wage "electronic jihad," attacking "enemy" websites to harm the enemy's morale and economic and military infrastructure. Many Islamist websites host discussion forums that discuss how to conduct such web-based offensives.

Finally, individuals acting alone can launch attacks as long as they have access to computer networks and the requisite skills. Deterring extremist individuals and collective non-state actors presents a challenging requirement. The ability to identify and target what adversaries most value—the fundamental principle underlying the traditional concept of deterrence—becomes problematic when they lack readily definable geographic boundaries and have ample opportunities for concealment. These conditions undermine the credibility of threats at retaliation.

In contrast to the more familiar terrorist organizations of the Cold War era, moreover, post-modern terrorists essentially pursue "destruction for destruction's sake." Whereas mass casualties were often considered a liability for "traditional" terrorist groups, post modern terrorists embrace catastrophic damage because it supports their broad goal of undermining the existing order. In this regard, Aum Shinrikyo in many ways represents the seminal post-modern terrorist group, as its leadership intended the attacks on the Japanese subway to precipitate the apocalypse. Death and destruction, not some political objective or cause, were the primary intent of the attacks. Similarly, the perpetrators of the Oklahoma City bombing did not seek some specific political concession, but rather aimed simply to strike a blow against the Federal Government as one step in its eventual destruction. Yet, thus far non-state actors have only infrequently employed unconventional weapons. Using conventional explosives—though often in unconventional ways—remains the favored mode of assault for terrorists since these weapons offer the easiest way to kill people.

Each of these three actors has different strengths and vulnerabilities. National governments are immune from certain pressures, such as arrest or capture, but are more exposed to retributory cyber attacks as well as diplomatic pressure and economic sanctions. Organizations are not tied down to any particular place, but are vulnerable to legal procedures and, in the case of terrorist groups such as al-Qaeda, to drone attacks. Individuals can more easily hide, but typically have the most limited capabilities to inflict damage or resist legal or physical actions.

When dealing with attacks emanating from another country, a defending state can use many of the traditional tools of statecraft. It can exert diplomatic or economic pressure on the state. If the state relies heavily on networks, those networks can be disrupted. But certain severe cyber attacks may be regarded as an act of war that warrants military retaliation.

In the case of an attack from a terrorist group, there may be little the defender can immediately do. If, for example, al-Qaeda were to mount a successful cyber attack from Pakistan against the US homeland, there is little left to deter them, as the United States is already attempting to kill or capture them anyway. If the attack is from a criminal organization or individual in a foreign country, the defender must demand that the country apprehend or destroy them. This will be a matter of diplomacy and law enforcement. Efforts are already underway to formulate a treaty regarding cyberspace, at least between Russia and the United States, but it has run into some difficulties. The US objectives are to promote extraditing and law enforcement options, while the Russians want to prevent a cyber arms race and outlaw various offensive weapons.[23]

When responding to each threat, the retaliator must keep in mind the different types of groups attacking the United States and their different objectives, capabilities, and vulnerabilities. This type of deterrence then is not an equivalence of mode, such as nuclear deterrence, but an equivalence of effect. Unlike MAD, it does not threaten an identical counterstrike, but is more similar to Massive Retaliation, where a different and more spectacular type

---

23. John Markoff and Andrew Kramer, "US and Russia Differ on a Treaty for Cyberspace," *New York Times*, June 27, 2009. *http://www.nytimes.com/2009/06/28/world/28cyber.html?pagewanted=all*.

of response is threatened. The situation becomes trickier in the case where the foreign government protects organizations or individuals linked to cyber attacks. Ideally, the defender would want to treat the group or individual as part of the government. An analogous case is where a country allows a certain terrorist or guerilla group fighting another country to reside within its borders. Under international law, the threatened country has the right to violate the borders of the harboring country to combat the terrorists or insurgents.

Unfortunately, assuredly linking a non-state actor to a state sponsor is difficult. In the well-studied examples of attacks conducted against Estonia (2007) and the Republic of Georgia (2008), observers widely believed that individuals within the Russian Federation were connected to the cyber efforts. Both cyber attacks coincided with highly emotional and public events (in Estonia's case, the controversial removal of the "Bronze Soldier" monument; in Georgia's, the August 2008 Russian invasion) involving Russia.[24] Although David Smith's chapter notes that the Russian authorities likely helped or encouraged these attacks (particularly in the case of Georgia), it has proven too difficult to establish a clear link between the Russian government and the attacks.[25] Instead, they were tied to the Russian Business Network, a cybercrime syndicate thought to be linked to some members of the Russian government.[26] If the government had used criminal networks to achieve its goals, it gave Russia a plausible denial. Similarly, China encourages "patriotic hackers" who target China's enemies but are not officially part of the PRC government.[27]

Hostile non-state actors do not have comparable assets to target. In the Cold War, the USSR was an empire with cities, a government, and power sources to protect. Deterrence was successful because they did not want to sacrifice these. If a cyber attack takes out a large portion of US infrastructure, the US cyber offense teams may not have a comparable asset to target. Against developed countries there may be such targets, such as in Russia or China. Against criminal or terrorist organizations though, perhaps the only target would be

---

24. Richard G. Zoller,, "Russian Cyberspace Strategy and a Proposed United States Response," Strategy Research Project, January 25, 2010, *http://www.dtic.mil/cgi-bin/GetTRDoc?AD=ADA522027.*

25. John Bumgarner and Scott Borg, "Overview by the US-CCU of the Cyber Campaign against Georgia in August of 2008," United States Cyber Consequences Unit (August 2009), *http://www.registan.net/wp-content/uploads/2009/08/US-CCU-Georgia-Cyber-Campaign-Overview.pdf.*

26. John Markoff, "Before the Gunfire, Cyber Attacks," *New York Times*, August 12, 2008, *http://www.nytimes.com/2008/08/13/technology/13cyber.html.*

27. Adam Segal "The Rise of Asia's Cyber Militias" *The Atlantic*, February 23rd, 2012, *http://www.theatlantic.com/international/archive/2012/02/the-rise-of-asias-cyber-militias/253487/.*

several computers. Here the sacrifice is worth it to the attackers, and deterrence is meaningless to them.

Proportionality and Escalation Control

It may be helpful to categorize cyber attacks along a spectrum by their *ends* rather than their cyber means. Put differently, they should be categorized and defined by what they aim to accomplish rather than the fact that the Internet was used as the vector of the attack. Understanding cyber attacks in this way is important because it can help determine appropriate cyber retaliatory equivalency.

In terms of responding appropriately for a cyber attack that does not inflict physical harm, it seems reasonable that attacks of that nature can be considered broadly either as espionage or hooliganism. If that is the case, then an adequate response should come from law enforcement agencies rather than from the military. Moreover, because no physical harm was inflicted, there is absolutely no reason to respond using military force. Indeed, the United States responded to a cyber attack that caused no physical damage with an armed response, it would probably be seen as disproportionate.

In a cyber attack that caused serious physical destruction, however, it might not even be possible to respond equivalently if the initial strike negated the defender's ability to respond with an effective cyber counterstrike. The DoD Strategy for Operating in Cyberspace hints at this issue, admitting that "Because degraded cyberspace operations for extended periods may be a reality and disruption may occur in the midst of a mission, DoD will fully integrate a complete spectrum of cyberspace scenarios into exercises and training to prepare US Armed Forces for a wide variety of contingencies."[28] The Pentagon is also planning to operate effectively in cases of degraded space and WMD-contaminated environments.

There is unlikely to be a war exclusively in the cyber domain any time soon. Rather, we are likely to continue to see "hybrid warfare" in which military operations use multiple domains of conflict. A hybrid cyber-conventional attack could include, for example, information attacks against 911 systems and other emergency services that coincided in time and place with a major physical bombing. Perhaps the most effective "hybrid warfare" campaign in history incorporating a major cyber component occurred during Russia's August 2008

---

28. Department of Defense, *Department of Defense Strategy for Operating in Cyberspace*, July 2011, p. 6, *http://www.defense.gov/news/d20110714cyber.pdf.*

war with Georgia. A 2009 report issued by the US Cyber-Consequences Unit documents how Russia apparently used patriotic hackers to supplement its conventional war against Georgia by employing a massive, well-integrated and pre-planned information warfare campaign against Georgia. The Unit's yearlong investigation of the Russian campaign drew on a variety of sources, including monitored Internet traffic, website caches, and debriefings of Georgian victims.[29]

In addition to ambiguous attribution, another problem with trying to apply an assured retaliation framework to the cyber domain is the uncertainty regarding the physical destruction, if any, a cyber attack might inflict. Except for a cyber attack that managed to disrupt a physical network, the amount of collateral damage inflicted in most cyber attacks will normally prove much less severe than that of even the most tailored and small yield nuclear strike. In addition, nuclear weapons typically contaminate environments with radiation. These properties make cyber strikes more usable as instruments of war than nuclear weapons (which have been employed in only one conflict more than six decades ago).

Cyber attacks can have physical effects, but this is not inevitable. For example, a cyber attack that was launched to acquire information from a secured system, such as a DoD or NSA database, could be considered as non-physical. Similarly, the Anonymous group seeks mostly to embarrass its victims rather than disrupt their critical operations. In the words of James Lewis, "These were political actions—cyber demonstrations and graffiti—spun up by media attention and copycatting."[30] But some cyber attacks aim to damage critical physical infrastructure. Yet, the distinction between physical and non-physical attacks can be imperfect since there would be some overlap between them. Furthermore, a "tit–for-tat" strategy may not (indeed, probably not) inflict equivalent damage on all parties. Cyber attacks do not have pinpoint accuracy and can have many ancillary effects. Anticipating the amount of collateral damage and the extent of the cyber counterattack's impact would be very difficult to judge in advance.

29. John Bumgarner and Scott Borg, "Overview by the US-CCU of the Cyber Campaign Against Georgia in August of 2008," United States Cyber Consequences Unit (August 2009), *http://www.registan.net/wp-content/uploads/2009/08/US-CCU-Georgia-Cyber-Campaign-Overview.pdf.*

30. James Andrew Lewis, "Cyber Attacks, Real or Imagined, and Cyber War," Center for Strategic and International Studies, July 11, 2011, *http://csis.org/publication/cyber-attacks-real-or-imagined-and-cyber-war.*

Conclusion

Defending cyberspace through a "tit-for-tat" deterrence strategy fails in several respects. First, the defender might not be able to convince the attacker that it will suffer more serious losses from an attack than the gains it might hope to attain, especially since an attacker can easily use proxies or other means of plausible denial. The difficulties of attribution limit the probability of retribution. The attacker knows that the defender probably will not identify the attacker with certainty. The defender will need to make clear in its declaratory doctrine and behavior that it is able and willing to respond even in cases of imperfect attribution.

There is no single answer to the problem of how best to deter cyber attacks. The model of perfect retribution, the "tit for tat" strategy, falls short in many cases. Yet, as discussed in another chapter, preemption has its own problems. An effective US cyber doctrine requires that the United States have the capacity and will to employ a wide variety of cyber and other elements of power in the cyber and non-cyber domains.

#CyberDoc: No Borders - No Boundaries

CHAPTER 12

Cybersecurity and Allies

David J. Smith

Allies in Cyberspace?

Last year, the US Department of Defense (DoD) named cyberspace as the fifth operational dimension, following land, sea, air and space.[1] One need not agree with all the Pentagon's policies to recognize that it makes a good point—we have truly entered an altogether new realm. Cyberspace is not like anything or anywhere else. However, like the high seas at the dawn of the age

---

1. Department of Defense, *Department of Defense Strategy for Operating in Cyberspace*, July 2011, *http://www.defense.gov/news/d20110714cyber.pdf*, accessed May 26, 2012.

Ambassador David Smith joined the Potomac Institute for Policy Studies as a Senior Fellow in 2005. In 2012, he became Director of the Potomac Institute Cyber Center. Amb. Smith has had a distinguished career in defense and foreign affairs, is an expert on international security issues, and in recent years has focused on the emerging field of cyber security. His other areas of expertise include US strategic missile defense, arms control, European security policy, and security relationships with China, Russia, and Korea. He also has in-depth expertise and experience in building stability and security in the South Caucasus region. Ambassador Smith is currently involved in a major project to assist Georgia in reforming its national security institutions, and serves as Director of the Georgian Security Analysis Center in Tbilisi. President George H. W. Bush nominated Ambassador Smith to lead the US-Soviet Defense and Space Talks on September 21, 1989. He was confirmed by the Senate and sworn in by Senator Bob Dole. He subsequently led the US team that worked to negotiate an agreement to allow deployment of defenses against the growing threat of ballistic missiles until the demise of the Soviet Union in 1991. From 2002 to 2005, Ambassador Smith was Chief Operating Officer of the National Institute for Public Policy, Fairfax, Virginia. From 1993 to 2002, he was President of Global Horizons, Inc. consulting on defense, international security issues and overseas business development. He previously served as Chief of Staff for Arizona Congressman Jon Kyl, Assistant for Strategic Policy and Arms Control to Senate Republican Leader Bob Dole, as professional staff for the Senate Committee on Foreign Relations and on the staff of the Joint Chiefs of Staff. He holds degrees from the University of Arizona, London School of Economics and Harvard University and is a Ph.D. candidate at Ilia State University in Tbilisi, Georgia.

of exploration or outer space today, cyberspace is uncharted and there are few, if any, navigation aids.

What awaits us as we boldly go where no human has gone before? On his *Carta Marina,* 16th century cartographer Olaus Magnus depicted, "Sea monsters, huge as mountains…seamen who anchor on the backs of the monsters in belief that they are islands often expose themselves to mortal danger."[2] And in our own time, the television series *Star Trek* conjured up the salt vampire, the silicon-based-acid-spewing horta and the telepathic reptile Melkotian.[3] Are we to face cyber perils imagined and real alone or with allies?

Although alliances have been a main feature of American strategy for 70 years, the United States has traditionally eschewed peacetime alliances. Do the cracks emerging among American allies, particularly among NATO allies, signal that the geopolitical forces that forged the alliances are shifting, maybe to the breaking point? Is it time for America to consider a return to its traditional pre-World War II stance? Or can a new community of cyber-interests reinvigorate old alliances or underpin new ones?

This chapter argues that the United States can and must face cyber challenges with allies[4] based upon six propositions.

- Effective action in a domain in which information flashes across international borders at the speed of light requires an international dimension.

- A community of interests, which must underpin any alliance, is emerging in cyber matters.

- As the still most powerful country in the world, and the country with the most to lose or gain in the cyber domain, the United States must take the lead in building upon the community of interests to reinvigorate old alliances, particularly NATO, and to forge new ones.

- In doing this, it can capitalize upon the strong bonds of friendship, shared values and common practices built up over seven decades of alliances.

---

2. Uppsala University Library, *Carta Marina, http://www.ub.uu.se/en/Collections/Map-collections/ Section-for-Maps-and-Pictures-map-collection/Carta-Marina/,* accessed May 26, 2012.

3. Lore Sjöberg, "Star Trek's Ten Cheesiest Classic Creatures," *Wired.com,* November 19, 2007, *http://www.wired.com/entertainment/hollywood/multimedia/2007/11/gallery_star_trek_ monsters?slide=1&slideView=3,* accessed May 26, 2012.

4. The term "ally" here means to associate or connect by some mutual relationship, which may or may not be a formal treaty or agreement.

- An emergent community of interests and a new mission is exactly what NATO needs at a moment when aspects of the Cold War community of interests that forged the alliance may be crumbling.

- There is an opportunity to forge a new alliance or coalition around the European Convention on Cybercrime and the concept of national responsibility.

The analysis presented here is couched in history and in realist or neo-realist terms to underscore that forging cyber alliances is altogether a matter of the mutual self-interest of like-minded nations without reference to maudlin idealism. Friendship, values and common practices can help build the edifice, but are insufficient to form its foundation.

No Eternal Allies

In a wide-ranging 1848 House of Commons foreign policy debate, Henry Temple, Third Viscount Palmerston, pronounced the most realist view of allies ever. "We have no eternal allies, and we have no perpetual enemies. Our interests are eternal and perpetual, and those interests it is our duty to follow."[5]

In general, Palmerston believed that England was "sufficiently powerful to steer her own course and not to tie herself as an unnecessary appendage to the policy of any other government."[6]

A half century earlier in America, George Washington had urged his countrymen "to steer clear of permanent alliances with any portion of the foreign world," not because we were in 1796 so powerful, but because "Our detached and distant situation invites and enables us to pursue a different course."[7]

Hans Morgenthau, father of the modern study of international relations and of its realist school, observed, "Whether a nation shall pursue alliances is a matter not of principle but of expediency. A nation will shun alliances if it believes that it is strong enough to hold its own unaided or that the burden of commitments resulting from the alliance is likely to outweigh the advantages to be expected."[8]

---

5. Hansard, Parliamentary debates, House of Commons, March 1, 1848, column 122. *http://hansard.millbanksystems.com/commons/1848/mar/01/treaty-of-adrianople-charges-against*, accessed May 20, 2012.

6. *Ibid.*

7. *The Address of Gen. Washington to the People of America on his Declining the Presidency of the United States*, 1796. *http://avalon.law.yale.edu/18th_century/washing.asp*, accessed May 20, 2012.

8. Hans J. Morgenthau, *Politics among Nations*, 7th edition revised by Kenneth W. Thompson and W. David Clinton, (New York: McGraw Hill, 2006), p. 193. The seventh edition is used here because it

He continued, "It is for one or the other or both of these reasons that, throughout the better part of their history, Great Britain and the United States have refrained from entering into peacetime alliances with other nations."[9]

A less quoted Palmerston passage indicates that the British statesman well understood the point that Morgenthau would articulate exactly a century later. "As long as [England] sympathises with right and justice," he said, "she will never find herself altogether alone. She is sure to find some other state of sufficient power, influence and weight to support and aid her in the course she may think fit to pursue."[10]

Insofar as allies might become necessary or desirable, Palmerston reasoned, England would find them in what Morgenthau, drawing upon Thucydides and Lord Salisbury, called a "community of interests." Morgenthau explained, "An alliance requires of necessity a community of interests for its foundation."[11]

By 1949, weary from two world wars and challenged by Soviet occupation of half Europe, Britain did not seem so powerful or America so distant. World events had forged the community of interests that underpinned the NATO peacetime alliance.

It is neither possible nor necessary here to review every indication that there are cracks in the community of interests that underpinned NATO from 1949 to 1991 or every argument for and against perpetuation of the Atlantic Alliance. With the demise of the Soviet Union, the adherence of a dozen post-Cold War NATO members and challenges such as the war in Afghanistan, the NATO community of interests has at least radically changed.

The question at hand is whether it is now in the interest of the United States to forge a new or renewed alliance to meet cyber challenges.

Eternal or not, We Need Allies

Just about every day, some or other news report underscores that cyber security is an international affair. Because the Afghanistan International Security Assistance Force is a NATO-led 50-nation coalition, this is a good place to start. Consider this passage from a recent Reuters story.

---

has been skillfully updated by Thompson and Clinton to show the enduring value of Morgenthau's work in the context of contemporary events.

9. *Ibid.*
10. Hansard, Parliamentary debates.
11. Morgenthau, *Politics among Nations* pp. 10, 194.

The Taliban have in recent months waged an intensifying information war with NATO forces in the country, distributing anti-government messages on mobile phone networks and using Twitter to claim largely improbable successes as most foreign combat troops look to leave the country by 2014. A day rarely passes without a Taliban spokesman using Twitter to claim the destruction of numerous NATO armoured vehicles and the deaths of scores of Western or Afghan security forces, with NATO quickly countering in its own Twitter feeds.[12]

Moreover, the numerous cyber events experienced by DoD, other national security agencies and defense contractors may be directed by major nation-states, but may appear to originate from IP addresses in Vietnam or Peru, routed through a half dozen countries. Most investigations require the assistance of other countries. It is an open-and-shut case for DoD to conclude, "Cyberspace is a network of networks that includes thousands of ISPs across the globe; no single state or organization can maintain effective cyber defenses of its own."[13]

And the point extends beyond the national security sphere. "Mala is to die for in those pigtails," said a posting on a now busted child pornography site. In this case, law enforcement officials in five countries, including the FBI, arrested people in four countries and rescued twenty children, crashing a secret child pornography news group. Part of the FBI's own report is worth reading in the context of this chapter.

> The operation began in January 2006 when an officer of the Queensland Police Services in Australia learned about the group. Since a number of the members were living in the United States, Queensland authorities came to the FBI that June; we launched our investigation two months later, working through our Innocent Images National Initiative. The officer who infiltrated the ring came to the US and worked with us directly through our International Innocent Images Task Force in our command center in suburban Maryland. We sent agents to Australia as well. Also participating in the investigation was the BKA Child Pornography Unit

---

12. Rob Taylor, "Taliban Website Hacked as Afghan Cyber War Heats Up," *Reuters*, April 27, 2012. *http://in.reuters.com/article/2012/04/27/afghanistan-taliban-hacking-idINDEE83Q05520120427*, accessed May 26, 2012.

13. Department of Defense, *DoD Strategy*, p. 9.

in Germany, the Child Exploitation and Online Protection Centre in the United Kingdom, and the Toronto Police Department in Canada.[14]

"The United States and our allies," says US President Barack Obama's *International Strategy for Cyberspace,* "regularly depend upon cooperation and assistance from other countries when investigating and prosecuting cyber crime cases."[15]

Plenty more examples could be brought to bear, but the point is clear—cyber security must have an international aspect.

We are already linked to our allies, so unless we are going to stop participating in coalition warfare, counter-terrorism, international law enforcement and more, we must have allies.

Moreover, as the DoD strategy points out, "Burden sharing arrangements can play to each nation's core strengths and capabilities; this will bolster areas where partners are less proficient, increase capacity, and strengthen collective security."[16] In some cases, the reverse may be true—particular allies may have a greater capability than we in some field, or they may even be able to do something that we cannot do. These observations pertain not only to national defense but also to just about every other sphere.

Finally, it is in our interest to bolster allied cyber security, particularly among less developed states because they may each hold a bit of our own cyber security—literally—on one of their servers.[17] Consider, for example, a naval port call or American law enforcement personnel operating abroad. Our host country could hold information critical to the protection of our people.

Consequently, it is unsurprising that this is already US policy.

Extending the principles of peace and security to cyberspace—while preserving its benefits and character—will require strengthened partnerships and expanded initiatives. We will engage the international community in frank and urgent dialogue, to build consensus around

---

14. United States of America, Federal Bureau of Investigation, "Major Child Porn Ring Busted," March 6, 2008. *http://www.fbi.gov/news/stories/2008/march/innocent_images030608,* accessed May 26, 2012.

15. White House, *International Strategy for Cyberspace: Prosperity, Security, and Openness in a Networked World,* May 2011, *http://www.whitehouse.gov/sites/default/files/rss_viewer/international_strategy_for_cyberspace.pdf,* accessed May 26, 2012.

16. Department of Defense, *DoD Strategy,* p. 10.

17. White House, *International Strategy for Cyberspace,* p. 13.

principles of responsible behavior in cyberspace and the actions necessary, both domestically and as an international community, to build
a system of cyberspace stability.[18]

And it is also DoD policy: "As international cyberspace cooperation continues to develop, DoD will advance its close cyberspace cooperation with its
allies to defend US and allied interests in cyberspace."[19]

NATO: Not an Eternity, but a Long Time

Perhaps we have no eternal allies, but 63 years—20 since the end of the
Cold War—is a long time in international politics. Although this chapter addresses allies in a sense broader and beyond formal alliances, it is worth
pausing for a moment on the potential of America's most venerable alliance.

Harvard Professor Stephen M. Walt argues that "There are deep structural forces that are pulling Europe and the United States apart." Just as some
Americans question the enduring value of the alliance, "even our traditional
allies have reason to worry about how we will use the capabilities at our
disposal."[20]

Nonetheless, he argues for renewing NATO's communities of interest to
face the post-Cold War challenges of terrorism, weapons of mass destruction,
the world economy and failed states. "There are, in short, plenty of areas
where continued cooperation would be desirable," he writes.[21]

Despite persistent centrifugal forces, there has been a sufficient force in re-
sidual communities of interest plus new ones to keep NATO going. For those
who want to continue that trend, this is precisely the moment—perhaps coun-
ter-intuitively—to load new missions on the alliance. Following Morgenthau,
states that perceive an interest in developing a strong cyber security regime
will band together if they must. History, common values, sentiment and even
common practices alone will not hold NATO together. However, "The ideo-
logical factor, when it is superimposed on an actual community of interests,
can lend strength to the alliance by marshaling moral convictions and emotional preferences to its support."[22]

18. *Ibid.*, p. 11.
19. Department of Defense, *DoD Strategy*, p. 10.
20. Stephen M. Walt, "The Imbalance of Power," *Harvard Magazine*, March-April 2004, p. 33.
21. *Ibid.* p. 34.
22. Morgenthau, *Politics among Nations*, p. 196.

Given the apparent community of interest in international cooperation in the field of cyber security and the considerable additional strength that 63 years of alliance brings, NATO is a good place to begin. Now we must build upon the community of interest. To put it in neo-realist terms, "In the quest for security, alliances may have to be made. Once made, they have to be managed."[23] In other words, beyond a community of interest, sustaining structures must be built.

NATO has been doing that since the 2002 Prague Summit, writes the Atlantic Council's Jason Healey. This was initially "at least partially in response to widely reported attacks on NATO organizations and alliance nations carried out by activists from Serbia, Russia and China during Operation Allied Force."[24]

However, the alliance's earnest involvement in cyber security came after the 2007 Russian cyber attacks against Estonia. Since the 2008 Bucharest Summit, NATO has launched a Cyber Defense Management Board, the NATO Computer Incident Response Capability (NCIRC), similar in concept to national computer emergency response teams like USCERT, and the Cooperative Cyber Defense Center of Excellence, symbolically located in Tallinn, Estonia.

Cybersecurity was seriously addressed by the so-called Albright Commission that formulated recommendations for NATO's new strategic Concept. The Commission warned, "The next significant attack on the Alliance may well come down a fibre optic cable," recommending that "Over time, NATO should plan to mount a fully adequate array of cyber defence capabilities, including passive and active elements."[25]

The Lisbon Summit, which approved the new strategic concept,[26] also set the alliance on a course to write a new cyber defense policy. The new

23. Kenneth N. Waltz, *Theory of International Politics,* (New York: McGraw Hill, 1979), p. 166.

24. Operation Allied Force was the 1999 NATO effort to expel Serbian forces from Kosovo, Jason Healey, "NATO's Cyber Capabilities: Yesterday, Today and Tomorrow," *Atlantic Council Issue Brief,* February 2012, pp. 1-2, *http://www.acus.org/files/publication_pdfs/403/022712_ACUS_ NATOSmarter_IBM.pdf,* accessed May 26, 2012.

25. Group of Experts on a New Strategic Concept for NATO, *NATO 2020: Assured Security; Dynamic Engagement,* May 17, 2010, *http://www.nato.int/nato_static/assets/pdf/ pdf_2010_05/20100517_100517_expertsreport.pdf,* accessed May 26, 2012.

26. North Atlantic Treaty Organization, *Active Engagement, Modern Defence,* November 2010, *http:// www.nato.int/nato_static/assets/pdf/pdf_publications/20120214_strategic-concept-2010-eng.pdf,* accessed May 26, 2012.

policy and an accompanying Action Plan were issued in June 2011.[27] They are, Healey writes, "By far the most important steps the Alliance has taken so far to mature its cyber capabilities."[28]

The current NATO policy focuses on the "protection of its own communications and information systems." However, it also recognizes that the alliance is dependent on the national systems of member states. Accordingly, "NATO will develop minimum requirements for those national networks that are connected to or process NATO information."[29] NATO Rapid Reaction Teams to assist member states under cyber attack should be fully operational this year.[30]

Perhaps most importantly, the NATO policy says, "Cyber threats transcend state borders and organizational boundaries. Recognizing the truly global nature of cyberspace and its associated threats, NATO and Allies will work with partners, international organizations, academia and the private sector."[31] According to the NATO Secretary General, Cyber Coalition 2011, a recent exercise, involved six partner countries and the European Union.[32]

In other words, NATO is becoming a platform for extra-alliance cooperation among like-minded nations and private organizations. Just one example is the Advanced Training Course in which IT managers from Afghanistan are studying cyber security at Turkey's Middle East Technical University (METU) in a curriculum jointly developed by NATO and Georgia and supported by Microsoft and Cisco. "This course should provide a tried and tested model for future cooperation between NATO and partner nations, and gradually become a real partnership tool for the Alliance," said Nazife Baykal, Informatics Director at METU.[33]

Although some will lament that NATO is not doing enough fast enough, there are three ready rejoinders to this claim. First, no member state, including the United States, is doing enough fast enough. Second, the debates taking place in the hallways of NATO headquarters largely reflect the debates in national capitals, including Washington. For example, NATO's focus on its

27. North Atlantic Treaty Organization, *Defending the Networks*, 2011. *http://www.nato.int/nato_static/assets/pdf/pdf_2011_09/20111004_110914-policy-cyberdefence.pdf*, accessed May 26, 2012.
28. Healey, "NATO's Cyber Capabilities," p. 3.
29. NATO, *Defending the Networks.*
30. Healey, "NATO's Cyber Capabilities," p. 2.
31. NATO, *Defending the Networks.*
32. Healey, NATO's "Cyber Capabilities," p. 4.
33. North Atlantic Treaty Organization, *Afghan Managers Train in Cyber Defence*, May 21, 2012. *http://www.nato.int/cps/en/natolive/news_86990.htm*, accessed May 26, 2012.

own systems while discussing how to protect critical infrastructure and share information among the alliance, member states and businesses is very reminiscent of current debates in Washington.[34] The third point is that it was ever so. Even during the heady days of the Cold War, Washington complained that NATO and some member states were not doing enough.

NATO is one of the mechanisms—and a good one—that the United States can use to build upon a community of interest to forge renewed and new alliances in the field of cyber security. We cannot ask the alliance to do more than it is capable to do, but that is not an argument against NATO or alliances in general. Doing more will require reliance upon ourselves or upon other arrangements.

The Limits of Beyond

Whether with NATO or any other form of international alliance, the United States must take care to recognize the limits. There is a point beyond which we cannot continue to badger NATO allies to do more about more things. And "Our Goal" as stated in President Obama's *International Strategy for Cyberspace* is likely overreaching:

> The United States will work internationally to promote an open, interoperable, secure, and reliable information and communications infrastructure that supports international trade and commerce, strengthens international security, and fosters free expression and innovation. To achieve that goal, we will build and sustain an environment in which norms of responsible behavior guide states' actions, sustain partnerships, and support the rule of law in cyberspace.[35]

As Morgenthau pointed out, an alliance "attempts to transform a small fraction of the total interests of the contracting parties into common policies and measures."[36]

Similarly, Waltz writes, "Alliances are made by states that have some but not all of their interests in common. The common interest is ordinarily a negative one: fear of other states. Divergence comes when positive interests are at issue."[37] Note that the goal articulated in the *International Strategy for*

34. James G. Stavridis and Elton C. Parker, "Sailing the Cyber Sea," *JFQ*, 2Q 2012, p. 5. *http://www.ndu.edu/press/lib/pdf/jfq-65/JFQ-65_61-67_Stavridis-Parker.pdf*, accessed May 26, 2012.
35. White House, *International Strategy for Cyberspace*, p. 8.
36. Morgenthau, *Politics among Nations*, p. 197.
37. Waltz, *Theory of International Politics*, p. 166.

Cyberspace is altogether a positive one. It is a nice ideal, but the United States is likely to encounter resistance to any concrete steps toward implementing it—it is the stuff of preambular language only.

Sweeping goals are not only likely to produce frustration. They may also doom an alliance. Morgenthau warned, "There exists a correlation between the permanency of an alliance and the limited character of the interests it serves; for only specific, limited interest is likely to last long enough to provide the foundation for a durable alliance."[38]

Of course, it is possible, although unlikely, that NATO will prove to be an exception to ages of history. Morgenthau wrote, "In its comprehensive objectives and the techniques used to accomplish them, NATO indeed moves beyond the limits of a traditional alliance toward a novel type of functional organization."[39] Perhaps it does.

Nonetheless, American policy-makers would be wise to heed the general observations of Morgenthau and Waltz, particularly under the strains that NATO's departure from Afghanistan is likely to produce. Furthermore, even if NATO has achieved some sort of ageless institutional status, it is unlikely to be replicated in new alliances outside the forge of world war and Soviet aggression. In either case, mind the limits.

One might also object that the staid, state-centric analyses of Morgenthau and Waltz are outdated in the cyber era in which foes may be other nation-states or hackers sporting Guy Fawkes masks. Things have indeed changed, but the actors in an alliance are still states, and human calculations have not changed nearly as much as electronic ones. Moreover, anyone who has been involved in practical politics can say that the observations on alliances offered by Morgenthau and Waltz are valid, even when the entity is not a nation-state. Mind the limits.

And there is one more limit to point out that is, the limit to what may be possible with countries like Russia and China. One dare not, in contemporary America, use the adjective adversarial to describe these countries, which in itself says so much about how little we understand the limits to cooperation with them.

Russia and China are rankled by their perception of a world that functions primarily according to rules made in Washington or Brussels. As with others, any alliance—in the widest possible sense—with Russia and China must be

---

38.   Morgenthau, *Politics among Nations*, p. 197.
39.   *Ibid.*, p. 531.

based upon limited interests, and with them, exceedingly limited interests. There are two reasons for this.

The first reason is that their leaderships are inextricably linked with all manner of cyber crime. Real law enforcement cooperation can occur only on particular matters and likely on a case-by-case basis. The second reason is that the quest for cyber security, and any alliances to further it, exists in the broader context of global geopolitics. Russia and China see cyber war as a viable tool in their geopolitical struggles. So long as tension remains, and so long as countries like Russia and China perceive that their current courses may lead to success, do not expect them to jump on the bandwagon of some sweeping western cyber security plan.[40]

We are better to talk to Russia and China, of course, but to be satisfied with what is possible. No amount of concessions or feel-good gestures will alter the fundamental geopolitical situation. We should continue to press them, but not abandon our positions in expectation of reciprocal moves on their part.

In this regard, a 2011 US-Russia agreement seems naïve. Howard Schmidt, until recently the US Cybersecurity Coordinator, writes on his White House blog:

> Both the United States and Russia are committed to tackling common cyber security threats while at the same time reducing the chances a misunderstood incident could negatively affect our relationship. We're actively working on doing so in numerous ways: through regular exchanges of information on technical threats to both sides like botnets; by better understanding each other's military views on operating in cyberspace; and by establishing 24/7 systems allowing us to communicate about cyber security issues via our existing and highly successful crisis prevention communications links between our two capitals.[41]

The preemptive concession to achieve this agreement was apparently to abandon our insistence that Russia adhere to the European Convention on Cybercrime, otherwise known as the Budapest Convention. Although all

---

40. In general, see Waltz, *Theory of International Politics*, pp. 125-127.

41. Howard Schmidt, "US and Russia: Expanding the Reset to Cyberspace," *The White House Blog*, July 12, 2011. *http://www.whitehouse.gov/blog/2011/07/12/us-and-russia-expanding-reset-cyberspace*, accessed May 26, 2012.

the measures that Schmidt describes are good and would be useful if implemented fully and reciprocally, for the two reasons mentioned above, they will not be. Meanwhile, Russia and China will continue to avoid the Budapest Convention while flogging their own international Code of Conduct.[42]

The bottom line is that the United States must pursue various cyber security alliances. However, both to preserve the alliances made and to define the realm of the possible, it must be aware of the structural limitations to those alliances.

What is to be done?

The United States must seek cyber security in conjunction with allies. We should build systems to afford mutual security, which may involve both passive and active measures. We should forge a global regime that fosters what we want to foster and does not preclude anything that we would not wish to preclude.

This requires getting our own policy house in order.

Then, on the military side, we should not squander the opportunity to use NATO as a foundation upon which to build. A lot of capability will be found there. In particular, we should use NATO's post-Cold War role as international security coordinator.

Many countries aspire to NATO membership and already cooperate with the alliance as if they were members. Many more are in some sort of association with NATO. Meanwhile, in the post-Cold War era, some like-minded countries are drawing close to the alliance in ways that were closed to them during the earlier period. And in the era of globalization, other like-minded countries around the world are increasingly cooperating with NATO. Other, ideologically more distant countries may wish to cooperate with the alliance for particular purposes, as they do in ISAF. This could be the beginning of a cyber security coalition that stretches beyond the alliance. Or it could be the foundation to various cyber security coalitions, assembled for various purposes and at different times.

Of course, whether NATO or some expanded coalition, the alliances will have limits. To accomplish tasks beyond those limits, the United States must

42. Wu Jiao and Zhao Shengnan, "Nations Call on UN to Discuss Cyber Security," *China Daily,* September 14, 2011. *http://www.chinadaily.com.cn/cndy/2011-09/14/content_13680896.htm*, accessed May 26, 2012.

either look to itself, to bilateral or fairly small coalitions, or to broader coalitions of the willing.[43]

In all these endeavors, American policy-makers must bear in mind that potential partners will view the United States and its motives through broader, geopolitical lenses.

On the law enforcement side, there is considerable potential because many countries are interested in protecting their data and networks and in fighting online fraud, child pornography, intellectual property theft, etc. This has been demonstrated by the increasing international cooperation among law enforcement agencies already underway. One example is the aforementioned case of cooperation on busting a child pornography ring.

There are many other examples such as cooperation between the United States and the Netherlands to take down the Rustock botnet or the cooperation among nine countries to halt the Megaupload file-sharing site for alleged copyright violations.[44]

Methods for further cooperation and communication should be developed as needed by law enforcement officers—we do not need to build bureaucracies for their own sake.

With regard to law enforcement, the warning about Russia and China bears repetition. We would be better off to make real progress with a critical mass of countries than to achieve watered-down consensus with the outliers.

One effort that would unequivocally serve American interests and draw considerable support would be to mount a campaign to gain signature, ratification and enforcement of the Budapest Convention. As President Obama's *International Strategy for Cyberspace* points out, wider adherence to the Budapest Convention would help countries update their cyber crime laws and provide an effective mechanism for cross-border law enforcement cooperation.[45] With only four non-European signatories, such an effort would be a great project for the United States and the Council of Europe jointly.

---

43. The term was coined by US President Bill Clinton in 1994 with regard to North Korea.

44. Robert McMillan, "With Rustock, a New Twist on Fighting Internet Crime," *PCWorld Australia*, March 18, 2011, *http://www.pcworld.idg.com.au/article/380266/rustock_new_twist_fighting_internet_crime/*, accessed May 26, 2012; and Ben Sisario, "7 Charged as FBI Closes a Top File-sharing Site," *New York Times*, January 19, 2012, *http://www.nytimes.com/2012/01/20/technology/indictment-charges-megaupload-site-with-piracy.html*, accessed May 26, 2012.

45. White House, *International Strategy for Cyberspace*, p. 20. For the text of the Convention and further information see Council of Europe, Treaty Office, *Convention on Cyber Crime*, open for signature November 23, 2011, *http://conventions.coe.int/Treaty/Commun/QueVoulezVous*.

A further step could be to begin to build support for national responsibility, a concept developed by the Atlantic Council's Jason Healey.[46] The idea is to get around the challenge of attribution by holding states responsible for what happens on their territory as a matter of policy. Although the concept could be enshrined by convention, this is unnecessary. It would be sufficient to assemble a critical mass of countries to adopt the concept as policy.

Together with the Budapest Convention, the concept of national sovereignty could be very powerful. Like-minded states could thus approach states from which any form of cyber malfeasance appears to emanate to demand cooperation. If cooperation is not forthcoming, they could assume either that the state in question was altogether irresponsible or complicit, either way resorting to appropriate means to deal with that state. Healey offers the example of a NATO country calling for consultations under Article 4 of the North Atlantic Treaty.[47]

The point for the purpose of this chapter is that there are some constructive steps in which the United States could lead that would galvanize many countries to action. The immediate objective would be to begin crafting a regime of cross-border law enforcement cooperation and national responsibility.[48] A corollary effect, however, would be to begin formation of a new alliance or coalition, or perhaps several, dedicated to cyber law enforcement. It would not look like NATO, but it would be a form of alliance and beneficial to the United States, nonetheless.

Conclusion

We are already linked to our allies in coalition warfare, counter-terrorism, international law enforcement and more, all of which require some cyber security cooperation. Moreover, cyber security is, by its nature, an international affair. There will be frustrations and limitations, however, it is in the

---

asp?NT=185&CL=ENG, accessed May 26, 2012. The United States signed this treaty at its inception, November 23, 2001; ratified September 29, 2006; and entered it into force on January 1, 2007.

46. Jason Healey, "Beyond Attribution: Seeking National Responsibility for Cyber Attacks," *Atlantic Council Issue Brief*, January 2012, *http://www.acus.org/files/publication_pdfs/403/022212_ACUS_NatlResponsibilityCyber.PDF*, accessed May 26, 2012.

47. *Ibid.*, p. 6.

48. On regime creation in general see Stephen D. Krasner, "Structural Causes and Regime Consequences: Regimes as Intervening Variables," in *International Regimes*, ed. Stephen D. Krasner, (Ithaca: Cornell University Press, 1983), p. 185; Robert Axelrod, *The Evolution of Cooperation*, (New York: Basic Books, 1984); Andreas Hasenclever, Peter Mayer, Volker Rittberger, *Theories of International Regimes*, (Cambridge: Cambridge University Press, 2002).

interest of the United States to have allies, and there is plenty of potential to cultivate them. Olaus Magnus's 16th century *Carta Marina* depicted sea monsters, red and green, devouring merchant ships. It also depicted merchant ships fighting each other, no doubt leaving control of the seas to the monsters. We should not let the cyber monsters win by failing to join forces with other like-minded countries.

CHAPTER 13

Providing for the Common Defense
The Responsibilities of the United States
Federal Government in Cyberspace

Ronald A. Marks

The Heart of the Challenge

Cyberspace and its access through the Internet is one of those issues which cut to the very heart of what we are as Americans. It directly challenges our citizens' desire for freedom from government's intervention against the requirement—the social contract—that our government has to protect all its citizens.

While Americans often point to the Declaration of Independence as our "founding document," it is essentially hortatory language declaring *what* we wish to become as a people. The Constitution of the United States is the document that provides the thesis statement, the foundation of law, as to *who* we are to be.

The Constitution set out the rules of the game. It lays out what roles the states would have. It also lays out the three separate, yet equal branches of the Federal Government. And it charged that Federal Government with the responsibility to "provide for the common defense and promoting the general welfare" of the people of the United States.

Ronald Marks is President of Intelligence Enterprises, LLC, a privately held management-consulting group. Mr. Marks also serves as Director of Battelle Memorial Institute's Cyber Doctrine Project. He is the author of the recently published "Spying in America in the Post 9/11 World," by Praeger Books. Mr. Marks spent 16 years with the Central Intelligence Agency. During that time, he served as a Clandestine Services Officer, Special Assistant to the ADCI for Military Support, and Senate Liaison to five Directors. Ron also served as Intelligence Counsel to US Senate Majority leader's Robert Dole and Trent Lott (1995-96). Since leaving government, Mr. Marks has been an executive with several defense contractors and software firms. He is a Senior Fellow at The George Washington University Homeland Security Policy Institute where he focuses on cyber related issues.

So what does this mean to us in cyberspace—what is the role of the Federal Government in dealing with an area, a space, undefined in physical limits yet affecting the daily lives of all Americans? Land, sea, air and space are tangible. What does providing for the common defense mean in cyberspace—one where borders are meaningless?

I argue that the role of the Federal Government in cyberspace should be to lead, guide and set rules for its people in cyberspace. As we provide laws and guidance for the safe and peaceful use of land, sea, air and space, only the Federal Government charged with the powers of the Constitution can do the job. Government is a "social good" done because no one in the private sector could profitably afford or have the "reach" and desire to do so. The Federal Government, by default and design must have that lead role.

How Fast the Expansion of Cyberspace

One of the primary challenges of cyberspace has nothing to do with its size or ubiquity in our lives. The challenge is one of the rapidity of expansion and its total lack of physical borders. While a part of our lives in 2012—comprising actions from banking to commerce to filing our taxes to sending an email to Grandma—we have really only been experiencing this remarkable phenomenon within the last ten years. For government, especially the Federal Government, built to chew and think over an issue, this is lightening speed. And, it has been slow to act.

At the beginning of the 2000s, the Internet from Washington's viewpoint was a private sector issue. Sure the military found it increasingly easy to use it as a way of transporting information to its far-flung efforts around the world. But the rest of the government was dealing with it in dribs and drabs—a website here, a computer or your desk that could handle "external e-mail." In short, it was a useful but not necessary tool.

That was not the case for the private sector that viewed it as a limitless frontier, an Internet tribute to Moore's law. For a business, from a "mom and pop" store through Wal-Mart, it meant the ability to interact directly with customers not in the immediate locale. It meant that a supply chain—moving goods from point A to point B and onward to the point of sale—could be charted, expanded and made more efficient.

For the private citizen, what started as the novelty of sending emails to friends and relatives became of cornerstone of daily life. A person could literally work from home thanks to the Internet. They could shop from home thanks to the Internet. And they could "surf" the web connecting with like minded people across the world on a given issue or "post" information showing everything from their children's birthday to the latest family pictures. They could reach across the world for information and contact. And, yes, they could indulge their vices from gambling to pornography.

The Child Is the Father of the Man

The Internet and the cyberspace it created is a child of the 1960s. And it carries with it the spirit of that era. The Internet was established by scientists in our national labs to share complex information more quickly and more easily. By the late 1980s, someone in Europe had figured out a way to share different kinds of scientific data across a World Wide Web.

The reader will note that while government employees may have been involved with this process, the spirit was one of total freedom without government interference. The government did not regulate this space. There was academic freedom and sharing of information in hopes of synergy and scientific finding.

The development of the personal computer industry from its roots in garages around the West Coast of the United States was done by spirited entrepreneurs who dismissed authority. They also believed the ability to share information freely and quickly across vast spaces was a good thing—a democratic way. And the idea of borders, national or otherwise, simply did not matter.

And so for its early life, for over twenty years, the Internet was unregulated save for loose organizations that would regulate Internet naming of email sights (e.g., .edu) and set some standard protocols.

The Federal Government Challenge

So the battleground has been set in cyberspace. On one side, you have a free wheeling cyber sector where freedom of speech, entrepreneurship and speed of action has marked their history. They enjoy one of the fastest rises of technology in American history—outstripping the immediate impacts of the telephone, the radio and even television.

On the other side, you have the Federal Government. It is not built for speed per the direction of the Founding Fathers. They did not want quick decisions driven through the spirit of the moment. They wanted deliberation.

You also have a huge Federal bureaucracy created after World War II and a tribute to the stove-piped structure of the era. Cross agency and departmental issues are difficult, at best. It is a slow adopter of technology and views unregulated space with suspicion fearing abuse. It, too, is living its role as "providing for the common defense and promoting the general welfare."

You additionally have a Federal Government that has separated the national and the international. We have dealt with—even felt comforted by— the relative safety of nation-state borders since our founding. The idea of the nation-state created in the 15th century Westaphalian world is smashed in a world where you can engage in commerce, providing of news and individual contact near instantaneously.

And, you have a big, ever expanding problem—the Internet and the cyberspace it connects are now so deeply ingrained in our commerce, our personal and government lives, we can ill afford disruption or crime. Yet, every day we hear about denials of service, hacking of personal or government information by individual criminals or nation-states or simple vigilantes. Cyberspace is the Wild West. And its citizens are vulnerable.

So what role for the Federal Government in cyberspace? I would argue that it is time for the Federal Government to step up as the leader, not the follower in cyberspace. Its duty must be to provide for the peaceful and safe use of the Internet.

The Internet and the cyberspace it accesses have become public utilities. They represent not a mere convenience but a public good, like electricity or transportation or water supply. The government regulates those for good reason—they affect all. And the Internet has now come to be that kind of good.

The government must also consider how it protects its citizens from "overseas" threats. As we have discussed, this is a space that knows no national borders.

How Far Does Government Go—At Home and Abroad?

The Constitution of the United States also serves as the template for the limits and uses of the power of the Federal government. Make no mistake, the Founding Fathers did not trust government. They had experienced the capriciousness of a king and parliament a continent away. The Federal Government would be the protector not the purveyor of rights. It would also be broken into three separate but equal branches of government. The rights of states would also be defined. Centralized power would be limited.

And thus we get into the debate when we regulate or oversee any industry or individual activity– how far does the Federal government go in terms of "proving for the common defense and promoting the general welfare" of Americans in cyberspace?

I would argue our Federal Government needs to set the definition of the responsibilities of the "cyber citizen." Businesses and individuals need to be protected with adequate security. The government needs to set those standards. The government needs to protect its citizens and itself from people outside the United States seeking to inhibit our systems, steal information or promote disorder in our land.

We also need to set standards that provide financial relief for the victimized—assuming they have followed the standards of safety required.

This will be a bitter pill to swallow for those used to the boundless freedom of the Internet. But let's face the ugly facts. This is no longer a small dimension of Americans' daily lives. It has become a wild and dangerous frontier. Only the Federal Government can provide for our common defense and promote the general welfare in this space.

How Do These Responsibilities Fit Into Our National Security Strategy and Structure?

Every President starts his Administration with some form of a National Security Strategy. It is the thesis statement of the President' overall security strategy for the nation. It sets overall goals and allows the military, the diplomats and the intelligence gatherers to set their goals and resource requirements to the policy of the President.

In the aftermath of 9/11, we now include homeland security in that strategy. It is an acknowledgement of the fact that our borders are porous and that providing for the "common defense" extends internally as well as externally. What happens at Bagram Air Base, Afghanistan could easily matter in Bellingham, Washington.

With the inclusion of homeland security and the international and domestic expansion of the Internet, cyberspace is now part of our National Security Strategy. The challenge is what position it should take in our National Security Strategy and structure. It is one we are still feeling out.

At Home and Abroad

During the Cold War, we focused on the external. We countered Soviet efforts overseas through our diplomats, sometime our military and always through our intelligence mechanisms. At home, the FBI focused on national security violations—primarily information gathering and potential sabotage by Soviet agents.

Also at home, we engaged in mass civil defense efforts with our population preparing for the unthinkable possibility of nuclear war with mass casualties. It was done pro forma—with bomb shelters and civil defense warnings. The exercise dropped off as the stalemate of the Cold War combined with the hopelessness of survival sunk into the populace.

In today's world of cyberspace, the potential attacks from within and without are limitless and quite personal. Our banking system, our utilities, our commerce—our daily lives as citizens—can be effected by hackers from anywhere on the planet. Such is the interconnectivity of the world. And, given the current unstoppable expansion, it can only get more connected.

I would argue that cyberspace is a borderless space that must be dealt with by the Federal Government both externally and internationally in tandem with other nations and unilaterally when need be.

The United States needs to be a leader in international fora relating to cyberspace—not just a follower. We have set the standards for international telecommunications. We have set the standards for international air travel. We have also set standards for efforts against organized crime and counterterrorism. We must set them for the protection of our citizens and government in cyberspace.

Cyberspace is much a dimension as land, sea, air and space. In each one, as the world's greatest super power, we have asserted our interests demanding and defining the supremacy of our power. We can ill afford to let this new dimension that so thoroughly directly effects our population to go without our dominance and control.

The Battle—Direct and Low Intensity Conflict

As Alfred Thayer Mahan discussed with the dimension of sea power in the late 1800s, a new space like cyber can invite challenges to our supremacy. Cyber lends itself to direct challenges to us through hidden confrontation and asymmetric warfare. It also does not simply stop at the power of a nation-state. Non-nation-states players from the organized (e.g., Hezbollah) to the less organized (e.g., Anonymous) currently have the power to take us on in this dimension and do great harm.

The definition of what constitutes that damage has caused some controversy. We are used to "booms and bullets"—damage that threatens life and limb directly. Cyberspace is more subtle, with damage to life and limb possible, but more likely indirect. No, cyberspace engagement is about blinding, impeding, and making us feel unsafe.

We have already seen the damage a nation-state can carry on in cyberspace conflict. Russia's efforts against Estonia and Georgia prove the point. For now, it is throwing sand in your face during a street fight. It is about blinding your net centric capabilities to carry on other aggressive offensive military acts.

The primary challenge of cyber conflict is that of low intensity conflict. The structure of cyberspace allows for anonymity and stealth. An agent of a nation-state or non-nation-state can pilfer our secret technologies and correspondence. They can degrade subtlety our military capabilities. They can spread confusion and discomfort within America attacking citizens' bank accounts or damaging the supply chain functions. Again, there are no borders here. And the actions can be directed simultaneously against the government and the citizen.

Who Are These Guys?

In the movie "Butch Cassidy and the Sundance Kids", the personable outlaws are chased for a long period by a faceless, relentless posse. Butch keeps asking "who are these guys?" And we can ask the same questions in cyberspace.

The unregulated and controlled cyberspace we live in today is one of infinite interconnection and complexity. Attacks like we discussed above can be routed through multiple servers that give anonymity to the culprit.

Determining motivations are also a problem. Lulzs often attack for the hell of it and to show vulnerabilities. Sometime they do it to embarrass companies like Stratfor who they dislike for political reasons. Still, what can you say are the motivations for Chinese attacks from an Internet café in Shanghai? Nationalism? Directed by the local government? How about both?

This is where our cyber defense and offense can be stymied. The solution is to accept the Herbert Simon solution of "satisficing." Satisficing means you take the best possible solution with the information available to you at that moment. It will be incomplete information. But in cyberspace, time is immediate and waiting for intelligence assessments takes far too long.

We need through our military, intelligence and law enforcement services to be willing to attack and arrest quickly those we can detect. Sometime we'll be wrong. A lot of times, we'll be right.

This is the justice that needs to be done in the Wild West of cyberspace. Like justice in our original Wild West, it will often be crude and sometime wrong. But, it needs to be done to send the message that America will protect its citizens and its government from harm.

How Should the Government Protect Itself?

For anyone who has toured England and visited the cathedrals, you cannot help but be struck by the wall of names of World War I dead. As horrific as World War II was to the British, the "Great War" was a shock to the Victorian superpower from which they slipped into a long, gradual decline.

The primary cause of their demise—beginning with the Great War—was they were caught in their own myths about the world around them. It was a rapidly changing world. Yet, they clung to Napoleonic notions of battle, expensive and large unproductive colonies and a fine sense of superiority of their motives and culture.

Let me argue that the United States appears to be in a similar way today allowing itself the indulgence of mid-20th century values in a time of quickly developing 21st century realities. In terms of the new dimension of cyberspace, Washington is dangerously adrift and behind the times with its response, due to bureaucracy that no longer suits our needs.

Stove Pipes in the Electric Age

The myriad of departments and agencies in the Federal Government are mind boggling yet somewhat logical in their design. As America grew, so did its government. And as we don't like government and don't trust government, it grew it bits and pieces. Each part of the government was designed to deal with a particular issue or problem.

With cyberspace, this Federal stove-piping and compartmentalization run into a brick wall. Cyberspace is all-inclusive in its reach. It touches civilians and the military sectors. It touches upon law enforcement and regulatory interests. It touches upon civil liberties and oversight of business practices.

A swift and coherent response from the Federal Government has been impossible. The players in this game range from the National Security Agency to the FBI to the Defense Department to the Justice Department, etc, etc. The White House has issued several cyber strategies in several administrations. All of them honored in word and not in the breach.

Defense Department Dominance

The military has had the greatest experience with cyberspace and has taken the lead in terms of both protection of its services and offensive capabilities. Being in the nascent stages of the Internet in the late 1990s, DoD has been anticipating and reacting to attacks upon it. This has come in especially handy as it is most vulnerable due to its "net centric strategy."

Spread over 150 countries, from military attaches to the large contingents Afghanistan and Korea, DoD was quick to adopt cyberspace as its own—a force multiplier. This allowed the military to move information about quickly and to the people downrange who needed it the most at the "pointy end of the spear."

However, DoD has been under constant low-level attack due, in part, to the vulnerability of an Internet that is difficult to totally secure. The Chinese, for instance, have done their level best to mine as much information as possible before increased security standards were put in place. And, DoD contractors remain vulnerable to the same kinds of mining.

DoD also recognized the offensive capabilities of the Internet. It watched carefully the efforts of China, Russia and North Korea carrying out low intensity conflict against any number of targets. It was equally aware and followed carefully the activities of the Anonymous and Lulz's of the world.

With that concern, in 2010, US Cyber Command was set up. This unit based out of the National Security Agency, was designed to engage both offensively and defensively in cyberspace. It also allowed one stop shopping for the DoD to coordinate its efforts across the services. It also tied in the Intelligence Community to DoD effort.

Cyber Command Trumps All

The single buttonhole and discipline of the DoD Cyber Command make it a "go to" place for cyber issues. However, this rubs against not only the bureaucratic grain of Washington, but also those who strongly fear military activities in the United States.

Another part of our Constitution not so directly pointed out, is a firm distrust of military taking action on US soil. After the Civil War, the Posse Commitatus Act of 1876 made even further assurances that would limit the military's role in the United States

There was also some wiggle room on this stance. During World War II and the 1950-60s period, Army Intelligence was quite active within the United States. However, the scars of Vietnam and Watergate burned deep into the early 21st century and scant military involvement took place in the United States.

After 9/11, the US military established a Northern Command to work the issues of cross border threat within the United States. However, it has never been strong and has been highly circumscribed in law and by a very nervous DoD who is reluctant to violate traditions and American instincts.

Cyber Command, however, is charged with dealing with a target that knows no boundaries. Thus, it has been placed in a position of collecting information both foreign and domestic and providing it to law enforcement and others throughout the government to take action.

This information gathering alone places it in a unique and powerful position in the current situation and in American history. It has also increased questions about who oversees it and what kind of information it gathers and maintains.

The Civilian Side—Not So Easy

The reader will note that I have dived deeply into a discussion of the defense/military response to the cyber challenge. On the civilian side of the Federal Government, the coordination chore has not so easy. In fact, it is a tangled mess

The players who wish to be involved—or should be involved—include everyone from the Federal Bureau of Investigation to the Justice Department to Department of Homeland Security. There have been great bureaucratic struggles between these organizations based on territory long divided or reformulated to reflect 20th century ideas of organization.

Even if they could get their collective selves together, there is another sticky interaction we referred to before—how do they interact with the military? The Constitution and the laws we have since developed make sure the separation is there. Efforts to modify and bridge this gap have been made in the counterterrorism side since 9/11. In cyberspace, much still needs to be done.

I would suggest that we allow the Department of Homeland Security to truly live up to its name and be clearly in charge of the cyber issue. Only it should have the mandate to reach across all agencies to direct the civilian government effort and coordinate appropriately and effectively with the military.

What Actions Should It Direct Its Cyber Citizens To Do?

As I have repeatedly noted, as expressed in their Constitution, Americans do not like or trust government. We view it as a necessary evil– until we need it. Need is usually defined in terms of government as a social good. No private sector concern would take on the issue as there is clearly no profit in it. And no individual group would take on the issue as they would not have the strength of law to enforce behaviors.

With these dilemmas, we are faced with the question of what the Federal government should expect from its private cyber citizens—private citizens, business and state and local government. And what, should they in turn, expect from their government. What is the social compact in cyberspace?

A Definition of Cyber Citizen

So what is a cyber citizen? Take the word cyber out of the question and we reach back to ancient communities since the dawn of civilization. The word we use—citizen—comes from the Latin term "civitas" meaning "community." And while there are many shades of definition, international law professor Virginia Leary has succinctly noted, citizenship is connoting "a bundle of rights—primarily, political participation in the life of the community, the right to vote, and the right to receive certain protection from the community, as well as obligations." Being a citizen is a contract between the governed and the governing and among the governed themselves.

The cyber community has been relatively unregulated since its early days. It was and, to a large extent, remains a territory of do what you want when you want. I would argue that is simply not sensible given the overall reach of cyberspace, the number of individuals involved and the importance to both our governance and commerce. Cyberspace is the Wild West and it needs to be tamed for the social good.

A cyber citizen has an obligation to his community. The obligation includes the use of proper security, the reporting of crime and theft and the willingness to abide by the common good. On the first point, we as cyber citizen have been extraordinarily sloppy in terms of our security. It has been estimated in a recent study by Verizon that three-quarters of leaks and such on the net come from inadequate or non-existent security. This might have been all right years ago in a less connected cyber world. That is not the case now. Whoever leaves the door open to the apartment building invites the thieves to come into the whole building—not just their apartment.

The second issue is a more "tender" one. Individuals tend to be better about reporting crimes than businesses; especially larger ones. Let's face it, a loss of information can and does affect trust. Why should I bank/buy/use your services if I can't keep my information safe?

If you are a business with stockholders, it also becomes a case of fiduciary responsibility. You owe the stockholders an explanation of why your system was insecure and what damage may have been caused to the overall valuation of the company because of this "malfeasance."

What Cost the Common Good?

Nobel Prize winning economist Herbert Simon came up with the concept of "satisficing." Its essence was the idea that with incomplete information and time restrictions, the individual or firm picked the best possible solution available to it—not the absolutely best possible solution. This is how people approach Internet security.

The use of cyberspace is growing higher. Most people don't have a clue as to what their security needs should be and what they need to do. They reach out to standardized solutions, such as a McAfee, and hope for the best.

They also fret over cost. In this sense, they are also the logical economic man. How do you balance and cost of security—dollars and time spent—versus the potential loss you might suffer by having no or less than 100% security. The management of this risk is one we do and businesses do everyday. And, not illogically, we tend to err on the side of keeping the costs down. For the individual, it is money out of their pocket. For the company, it is another expense they must endure cutting profitability.

What Should the Federal Government Do For Its Cyber Citizens?

I believe it is time to treat the Internet as a public utility such as water, gas, electricity or roads. As the Federal Government is obliged by the Constitution to "provide for the common defense and promote the general welfare of its citizens", then cyberspace fits this role perfectly.

First, Washington must set minimum-security standards on the Internet. I would recommend expanding the Federal Communications Commission to do this. The freedom loving and relatively unregulated Internet providers are going to scream bloody murder about this. By they are cyber citizens and owe their society the safety of their product. Minimum standards of security must be set and enforced.

Second, the Federal Government must see to it that "streets" of cyberspace are safe. Legal penalties must be imposed on miscreants who violate this space. We send people to jail for stealing cable television or polluting our water supply. Why should we tolerate someone messing with our Internet?

Third, the Federal Government must find some way to compensate and encourage people to "pay their Internet tax" of security. We allow for mortgage deductions. Perhaps it is time to allow for Internet security deductions. And, perhaps, allow private companies some type of financial ceiling on damages they may incur from the failing to provide adequate protection to their customers.

Being cyber citizens means we have an obligation to each other. Imposing rules internationally is difficult if not impossible. However, we American cyber citizens owe our fellow cyber citizens the rights and privileges of being a citizen.

What Are The Checks And Balances in Cyberspace?

While the Federal Government may impose rules on the cyber system, it also owes it citizen's protection from potential abuse—from both itself and private concerns. We, as Americans, value our freedom. We need protection in cyberspace. But we also cannot afford to allow "Big Brother" to creep into the system.

The concept of Big Brother is the boogey man of the Internet world. In China and Russia, the central government controls the Internet. We fear that type of control and should. We have a track record in this country of abuse when power is centralized and there are no checks and balances on that power.

The most recent example came in the 1950-60s. The FBI, under Director J. Edgar Hoover, kept us safe from communist agents in America during the Cold War. It also kept information and spied on citizens and organizations that simply were in no sense threats.

So who regulates the regulators of cyberspace? And who regulates those who use cyberspace to collect information on cyber citizens?

Inside and Outside

The first great regulator of cyberspace is the cyber citizen himself or herself. Unlike the 1950s, we do not live in a time of repressed expression. Cyberspace is filled with opinion and the exercise of free speech. Short of the government actually closing down the net in time of war, that is unlikely to change. Abuses are reported constantly and the embarrassed are either closed down or investigated by the authorities.

So who is regulating the authorities? That is were the trouble begins. Cyberspace has been unregulated because of its history of "freedom" but also because of the speed that it came upon us. We are more deeply committed cyber citizens every day—like it or not. The government has not come close to keeping up. Now, we must keep an eye on its catching up too fast and overreacting.

The second great regulator—and the standard bearer under our Constitution is the Congress. I realize that elicits a groan about an institution that barely captures a 10% confidence level among the average America. But, they are charged with setting the laws of the land. They do have the system of oversight. They are beholding to the people every two and six years in election. And we can communicate with them at will.

The third great regulator of the Internet is outside organizations ranging from the American Civil Liberties Union (ACLU) to the US Chamber of Commerce. While it sounds like these are strange bedfellows, they are not. Both want some regulation of cyberspace for clarity of responsibility. Both fear what the government may impose on them. Both are concerned over how information obtained in cyberspace is used and stored.

The fourth and greatest regulator is our court system. We could, of course, set up some type of public-private citizen's board to oversee the net. However, theses types of boards—such as the President's Intelligence Advisory Board—tend to be benign and sometimes ineffective.

The court system of the United States is part of the Constitution and equal to its other branches in the Executive and Legislative Branches. Unlike the 1950s, we are a far more litigious society today far more willing to get in and sue if we feel aggrieved or violated. This behavior applies to the Internet.

Bottom line: Our freedom in cyberspace will be overseen through the constitutional process and through our own diligence—enhanced, in fact, by the Internet and cyberspace. But, ultimately, it is up to us to be diligent cyber citizens. This is our right and our obligation to ourselves.

CHAPTER 14

The Brave New World of Cyber

Timothy R. Sample, Michael S. Swetnam, Kathryn Schiller Wurster

What if you woke up tomorrow and found that the balances in your online bank account were off just enough to make you question their veracity? What if that happened that same morning to everyone having an account in the same bank? What if many of these account holders tried to withdrawal their money in an attempt to safeguard it? What if it happened to multiple banks at the same time? What if an "attack" by a foreign corporation on a United States Government computer system was so extensive that it might be considered an act of "war?" Who responds and under what laws; Cyber Command or the Federal Bureau of Investigation? What if we found out that a state-sponsored company was going to "attack" us? Is that a Title 10 or Title 50 preemptive response? What if two corporations launched significant cyber attacks on each

Timothy R. Sample is the Vice President and Sector Manager for Battelle Memorial Institute's Special Programs Organization. Prior to joining Battelle, Mr. Sample served as the President of the Intelligence and National Security Alliance (INSA), a non-profit public policy and advocacy forum for intelligence and national security. Mr. Sample joined INSA after a position at General Dynamics Advanced Information Systems as the Vice President for Strategic Intelligence Strategies and Programs. Prior to General Dynamics, Mr. Sample had 30 years of intelligence and policy experience as both a supplier and user of intelligence. He served on the House Permanent Select Committee on Intelligence (HPSCI) for nine years, achieving the title of Staff Director from June 2000 to May 2003. Mr. Sample's experiences prior to Congress have included service as both an intelligence and imagery analyst in the Central Intelligence Agency. He has held senior government positions including Deputy US Negotiator for the Strategic Arms Reduction Talks (START I) when it was signed in 1991, and the Executive Director of the Director of Central Intelligence's Nonproliferation Center. His military background includes service in intelligence units within the US Air Force. Beyond his employment with General Dynamics, he has additional business experience, having worked on information processing and telecommunications technologies at GTE Government Systems and as the co-founder and first President of the Potomac Institute for Policy Studies.

other over control of market share or influence on a host government? What if a country began issuing Letters of Marque and Reprisal to corporations? What if a country launched a dedicated denial of service (DDoS) attack on the US State Department in an attempt to dissuade communications with a dissident group? What if that country instead altered the State Department message in ways favorable to that country's message and control of the population?

These types of "What if" scenarios are the subject of this chapter. On the surface, some of these scenarios seem too far–fetched in today's society to be considered. But the fact is cyber technology has fundamentally changed the conduct of life in the modern age and such scenarios are more plausible today than they were just a decade ago. Moreover, one can argue that with each passing year and technological advancement, such scenarios may well be more certain a decade from now. In the case of United States (US) law and our ability to keep pace with cyber developments, one can argue that these issues face us today and we are behind in our response. And as we consider a doctrine for the cyber era, there is a requirement to at least debate such scenarios in order to either be prepared to face them, or to take steps to prevent their occurrence.

Michael S. Swetnam was co-founder of the Potomac Institute for Policy Studies in 1994. Since its inception, he has served as Chairman of the Board and currently serves as the Institute's Chief Executive Officer. Mr. Swetnam is currently a member of the Technical Advisory Group to the United States Senate Select Committee on Intelligence. In this capacity, he provides expert advice to the US Senate on the R&D investment strategy of the US Intelligence Community. He also served on the Defense Science Board (DSB) Task Force on Counterterrorism and the Task Force on Intelligence Support to the War on Terrorism. From 1990 to 1992, Mr. Swetnam served as a Special Consultant to President Bush's Foreign Intelligence Advisory Board (PFIAB) where he provided expert advice on Intelligence Community issues including budget, community architecture, and major programs. He also assisted in authoring the Board's assessment of Intelligence Community support to Desert Storm/Shield. Prior to forming the Potomac Institute for Policy Studies, Mr. Swetnam worked in private industry as a Vice President of Engineering at the Pacific-Sierra Research Corporation, Director of Information Processing Systems at GTE, and Manager of Strategic Planning for GTE Government Systems. Prior to joining GTE, he worked for the Director of Central Intelligence as a Program Monitor on the Intelligence Community Staff (1986-1990). Mr. Swetnam was also assigned as the IC Staff representative to intergovernmental groups that developed the INF and START treaties. He assisted in presenting these treaties to Congress for ratification. Mr. Swetnam served in the US Navy for 24 years as an active duty and reserve officer, Special Duty Cryptology.

Considering the Revolutionary Impact of Cyber

There are many aspects to the term "cyber." At a very general level, though, there are three basic components to consider when discussing a threat or a doctrine. First is the domain itself. This is cyberspace. It is the collection of networks and systems that form the environment in which the transfer of data happens. Anything connected—physically or virtually through wireless methods—is, by extension, part of cyberspace. Second are the mechanisms that allow access to cyberspace and govern the transfer of data. The Internet is the most prominent source of access, but there are also a variety of wireless communications networks that allow transfer of data into the Internet. The transfer itself is governed by software and "tools." In most cases, this software is standard and allows links between individual "nodes" within cyberspace. In some cases, this software is being developed and deployed with malicious intent and results. Such software can be activated immediately upon employment, or sit idle and undetected until activated. The third component is the information itself. And at the root of many of the "What ifs" described above is the access and control of information.

Dependency on the Internet by governments, companies, academia, scientists, militaries (especially the US military), and individuals (including various groups of individuals), has grown in unimaginable ways in a very brief period of time. In fact, heretofore disparate groups of individuals have utilized the Internet to form additional links worldwide that might never have been possible. The Internet gives the power of communication to a single voice, enhancing its influence. In an article published by the *New York Times*,

Kathryn Schiller Wurster is Chief of Staff in the Office of the CEO at the Potomac Institute for Policy Studies. As Chief of Staff, she provides critical, high-level support to the CEO/Chairman of the Board of Directors and the other Corporate Officers, and serves as a liaison to the Board of Directors and Board of Regents. Ms. Schiller Wurster exercises coordination authority on behalf of the CEO and the CEO's Office. In addition, she helps advance the organization's strategic priorities, manages the planning and operations of the CEO/Chairman, and works frequently with the organization's senior leadership and staff across all functional areas of the organization to manage projects and provide strategic support. Ms. Schiller Wurster is currently supporting the Defense Microelectronics Activity on strategic planning efforts, supply chain risk management and trust issues for microelectronics parts. Her past research projects have included work for DARPA, DDR&E, Air Force, Congress, and other agencies. Ms. Schiller Wurster helped launch the Center for Neurotechnology Studies (CNS) and participated in drafting the National Neurotechnology Initiative legislation, and continues to assist CNS with seminars and workshops on ethical, legal, social and policy issues related to neurotechnology.

Vint Cerf, Vice President and Chief Internet Evangelist for Google addressed the enabling nature of technology related to the "Arab Spring," noting that, "Though the demonstrations thrived because thousands of people turned out to participate, they could never have happened as they did without the ability that the Internet offers to communicate, organize, and publicize everywhere, instantaneously."[1] Like it or not, the utilization of cyberspace forms the basis of almost every human endeavor today involving information, communication, or automated processes. Modern society is rapidly becoming as dependent on cyber technology as we are on food, water, and air for survival.

So, cyberspace and its associated technologies are inventions by mankind that totally change the way humans interact and live. Traditionally, we speak about science and technology revolutions as human events where the invention of a key technology radically changes the course of human history. Clearly the invention of the wheel, ca. 3500 BC, changed almost all aspects of human commerce. This simple technology empowered early societies to move large amounts of materials, food, and other resources across greater distances. This technology led to massive changes in man's ability to build, gather in towns and societies, engage in commerce, and expand the influence of civilization.

Much later (ca. 1440 AD) the invention of the printing press changed the history of the modern world and made possible the accessibility and rapid expansion of knowledge and education. The subsequent rapid advance of thought, governance, art, and an explosion in the advancement of science and technology can be traced to the printing press as a key enabling invention.

The invention of mechanized and industrial processes, in the late 18th century, along with steam and later gasoline engines, brought about massive changes in the quality and type of life in the modern world, and the "industrialized world" was born.

The invention of nuclear weapons, radar, and modern cryptology changed warfare in the 1940s and 1950s and led to the development of technologies such as television, microwaves, transistors and, later, microelectronics. These enabling inventions, in turn, led to the development of computing, the Internet, and the information revolution.

Clearly, the invention of modern digital communications technologies has brought about changes in almost every aspect of society, including in the way we get information, interact socially, and conduct business and commerce.

---

1. Vinton G. Cerf, "Internet Access Is Not a Human Right," *New York Times*, January 4, 2012, *http://www.nytimes.com/2012/01/05/opinion/internet-access-is-not-a-human-right.html.*

The changes brought about by this technology are more than just increases in efficiency, or greater outputs. The changes, empowered by cyber technologies, are revolutionary in nature and enable entirely new forms of social and economic activity.

Thomas Friedman's "The World Is Flat: A Brief History of the Twenty-First Century"[2] is a good reference on the many revolutionary effects of these technologies. Examples include the vast changes this technology has on business affairs. When personal computers appeared in the early 1980s, as word processors, people predicted vastly increased efficiency because secretaries would be able to produce and correct documents much more easily. There have been vast efficiencies realized, but for different reasons; instead computing replaced secretaries altogether. Today there are far fewer secretaries, stenography is no longer taught in schools, and typing pools have disappeared. Today, a busy executive can dictate a letter to his cell phone or iPad between meetings and have it delivered by email. Entire businesses have gone out of existence, including companies producing typewriters, carbon paper, and correction fluid. Instead of creating incremental efficiencies, computer technologies revolutionized the way business is done.

Computer technology has also fundamentally transformed the global economic system. Twenty years ago, building an international company required the capital investment necessary to construct shipping, receiving, repair, and customer service capabilities in the countries one wished to do business. Today even the smallest privately owned shop in the United States can do business internationally by employing FedEx, UPS, and the Internet.

The technology has not merely caused an evolutionary effect by increasing the speed and throughput of an existing process. It empowered the creation of entirely new processes such as "just in time delivery," customer service by international centers rather than local affiliates, and out-sourcing of capabilities not core to the mission of the enterprise. That is revolutionary.

Clearly cyber technologies are having a similar revolutionary effect on warfare. John Boyd developed the concept of the OODA Loop (observe, orient, decide, and act), the cyclical process where a commander continuously assesses the situation, decides on a course of action, and acts, and posited that one could gain an advantage by completing this loop faster than one's

---

2.   Thomas L. Friedman, *The World is Flat A Brief History of the Twenty-first Century* (New York: Farrar, Straus & Giroux, April 2005).

opponent.[3] This process has been greatly sped up by cyber technologies, which allow a commander to get a better picture of the situation, to act more quickly, and to assess the effect and act again if necessary. Cyber technologies can increase the pace and effectiveness of this process, but this is an evolutionary effect, not revolutionary, since it simply improves upon an existing process.

However, the truly revolutionary effects of cyber technologies will be something entirely different. Cyber techniques could be used to vastly change the situational awareness perceived by the enemy so that he is deceived into action he would otherwise not consider. One could imagine a cyber scenario where a combatant has gained control over the enemy's information systems. One option would be to shut down the enemy's systems at this point and force him to revert to old ways of doing business. An alternative strategy might be to subtly change the information in his systems without disrupting normal operations, to convince the enemy that the war is proceeding in an entirely expected way. One could then easily maneuver one's enemy into a certain defeat.

Psychological warfare and propaganda have been a part of military and diplomatic strategies throughout recorded history. Imagine a world, however, where dominant control of the information space would allow an actor to vastly change and alter the situation as seen by another actor. This is the ultimate in deception and information warfare. It is empowered and made possible by ubiquitous information systems that touch every part of modern society.

If one were able to gain information superiority over the key systems of an adversary in warfare, why wouldn't one use this same technical capability to change the perception of the leadership or even the population of the adversary to potentially prevent kinetic response? Information dominance could be used to ensure that the leadership or population of a target country saw only information that spoke to the inferiority of their force, the impossible situation they were in, and the ultimate need to surrender.

Fighting against an enemy with such capabilities would mean being engaged in a conflict where the battlefield is defined by the veracity of the information on which we depend, rather than on the lethality of our kinetic weapons. Kinetic weapons will likely always play a role in conflict, as a tool to enforce demands or punish when needed, but information and misperception

---

3. "A Discourse on Winning and Losing: Introducing Core Ideas & Themes of Boyd's 'Theory of intellectual evolution and growth'," Col Dr. Frans Osinga. Briefing presented at Quantico, VA. July 13, 2007. *http://www.au.af.mil/au/awc/awcgate/boyd/osinga_boydconf07_copyright2007.pdf*

would become the primary tools of warfare. One can further envision a world where powerful nation-states battle in cyberspace over the control of information and its dissemination to the masses, and rarely, if ever, resort to kinetic weapons. That would be revolutionary!

One can envision even more revolutionary concepts about the impacts of a cyber-enabled world. Can we imagine a world where the flow and content of information can be sufficiently controlled or influenced to cause the rise of mass movements that would overthrow governments, change or alter the political landscape, or alter a population's support for war or peace? As previously noted, have we seen the first real example already in the Arab Spring? If a major nation-state or world power were able to understand, create, and control the phenomena of "going viral", how could it be used? In such a world would we be able to tell that information was being manipulated on a broad scale? Clearly this type of alternative universe would first require an entity or nation-state to gain control of the information superhighway, or the deep understanding of the mechanisms of information dissemination. Or would it?

Along with the potential impact of cyberspace and cyber technologies, and the vulnerabilities that are becoming discussed more openly in the public domain and are highlighted in this book, are the effects emerging related to our current laws, processes, and government structures, our expectation of privacy, and potentially on the influence of governments themselves.

Is Cyber War, War?

It can be argued that a cyber war is no more a war than a war on terrorism or a war on drugs. Would we characterize the next war as a "water war" if one of the main tools of warfare were the denial of water to a population? Possibly. But wouldn't it be more correct to characterize water warfare, cyber warfare, even terrorism as a tool and technique of warfare rather than a war unto itself? Probably.

In that context, the utilization of cyberspace for "attacks" applies to the use and application of tools and techniques of war. Over time, generally accepted "rules of war" have been developed which limit how war may be conducted. Modern international humanitarian law is based on formal treaties such as the Geneva Conventions and the Hague Conventions, along with other rules of conduct called customary law. It is considered against these "rules of war" to deliberately target civilians, torture prisoners of war, or use biological and chemical weapons.

A central principle of this body of law is the concept of distinction: "all sides in a conflict must distinguish between legitimate military targets on the one hand and civilians and civilian objects on the other."[4] Under these rules, action such as denying water to a civilian population would be considered inhumane and an illegal act of war.

Is the denial of information/cyber technologies on which modern society depends a legitimate tool of war? If denying these technologies causes thousands or millions of civilians to suffer or restricts their access to basic necessities, would it be called an illegal act of war? If one accepts the concept of distinction, then the use of cyber tools in warfare would be limited to targeting military elements. Broad cyber attacks that targeted the general population or the civilian infrastructure of a country could be considered illegitimate or even inhumane acts of war. For example, if a cyber "attack" resulted in physical damage to our electric grid or our ability to supply water to a population, is that an illegal act of war? Does the distinction change depending on whether this occurs after a formal declaration of war has been issued between two countries?

Applications of Cyber Technologies in War

Clearly the US military is deeply dependent on cyber technologies for the operation of its war fighting capabilities. Almost every aspect of US military operations today use and depend on modern information technologies. These technologies not only enhance our military capabilities, they allow for accuracy, precision, and force multiplication that is beyond the imagination of war fighters of old. However, this dependence on cyber technologies also creates targets, vulnerabilities, and an arena for warfare that did not exist before.

Since the vast majority of our potential enemies also depend on information technologies, these technologies can become an area of opportunity. Using cyber technologies to attack an adversary's cyber dependent systems is a new and exciting war fighting capability. Targeted attacks using this technology might include a spectrum of attacks from the command and control systems of the enemy to individual weapons systems.

One can imagine using cyber technologies to attack the infrastructure that underpins and supports the military capabilities of the country or region one

---

4.   International Committee of the Red Cross. "International Law on the Conduct of Hostilities: Overview," Oct. 29, 2010, *http://www.icrc.org/eng/war-and-law/conduct-hostilities/overview-conduct-of-hostilities.htm.*

is opposing, thereby decreasing the enemy's ability to resist or wage warfare. Harkening back to the previous discussion on "distinction," an issue apparent in such a capability is that more and more today, a country's infrastructure that supports its military and that which supports its general population is one and the same.

Many envision cyber attacks as part of the full spectrum of warfare. We could well use these technologies long before actual kinetic warfare breaks out. These techniques and capabilities could help prevent actual war, assist in the build-up to war, and increase the effectiveness of war itself. The application of cyber technologies and techniques in pre-war/conflict scenarios is of particular interest. These types of capabilities could provide the opportunity to change the international scenario in ways that either prevent conflict or work to ease international tensions.

It is important to note that cyber technologies provide much more than just a weapon. First and foremost, cyber technologies enable collection of intelligence on the adversary's infrastructure, command and control systems, capabilities, and sometimes even intentions. Cyber technologies are a new growth field in the intelligence collection business. Intelligence collectors can steal the war plans of an adversary by breaking into his computer rather than having to venture a risky effort to physically break into his secure head-quarters. The insights, directions, and visions of our potential adversaries are available through creative exploitation of their computer systems. In the past, critical intelligence was collected by recruiting spies in the adversary's camp, breaking into the enemy's files, or intercepting communications. Computers make life easier and more productive for all, but they also provide a central file of comprehensive information that can be reached and accessed by others on a global scale. Computers are a "one-stop" mega-supermarket for the intelligence collector!

The same technology that allows an intelligence collector to get inside an adversary's computer to read his mail, also allows one to destroy or vastly alter the data on that computer. The technology can also be used to very carefully change how systems function; not just disabling a system, but changing the timing or effectiveness of the system so that it functions in very different ways from its intended use. If thoughtful, the computer network exploiter can not only use the technology to gather data and information, but change the way the system provides this data to its owner, thereby changing the owner's view of the data and information in the system. This subtle use of cyber technology to control an adversary's information flow is potentially much more powerful than simply disabling an enemy's computer or stealing their information.

This same technology can also empower protection of cyber assets. If one develops the capability to exploit computer networks, one has put in place the capabilities to track those who wish to do harm to his systems. Being able to recognize and deal with threats before they enter one's own system is a key enabling concept in computer network protection or defense.

Cyber as a Form of Unconventional War/Covert Action

Cyber warfare should be defined as a type of unconventional warfare and covered by the legal definitions of covert action. Unconventional warfare, or covert action, is the targeted application of force into an adversary's (or potential adversaries) territory to gain an outcome or affect that could not be achieved by other means. Covert action often includes the need for "plausible deniability". One wants to apply a level of force inside the sovereign territory of another country that might easily be considered an act of war, without the action being attributed to the country of origin.

This type of warfare has been generally successful for many decades, often achieving national objectives such as bringing about a change of government without a declaration of war. However, there have been some very notable embarrassments, including the Bay of Pigs during the early Kennedy Administration and the Iran-Contra fiasco during the Reagan Administration.

Following the Iran-Contra scandal, which included the indictment of several White House officials for lying to Congress about these activities, Congress passed legislation that required the President to issue a "finding" and report it to the US Congress within 48 hours of his approval of a covert action (Title 50 USC, § 413B[5]). In general, the law requires that when the President decides to embark on a covert effort utilizing the unique authorities given to the Intelligence Community, he must have a clear foreign policy objective and must notify the Congress in writing (called a "finding") and then keep Congress informed throughout the effort. The law very carefully describes what is considered a covert action and what is not.

---

5. Presidential Approval and Reporting of Covert Actions, 50 USC § 413b. *http://www.law.cornell.edu/uscode/text/50/413b.*

The law defines covert action:

"As used in this subchapter, the term "covert action" means an activity or activities of the United States Government to influence political, economic, or military conditions abroad, where it is intended that the role of the United States Government will not be apparent or acknowledged publicly, but does not include:

(1) activities the primary purpose of which is to acquire intelligence, traditional counterintelligence activities, traditional activities to improve or maintain the operational security of United States Government programs, or administrative activities;

(2) traditional diplomatic or military activities or routine support to such activities;

(3) traditional law enforcement activities conducted by United States Government law enforcement agencies or routine support to such activities; or

(4) activities to provide routine support to the overt activities (other than activities described in paragraph (1), (2), or (3) of other United States Government agencies abroad."

Note Section (1) of the definition above. If it is determined that the "primary" purpose of the effort is intelligence or maintenance of security, then the action is not considered cover action even if acts of war are included.

The question of whether cyber attacks can be considered covert action, and thereby subject to US Law (Title 50 USC 413B) have been debated in the last couple of Administrations. Some have held that cyber attacks have not been defined by international law as acts of war and, therefore, are not subject to the need for a Presidential Finding and reporting to Congress. This view was held by the Bush Administration throughout the early 2000s. On the other hand, the Obama Administration has argued in international forums that cyber attacks are acts of war.[6]

6.   William J. Lynn III, "Defending a New Domain: The Pentagon's Cyberstrategy," *Foreign Affairs*, *http://www.foreignaffairs.com/articles/66552/william-j-lynn-iii/defending-a-new-domain.*

In 2011, the Obama Administration issued a cyber strategy document that declared the US position that a cyber attack on US assets or infrastructure would be considered an act of war and would be met with a proportional response, not necessarily cyber in nature.[7] In other words, an attack on the IT infrastructure of the United States may be met with a kinetic response.

Blurring of the Lines between Foreign and Domestic Surveillance

When the cyber action that is being contemplated involves action in the United States or against US assets, the relevant authorities include Title 50 and Title 19. The technical capability and authorities embodied in the National Security Agency (NSA) and the US Cyber Command must be "teamed" with the capabilities and authorities that have been granted to the Department of Justice, the Federal Bureau of Investigation (FBI), or the Department of Homeland Security (DHS). This system is problematic at best.

The NSA does not have any authority to collect inside the United States without a court order. The Foreign Intelligence Surveillance Court (FISC) was established to review electronic surveillance requests for foreign targets operating within the United States. The court is composed of eleven federal judges that review requests from the Department of Justice for warrants to tap the phone of suspected terrorists, foreign spies, or others, where a clear threat to the security of the United States can be justified to the court. The Attorney General can also authorize emergency surveillance and then must notify the court within 72 hours.[8]

The original Foreign Intelligence Surveillance Act (FISA) dates back to 1978 but has been modified in the last decade to reflect the new technical and threat environment. After the terrorist attacks of September 11, 2001, the USA PATRIOT Act expanded the authorities of the FISA legislation to cover activities by suspected terrorists that were not backed by a foreign government, as more traditional intelligence activities.

The USA PATRIOT Act was amended in 2005 to grant the authority to use National Security Letters (NSL) to obtain information on US citizens, and judicial review was added; in 2010, "the FBI made 24,287 NSL requests (excluding requests for subscriber information only) for information... pertaining

7. White House, *International Strategy for Cyberspace: Prosperity, Security, and Openness in a Networked World,* May 2011, *http://www.whitehouse.gov/sites/default/files/rss_viewer/international_strategy_for_cyberspace.pdf.*

8. 50 USC Chapter 36, § 1803 and § 1805, *http://www.law.cornell.edu/uscode/text/50/chapter-36.*

to 14,212 different United States persons."[9] The Protect America Act of 2007 further amended FISA to allow domestic wiretapping of communications that begin or end outside the United States, without supervision by the FISC.[10] The use of the FISA Court to authorize the interception of communications and collection of intelligence on US citizens has been the subject of some significant discussion.[11]

It should be noted that the technology necessary to intercept phone calls, emails, etc., in the modern age of the Internet is exactly the same technology used by the NSA to collect foreign intelligence. Further, because of the structure of Internet routing, there is no longer any clear distinction between foreign and domestic communications. An email sent by an American citizen from Arlington, Virginia could well transit the Atlantic Ocean before returning to the United States, where it gets delivered to a US citizen. Collection assets that are authorized under US Title 50 and are pointed overseas today routinely see emails, data, and even phone calls from US citizen to US citizen within the United States. How, then, is the US Government going to ensure that the privacy of its citizens is not violated without court order?

To confuse the issue further, the authority and mission of protecting homeland security is held by DHS, not DoD or the Intelligence Community. If DHS is to fully embrace its responsibilities, it will need to monitor the Internet, inside the United States, to ensure that our country and its infrastructure are not being attacked. Once again, the technology to accomplish this mission is exactly the same technology that the NSA, and now the US Cyber Command, deploys to address the need for foreign intelligence collection, cyber warfare, and cyber defense. If we are uncomfortable with the NSA and the Intelligence Community collecting and monitoring within the United States, should we recreate this technology in DHS? Would the two separate cyber activities interfere with each other?

From a technical perspective, the creation of two separate systems makes no sense. The Internet is not divisible by national boundaries, so if one is on the Internet in the United States, one is on the Internet globally and vice versa.

---

9. Department of Justice Memo, Report to Congress on 2010 Electronic Surveillance Activities, April 29, 2011, *http://www.fas.org/irp/agency/doj/fisa/2010rept.pdf.*

10. Public Law 110-55, *http://www.gpo.gov/fdsys/pkg/PLAW-110publ55/pdf/PLAW-110publ55.pdf.*

11. See, for example, "The Foreign Intelligence Surveillance Act: A Brief Overview of Selected Issues," Elizabeth B. Bazan. Congressional Research Service, Feb 8, 2008, *http://fpc.state.gov/documents/organization/101789.pdf.*

The traditional separation of foreign and domestic intelligence collection is rapidly disappearing in the age of the Internet.

Freedom of Information

The First Amendment to the US Constitution guarantees freedom of religion, speech, and press. A quick reading of the Federalist Papers of the late 1790s shows that the framers of our constitution believed strongly that a free and open public discussion and debate were essential to the maintenance of a democracy. The founders also claimed that the open flow of information and speech would empower a population to seek freedom and a democracy.

The strength of this system was demonstrated by the Soviet Union, which attempted to close off the flow of information into and out of their country in an effort to control the population's knowledge of the rest of the world. The increasing flow of information about the rest of the world into the Soviet Union was considered a major factor in its collapse.

Modern versions of this attempt to control information can be found in China and Iran, where the governments are attempting to control the flow and substance of information going in and out of these countries. The full extent and effectiveness of these measures is difficult to measure, as in both cases there are economic considerations that make external contact by the middle as well as the ruling class beneficial. The ultimate example of a government's lock on information control is North Korea.

Further, Russia has declared that it considers the information networks by which their population receives information, news, and data as a part of its sovereign territory: "Russia retains the right to use nuclear weapons first against the means and forces of information warfare, and then against the aggressor state itself."[12] In 2000, Putin published an Information Security Doctrine that "empowers the state to control information to: protect strategically important information; protect against deleterious foreign information; and inculcate patriotism and values."[13]

---

12. V.I. Tsymbal, "Kontseptsiya 'Informatsionnoy voyny' (Concept of Information Warfare), Russian-US conference on "Evolving Post-Cold War National Security Issues," Moscow, September 12-14, 1995, p. 7.

13. Information Security Doctrine for the Russian Federation. Approved by President of the Russian Federation Vladimir Putin on September 9, 2000, *http://www.mid.ru/bdomp/ns-osndoc.nsf/1e5f0de 28fe77fdcc32575d900298676/2deaa9ee15ddd24bc32575d9002c442b!OpenDocument.*

In other words, a nation's, society's, or group's information systems are considered "national assets" and have the same status as the physical territory and citizenry of the nation. Then, by the commonly accepted rules of war, if one nation-state attacks, alters, or exploits another's information territory, one has committed an act of war just as if one had invaded the physical territory of another country. Although the United States has published an *International Strategy for Cyberspace*[14] that states an attack on our cyber infrastructure would be considered an attack on our country, it has not made a declaration, like the Russian's, that information systems are to be considered part of a country's sovereign territory.

This concept of information space being sovereign territory is even more important in cases such as the Arab Spring, where information technology enabled communications and expression of discontent in countries that were subjected to central control. A predictable reaction has been the almost total isolation of countries like Syria in an attempt to clamp down on external influence and information about the brutal government reaction to protest. Another result is the effort to define "rights" in this regard. On June 29, 2012, the United Nations General Assembly Human Rights Council passed a resolution that, "Affirms that the same rights that people have offline must also be protected online, in particular freedom of expression, which is applicable regardless of frontiers and through any media of one's choice, in accordance with Articles 19 of the Universal Declaration of Human Rights and the International Covenant on Civil and Political Right..."[15] In response to the Special Rapporteur's report that underpinned the resolution, Google's Vint Cerf argues that a debate over this issue, "...however well meaning, misses a larger point: technology is an enabler of rights, not a right itself..." but acknowledges that, "While the United States has never decreed that everyone has a "right" to a telephone, we have come close to this with the notion of "universal service"—the idea that telephone service (and electricity, and now broadband Internet) must be available even in the most remote regions of the country. When we accept this idea, we are edging into the idea of Internet access as a civil right, because ensuring access is a policy made by the government."[16] Cerf makes a key and critical point that relates both to

14. White House, *International Strategy for Cyberspace: Prosperity, Security, and Openness in a Networked World*, May 2011, *http://www.whitehouse.gov/sites/default/files/rss_viewer/international_strategy_for_cyberspace.pdf*.

15. United Nations General Assembly, Human Rights Council, A/HRC/20/L.13, 29 June 2012.

16. Cerf, "Internet Access Is Not a Human Right," January 4, 2012.

access and, by extension, the issue of sovereignty, by stating, "Yet all these philosophical arguments overlook a more fundamental issue: the responsibility of technology creators themselves to support human and civil rights. The Internet has introduced an enormously accessible and egalitarian platform for creating, sharing, and obtaining information on a global scale. As a result, we have new ways to allow people to exercise their human and civil rights."[17]

Freedom of Information...Influence

Along with the issue of the free flow of information is the reality of influence. Scores of large companies have already compiled vast repositories of data on individual demographics and buying habits, through frequent buyer cards, discount clubs, supermarket memberships, gas stations, and credit cards. These businesses routinely collect data on buying habits and have developed sophisticated algorithms to describe and predict an individual's likes, dislikes, political leaning, geographical location, income level, ethnic background, marital status, and whether one is pregnant, and use this data for targeted marketing campaigns.[18]

Similar techniques could easily be used to send an individual targeted information, for instance designed to speak to some political movement or social injustice, that can be predicted to have a certain effect. Could such a marketing effort create or help fuel a Tea Party or an Occupy Movement? These types of targeted marketing efforts have proven very successful in influencing behavior, selling everything from cars to soap. Why not political bias? Of greater concern is the security of our election data in this regard. The result of the 2000 Presidential election was held in abeyance, with the decisions grounded on so-called "hanging chads." As our election system becomes more technologically advanced, might someone "hack" in and create electronic "chads" in an attempt to confuse, or perhaps, change the results. A perhaps more plausible scenario might be modification of poll date just before and during Election Day in an attempt to influence voter turnout. If this was done at the hands (or under the direction) of a foreign government, how would we respond?

As mentioned previously, our Founding Fathers and generations since have believed that the free flow of information would empower a population and

---

17. *Ibid.*

18. Charels Duhigg, "How Companies Learn Your Secret," *New York Times.* February 16, 2012, *http://www.nytimes.com/2012/02/19/magazine/shopping-habits.html?pagewanted=all.*

strengthen a democracy. Implicit in this view is the concept that the free and uncontrolled flow of information would help sort out fact from fiction and flush out biases, inaccuracies, and falsehoods. It would seem that the freer the data and information flow, the more rapidly facts would be sorted from fiction. However, we have yet to determine whether the exponential increase in information flow provided by the Internet will have this effect.

In the old days, BI (Before the Internet), the process for sorting fact from fiction was fairly well refined. Since the printing press was invented, printed information has been held to a higher standard than "word of mouth". The process and expense of printing a newspaper was high enough that some care was taken to ensure that the information presented was accurate. Journalistic ethics was seen as a foundational element to a newspaper's success, in that it built the trust that made people buy it and use it as a knowledgeable source—and veracity of fact was the key to trust. Retraction of bad information was the norm and embarrassing enough to force major efforts to ensure accuracy. Stories and sources were always back checked and verified. Books, which cost even more to print and correct, were given an even higher level of review. The result was a world where information was referenced, cataloged, carried an ISBN, and printed by reputable news organizations. The resources needed to produce books, magazines, and newspapers meant that there were a limited number of authoritative sources of information.

Today, AI (After the Internet), anyone can write, publish, and disseminate a book, newspaper, blog, etc. electronically for the cost of a home computer system, iPad, or even a smartphone. Fact checking, referencing, and publishing corrections are still important to some authoritative sources, such as large publishers of books and newspapers, but there are a vast number of information sources which do not abide by the same standards. The great experiment is Wikipedia. Here, information can be changed, biased, and altered by anyone, yet many argue that the "wisdom of crowds" suffices—that when incorrect or biased information is detected rapidly by unbiased sources, it is quickly returned to a neutral state. Whether one believes the latter argument, the issue remains as to the rapidity in which bogus or biased information can be identified. Moreover, there is a dynamic that must not be overlooked; that we are writing history "on the fly," and in near real time. As one can find several examples where there is more than one history to almost any event, such a dynamic may well be problematic.

In this age of exploding information and data, how is one to sort the good from the bad? How does one measure trustworthiness or veracity on the

Internet? If a foreign (or domestic) actor were intentionally spreading biased information on the Internet, how would it be detected? To some degree, the vast scale of the Internet may mean that there is always someone out there who will detect bias and uncover the truth. This scale and complexity means that there are always dark corners where information can hide, for better or worse. But there is the potential for cyber technologies and weapons to prevent identification of misinformation or to squelch or discredit individuals who claim to find it.[19]

A clearly frightening alternative universe would be one where scientists have come to understand the phenomena of things going "viral" on the Internet. There are several academic research efforts in this area now, primarily in the areas of marketing, psychology and sociology. If one knew how to create an Internet "movement"; cause an idea, concept, or piece of information to go viral and spread across the Internet (and, therefore, the population of the modern world), how could this be used to affect popular opinion, the political system, or other areas? The fact that it would happen at astonishingly fast speeds is enough to cause one great concern.

Information, Influence, and the Corporation

The issue of the corporate world's participation in cyberspace is significant and multifaceted. Those corporations that have direct responsibility for the Internet have certain decisions ahead that include their responsibility to ensure access, as well as an individual's "rights," and what incentives are needed to balance security with shareholder value. Here, however, we want to discuss the corporations' role and potential actions that might contribute, or possibly detract, from the directions and ambitions of governments.

Regardless of the continuous discussion and planning for a "Cyber War," many corporations feel that they are already on the battlefield and that the Cyber War has begun within the economic environment. We continue to read about cyber attacks on corporations, especially leading to the theft of Intellectual Property (IP). As reported by Foreign Policy, General Keith Alexander, Director of the National Security Agency and Commander of Cyber Command, in an address to the American Enterprise Institute, stated that, "US companies lose about $250 billion per year through intellectual property theft, with another

---

19. Gregory Korte, "Misinformation Campaign Targets *USA TODAY* reporter, editor," *USA Today*, April 19, 2012, *http://www.usatoday.com/news/washington/story/2012-04-19/vanden-brook-locker-propaganda/54419654/1.*

$114 billion lost due to cyber crime, a number that rises to $338 billion when the costs of down time due to crime are taken into account." He declared this to be the, "greatest transfer of wealth in history."[20] And when your bottom line is the bottom line, such losses cannot go unheeded over time.

Moreover, the issue of influence weighs greatly within this "war" in that most large corporations have footprints in many countries and their relationships with foreign governments as well as their own are evolving. Author Thomas Friedman recounts a period in recent history when a significant amount of tension—and resulting nuclear "saber rattling"—was occurring between India and Pakistan. As Friedman's interviews indicate, the situation was quickly curtailed when a group of Indian business leaders went to the Indian Government and told them to quit because it was undermining their businesses and, thus the Indian economy. In this case, they argued, their business growth was based on trust and stability, and that such government actions negatively affected both.[21]

For the past few years, there has been a continuous "battle" between Google and the Chinese Government over censorship. A variety of "tit-for-tat" moves by both have resulted in Google's need to move its servers to Hong Kong, out of China's sensors reach, but with what could be continued retaliatory actions by Google to highlight, and ultimately influence, the Chinese Governments censorship policies and actions in order to further open up the Chinese market. One recent, albeit subtle, change in software, now warns users in China when they are likely to be kicked off or blocked from a site based on certain search terms or parameters.[22]

And as a corporation's influence and its technology increases, at what point might a corporation be in position to do a government's bidding? Today, cyber technology principally resides in the corporate sector. Although the US Government (principally NSA and Cyber Command) develop advanced tools and techniques, much of the underlying technology still comes from industry. Today, a large corporation under attack either can or soon will be able to utilize technology to "attribute" such attacks. The question is, then what? Today, US companies enlist the support of government to respond. Often times that response is more defensive in nature—identification of the

---

20. Josh Rogin, "NSA Chief: Cybercrime constitutes the 'greatest transfer of weath in history,'" *Foreign Policy*, July 9, 2012, *http://thecable.foreignpolicy.com/posts/2012/07/09/nsa_chief_cybercrime_constitutes_the_greatest_transfer_of_wealth_in_history.*

21. Friedman, *The World is Flat*, April 2005, p. 591-593.

22. Michael Wines, "Google to Alert Users to Chinese Censorship," *New York Times*, June 1, 2012.

source or the malware in order to attempt to fix the software vulnerability and prepare for the next attack. But at what point does a company take a more direct, offensive stance both to protect its resources and market share and, in some cases, our national security?

On March 16, 2011, Microsoft announced that it had successfully taken down the Win32/Rustock botnet. As described in a Microsoft Security Intelligence Report, Microsoft enlisted the support of other industry, academia, and the government (principally law enforcement) in the effort, which had started a year earlier. In 2010, Microsoft asked for, and received, a court order that allowed for the shut down a number of malicious domains, to include a John Doe lawsuit against the anonymous operators of the Rustock botnet. The court order included a seizure order, which allowed Microsoft staff, escorted by US Marshals, to physically capture evidence onsite, and take some of the infected servers from hosting providers for analysis. Additionally, with help from upstream providers, Microsoft successfully severed the IP addresses that controlled the botnet, cutting off communications and disabling it."[23]

As the level of corporate technology, access, influence, and alacrity increases, the Microsoft example brings about an interesting option. Might the United States again consider issuing 21st century Letters of Marque and Reprisal? A Letter of Marque and Reprisal is a commission granted by the government to a private individual (or in this case a corporation) to take the property of a foreign state, or of the citizen or subjects of such a state as a reparation for an injury committed by such a state, its citizens or subjects. Such an option, which is specifically called out in the Constitution and within the responsibilities of Congress, would create corporate privateers that, would have authority to take whatever actions necessary to protect our national security by identifying, locating, and neutralizing cyber threats on their own. The United States has used Letters of Marque and Reprisal before. In 1812, they were issued against Britain. The most recent example occurred in late 1941 and early 1942 right after the Japanese bombing of Pearl Harbor. In this case, the Goodyear Blimp *Resolute* was operated as an anti-submarine privateer based out of Los Angeles. It patrolled the seas for submarines armed with a rifle and a civilian crew.[24]

---

23. Microsoft Security Intelligence Report, Special Report, *Battling the Rustock Threat*, 2011.
24. Rendall Brown for the LTA Society, "A Brief History of the Wingfoot Lake Airship Base," *http://www.goodyearblimp.com/history/wingfoot.html*.

On first blush, taking such steps may seem irrational and not something the United States would do, especially when there must be consideration that other countries could do the same. But, what if persistent threats came from a private corporation or attacks came at a pace whereby our government structures simply could not keep up? Regardless of what we think today, threats like these must not be ignored and solutions like a Letter of Marque must not be foreclosed as an arrow in our national security quiver.

Unfortunately, the most near-term direct threat to our national security and to our livelihood from corporations may be open, direct, and legal. Creating a monopoly of access to the world's communications systems could provide a government access that it otherwise might not realize. Such is the concern related to China and two Chinese companies; Huawei Technologies Co., Ltd and ZTE Corporation. These two companies, since 2000, have successfully acquired or won service contracts that provide "pervasive access" to 80% of the world's telecommunications, according to recent reporting by WND.[25] According to the reporting, these two companies "give the Chinese remote electronic "backdoor" access through the equipment they have installed in telecommunications networks in 140 countries. These Chinese companies service 45 of the world's 50 largest telecom operators." If the reporting is true, a massive surveillance and access system for the Chinese may already be in place.

Anonymity and Privacy in the Information Age

Many assume that privacy is a right that our government should guarantee. Yet it is not mentioned in our constitution and is an interesting point of law. "The right of privacy is restricted to individuals who are in a place that a person would reasonably expect to be private (e.g., home, hotel room, telephone booth). There is no protection for information that either is a matter of public record or that is voluntarily disclosed in a public place. People should be protected by privacy when they "believe that the conversation is private and can not be heard by others who are acting in a lawful manner."[26]

Today many governments at multiple levels are installing cameras liberally across areas of their jurisdictions. The intent is to catch those who break the law or engage in activity that disturbs the peace. This includes the ability to

---

25. Michael Maloof, "China: 'Pervasive Access' to 80% of Telecoms," July 1, 2012, *WND*.
26. Am.Jur.2d *Telecommunications* § 209 (1974).

locate a potential "suspect" after a terrorist event to enforcement of traffic laws. Stores and malls are also installing cameras and surveillance equipment from the parking lots to the dressing rooms. Even modern offices are being equipped with cameras and monitoring equipment. Unmanned aircraft are increasingly being used to monitor our border as well as compliance with state and local laws. And the use of such vehicles is increasingly being debated.

It is becoming increasingly difficult to move through the modern world without coming under surveillance of some kind. In addition, as previously noted, our buying habits are tracked and analyzed via the myride of frequent buyer programs that we all sign up for (and sign away our rights concerning the use of this data).

It is said that modern frequent buyer programs are so good that most supermarkets produce specials and coupons for buyers specifically tailored to their buying habits. Is it really a mystery that you get a coupon printed out at the register upon check out for a grocery item that you often purchase, either for your next purchase or from a competitor's product in hope you will try it and switch? Is it really a mystery that you get in your mail a coupon or notice of an impending oil change need for your car? This data, combined with what is already available on the Internet on most people (phone numbers, addresses, schools attended, work history, etc.) is enough to provide a very clear and accurate view of those living in the modern world. Clearly there are places, in rural parts of the world where automation, the Internet, and modern communications systems have not penetrated. But most of the industrialized world is very "connected."

The effects of this on anonymity and privacy are obvious. If one chooses to live in and use the services of our modern world one will leave a set of fingerprints everywhere that clearly identify what one eats, where one travels, what one buys, and what entertainment he or she prefers. What modern automated profiling software can predict from this information is astounding.

But, most of us, whether we fully realize it or not, grant permission to these companies that are collecting and using this data when we sign up for the service, whether it is a frequent buyer program, credit card, or computer/iPad/iPhone app. We have granted one company access to one stream of data about us. When more than one company share this data, our rights to protect or hold private information about us is greatly compromised.

Few today seem bothered by these facts. Most take it for granted that the data is collected and used for the purposes of making the service better, which is often the case. Many like the fact that stores know what you want, Amazon and others direct you to books similar to those you bought before, and that credit card companies can spot suspicious behavior. Almost no one thinks about the use of this data for purposes other than those listed above.

The issue here is who is collecting and utilizing the information? In the United States, we take for granted that a retail merchant or other commercial business is doing this, in part, because we have granted them permission (again, whether we fully realize it or not). We are very much less inclined to grant that capability or authority to a government, especially the Federal Government. But what if there was an organized effort to use or borrow this data from these commercial entities to properly analyze the data so that we might be able to discover those who are plotting crimes before they were actually committed.

Such an effort was contemplated by the Defense Advanced Research Projects Agency (DARPA) in the early 2000s. It was called the Total Information Awareness (TIA) Program which, under Congressional review and highly charged, political media pressure was ultimately disbanded. The program sought to collect masses of financial and other data on the buying habits of as many as could be looked at. It was postulated that, just as credit card companies track fraudulent activity with this data, this system could identify and track the activities that were indicative of terrorists hiding in the United States.

In this case, a significant mitigating factor that played into the oversight calculus was that the Federal Government, and in this case specifically the Department of Defense, would be reviewing and analyzing its citizens' information, and thus, would be infringing on the citizens' rights to privacy. But in today's world, have we prevented ourselves from preventing the next major terrorist attack? At what price is freedom and privacy? And what is to prevent some other group that does not enjoy aggressive oversight, from building such a capability?

Today it is fair to conclude that anonymity and privacy in the information age, for those who chose to live in and partake of its benefits, are becoming increasingly difficult, if not impossible. Obviously, this trend could well lead to abuses that threaten the civil liberties we hold most valuable. But to stand on past precedent or ignore the impact that technology has made, only serves to ignore the reality of the new environment in which we live.

Conclusion

"Then you will know the truth and it will set you free."[27]

The impact of cyberspace and the tools that enable its use in today's world, has changed the landscape of life, and the development of doctrine will require a broader understanding of the ubiquitous nature of this technology.

In particular, we will need to rethink and/or revalidate the legal authorities that we have created in the past for the conduct of intelligence, defense, warfare, crime protection, and civil liberties protection. Cyber technologies provide capabilities and threats that require new and expanded ways of accomplishing all of these missions.

Might it be in our interest to consider a cyber doctrine for the United States that states that "any individual, country, or power that is intentionally biasing the free flow and content of information against our nation is committing an act of war"? Clearly the ideas that freedom of speech and information will set us free and keep us so, are inadequate. We also need a guarantee information is freely flowing, not altered, and that we have some way of telling the author and their agenda.

Finally, adapting to and managing a world that provides little anonymity and only modest privacy is clearly a new challenge for mankind. The full impacts and implications are difficult to understand and articulate at this point. Clearly, we are facing a world where all personal activities and actions (good and bad) will be available for all to view and judge. We are either facing a new reality where one can be "labeled" early in life and have little chance to change the label, or we will create a much more tolerant society than man has ever created before.

---

27. The Bible: John 8:32: ver 36.

CHAPTER 15

Report of the Conferees

The Battelle Doctrine Project included the commissioning of several papers as the foundation for studying aspects of a national doctrine for the cyber era. These papers were supplied to a selected group of individuals, who were then invited to discuss and debate these issues at The Founders Inn, Virginia Beach, Virginia, on June 7-10, 2012. At the close of their discussions, the participants of the conference reviewed as a group key points and a statement summarizing the robust debate. The statement represents general agreement, but not necessarily complete consensus. It does not represent the views of any institution with which participants are affiliated.

Why A New Doctrine?

Cyber is a dimension that not only touches governments, but also has become nearly indispensible to private industry and individuals around the globe. It is a place of science, education, influence, perception, and persuasion, and, especially, of commerce on an international scale that relies on the fundamental assumption that the means to conduct business and sustain an increasingly interconnected world population, the Internet, will always be at hand and functioning. For the United States, the challenges are especially pressing in that, more so than any other country, our reliance on the Internet has become so great that we have become one of the countries most vulnerable to abuse, theft, and attack. Well-directed, sustained, low-level cyber attacks—planned or unplanned—could result in significant damage to our existence as a viable world leader and a world economic power. One can postulate a time in the not-too-distant future when the Internet itself becomes our most critical infrastructure. The threats and challenges of the era of Containment were macro. The threats and challenges in the era of cyber are micro; they appear in our very homes, businesses, and governments.

A principal role of the United States Government, as stated from our Constitution, is to provide for the common defense. What is often overlooked is the second charge, to promote the general welfare of its citizenry. Rarely

245

does this responsibility loom as large as it does now in addressing our evolving reliance on the Internet for our future livelihood, and possibly existence of our societies, as we know them. We urge our government to respond to this second responsibility by developing and articulating a new national doctrine for the cyber era, a statement that describes national priorities and responsibilities for the use and protection of the Internet in peace and during conflict. Establishing a national doctrine is a role that the Federal Government can play well, and what it has done in at least eight cases since the founding of our country.

Today because of the pace of technology and its availability and acceptance worldwide, our policies and strategies are being relegated to statements that address symptoms or immediate problems encountered rather than setting forth a framework whereby government entities, businesses, and individuals can understand and share in their roles and responsibilities, collectively, in protecting our nation's Internet-based security. As is often the case with difficult issues, the debate has developed into an "either/or" approach between sharing information with the private sector and regulating that sector to enhance security. Moreover, while several individuals within government have been given "lead" roles for various aspects of cybersecurity, no one is truly in charge.

As General Michael Hayden, former Director of both the National Security Agency (NSA) and Central Intelligence Agency (CIA) said in a Strategic Studies Article in Spring 2011, "[r]arely has something been so important and so talked about with less clarity and less apparent understanding than this phenomenon." He further noted that he had been "unable (along with my colleagues) to decide on a course of action because we lacked a clear picture of the long term legal and policy implications of any decision we might make."[1]

We, in this conference forum, believe the cyber domain provides unique challenges for our nation that will increase in their complexity throughout this century. It is an entirely new dimension, without borders or boundaries, and the barriers for entry into the "club" are relatively low and do not apply just to nation-states. Cyber has no American Air Force, no British Navy, nor Russian Army controlling the field. Instead, it is populated by billions of computers and network appliances controlled by individuals, organizations, and Internet service providers. Its size and impact are expanding at a rapid rate

---

1.   Gen. Michael V. Hayden, USAF, Retired "The Future of Things 'Cyber,'" *Strategic Studies Quarterly,* Spring 2011

and it involves players ranging from nation-states, to non-nation-states like Al Qaeda, to "flash mob" entities like Anonymous, and to individuals.

In other domains, the human race principally has "tamed" the natural elements, utilizing man-made technology to effectively use each domain to man's advantage, while respecting some natural forces that simply cannot be avoided. Cyber, on the other hand, is a man-made domain that is principally managed by private entities and corporations. Its technological "natural elements" are constantly evolving at the pace of scientific and engineering innovation. And, due to its complexity, we do not yet understand the "natural forces" that are reflected in the Internet. The Internet was designed to be robust. Security, which was not a concern when it was designed, has become an overriding issue. We have observed incidences where actions or changes create significant unintended consequences. The pace of software technology development, and injection, suggests that there are few "constants", and that a level of ambiguity is a key "natural element".

The conference group noted that the United States faces a number of global challenges. Some are difficult to discuss because they highlight national shortcomings or are issues that are easily politicized. Others are difficult because they do not fit easily into comfortable conventional approaches or, in some cases, have no clear answers. Also today, since damage to or via the Internet is not seen to pose a threat that is equivalent to a significant kinetic attack or to constitute an immediate existential threat, it is easier to gradually ring the warning bells instead of formulating a realistic response, a situation similar to that existing on September 10, 2001. Although some of these harsh realities and uncomfortable truths will be explored further in this paper, it is important to identify the key truths at the outset.

- *The President must take the lead in articulating a national-level doctrine for the cyber era, building momentum for it, and implementing it. The issue is so overarching and significant that it cannot be relegated to a "coordinator" or "czar" who has the ear and direction of the President, but little actual authority or capability to effect change. Rather than looking at cybersecurity as another significant challenge among many, the President must consider that addressing the cyber domain is every bit as important, significant, and daunting as Britain's need to "rule the waves" in the 18th and 19th centuries, or our decision to view presence in the Western Hemisphere by European nations as impinging on our national security, resulting in the Monroe Doctrine.*

- *We are drowning in information and starving for wisdom. Decisions regarding cybersecurity today are driven more by hypothesis and anecdotes than by science, data, or facts. With a perceived need to show a responsive government combined with varying real-world threats, we are promulgating policies, strategies, authorities, legislation, and activities that are largely disconnected from reality. The fundamental decisions about who we (America) should be in this era are little debated and rarely being made on a strategic level.*

- *The threats we face today in the world—economically and militarily—are non-traditional, asymmetrical, and not necessarily obvious. If there is ultimately an existential threat to the United States via cyber means, it is likely to manifest itself in a "death by a thousand cuts" more so than a Cold War-like nuclear exchange. That, however, could change in the future. Although today the United States is believed to have better cyber "tools" at its disposal, other countries (and their businesses) are approaching the dynamics of influence via cyber with more alacrity, regardless of the sophistication of their "tools."*

- *Given the inherent complexity of the cyber dimension, the traditional constructs of nation-states and their influence may be blurred in the future. Even today, corporations may well have better access and more influence in certain countries than does our government. It also is becoming impossible to segregate civilian and military sectors due to the pervasive use of the Internet by the military.*

- *The security of our economy is now intrinsically linked to private companies. Re-tooling of the infrastructure by the government (as some have posited) will most likely fail in the contemporary political environment. Moreover, in the current economic environment, we do not have the funds to rebuild a network, let alone create an entirely new network.*

- *The United States Government's leadership role must change. Due to our reliance on the Internet and, thus, our vulnerability, there is clearly a need to lead on an overall national and international scale. That said, the Government must come to grips with a doctrinal implementation strategy that recognizes the dynamics of interacting with the civil and business sectors; in military parlance, knowing when to be the supporting or the supported command.*

- *From a military standpoint, cyber is currently not viewed as a stand-alone capability; rather it is expected be used in conjunction with other forms*

248

of warfare. As the sophistication of tools increases, this could change. A limitation on the use of cyber to retaliate is that attribution is very difficult to obtain. Attackers can use proxies to hide their origin since we do not have the experience to correctly predict collateral damage, this also constrains retaliation. From a strategic standpoint, counter/countermeasure parries in the nuclear arena were measured in years and decades. In the cyber age this is now calculated in minutes and seconds. That said, at least today, the cyber battle space does allow one crucial luxury to avoid escalation—time. This, however, requires that networks be resilient.

- *The private sector is not providing cybersecurity at an acceptable level, nor is it incentivized to do so. Cybersecurity cost money and, generally in the eyes of companies, there currently is not enough market demand to warrant the expenditure internally, or to pass it on to their customers. In times of national crisis, although one option might be to declare "marshal law" on companies composing our critical infrastructures, no one currently believes that the Federal Government can provide security at an acceptable level either. In all likelihood, incentives for companies to enhance cybersecurity to acceptable levels will come from incidences whereby clients lose trust in the company's ability to perform and to protect the client's information. Consequently, a requirement for "open disclosure" of information related to penetrations and attacks has, in some areas, been an effective incentive.*

- *In general, the American public is not attuned to the threats we face as a nation from cyber attacks. Although generally familiar with identity theft and media-reported intrusions of companies' databases, most Americans normally do not see the personal impact or potential effects and tend to trust in the information they receive either in emails or in Internet queries. If abuses of the Internet cause Americans to lose faith in information received via it, this could, over time erode the American democratic system. As, at its core, America is a country founded on self interest, it is incumbent upon the government to find the best way to influence and incentivize its citizens in a meaningful and personal way. A cyber civil defense should be an organizing principle.*

- *Because of the nature of the threats imposed within the cyber domain, a strong US Intelligence Community remains absolutely critical to our nation's security, especially when direct conflict may not occur. The use of counterintelligence, misdirection and other offensive operations will be crucial in determining the direction of the information age, and a savvy, agile community must be focused on motive and intent, with the ability to find individualized threats wherever they may reside.*

- *As a nation, we also tend to be reactive with our legislation. Consequently, we too often find ourselves "fighting the last war" legislatively, as we respond to national events or emergencies, even when looming issues may call for preemptive action. There are few lawyers within the Executive Branch who are willing to promote changes to our laws without significant justification; often found in the aftermath of a crisis. This was true after the terrorist attacks on September 11, 2001, and is true today. The introduction of the no borders/no boundaries activities that cyber technologies allow places significant pressure on our existing legislation and legislative processes that is yet to be realized. The cyber world effectively blurs our traditional legal tenets (that are based on location of event rather than point of origin), the separation between intelligence, military activities, and law enforcement, and the interactions between government and industry. Like other "hard problems" of this era, cyber issues cross the jurisdiction of several Congressional committees, making changes an invasion of each committee's existing authority. Both houses of Congress have worked hard to produce various pieces of legislation that address various aspects of current problems. Without judging the effectiveness and value of one piece of current pending legislation over another, what is needed is a truly holistic review and assessment of existing laws, and a subsequent legislative campaign to fully address the cyber challenges within the construct of a national-level doctrine. Legislation, policy, strategy and process must all come together within a framework if we are to be effective in protecting our national security. Finally, the pace of technology and subsequent decision making in the cyber era directly challenge our constitutional process of checks and balances, as our bodies of Congress are, by design, meant to be deliberative in a timeframe that was not foreseen by our founding fathers. Over the next decade, this may significantly increase the tensions between the Executive and Legislative Branches, more so than at any other time.*

- *It would be unfortunate if it took a cyber event akin to the bombing of Pearl Harbor or the terrorist attack on September 11, 2001, to effectively wake up the American government and its population to the constant, persistent, and significant threats they face, and to act with the same determination and sense of purpose as we did with our entry into World War II.*

Consequently, we believe, in the final analysis, it is incumbent on the government of the United States to act now to openly debate the issues and subsequently to articulate and implement a doctrine that leads our government, our businesses and our citizens safely into this brave new dimension of the 21st century. This is not an easy or simple task and it is made more difficult because the government cannot simply dictate our actions, but must delicately balance roles between government and industry and be flexible enough to adjust as situations rapidly evolve.

As with the development of the doctrine governing the nuclear age, the scientific and policy communities must help government in developing the thoughts and foundations of a doctrine considering the impact of cyber technologies. For this reason, Battelle began this project and will continue with this effort over the course of the next several months. The goal of this conference was not to emerge with a doctrine. Instead, the goals were to debate the issues that a doctrine should consider and to begin identifying a broad framework from which a doctrine might be developed.

Such a framework might begin with the following major points:

1. The United States views the Internet as a critical component of its national security, and wishes to enforce a secure and peaceful cyberspace.
2. In doing so, the United States will take the lead internationally in cooperation with, but not subject to, other nation-states' desires.
3. The United States Government, in cooperation with the private sector and individuals, will work to pursue a reasonable set of rules for safe use and development of cyberspace.
4. The United States will use all offensive and defensive means to protect its citizens and interests in cyberspace.
5. The government of the United States will work in cooperation with its academic and corporate sectors and citizens to establish a firm understanding of citizenship in the cyber age.

How We Structured the Conference

The conference was composed of both practitioners and laymen from government, business, and academia to provide the true breadth and scope of the current cyber situation. The discussions were aided by a series of papers commissioned for the conference and supplied to the participants in advance. These papers provided a robust background, including the nuances associated with very complex issues. The conference itself was then conducted in five plenary sessions:

1. Attribution and National Defense
2. Cold War Paradigms Revisited
3. Harsh Realities and Uncomfortable Truths
4. Roles and Responsibilities
5. A Framework of Doctrine

The goal was not to drive to consensus, but to ensure reasoned debate, exchange information, and viewpoints, and to come to general agreement on areas that a national-level doctrine must address.

What Is a National Doctrine?

The Merriam-Webster Dictionary definition of doctrine is quite simple: doctrine is "a statement of fundamental government policy especially in international relations". But in reality, it is more than that. A national doctrine represents our beliefs as a nation. It tells us: Who we are? What we are protecting and how? What we are not protecting? A national doctrine becomes the bedrock of all government national security actions and priorities. As national security expert, Frank Sempa, has noted, "a national security doctrine serves as a guide by which leaders conduct the foreign policy of a country."[2]

In other words, our diplomacy, our military, our intelligence gathering, and our law enforcement are best guided by a clearly articulated doctrine. A doctrine also informs and enlightens the American people providing them a "framework of understanding" about the challenges to their national security. It even allows them to take positive action, such as civil defense, to support a doctrine.

The military, for example, has been brilliant over the years in establishing military doctrine; how every aspect of activity, from concepts, to planning, to acquisition, to training, to deployment of forces, can be brought together in a cohesive fashion to achieve true "joint" war fighting operations, for example. With that, is the understanding that military deployment ultimately supports an overriding American national security doctrine.

---

2. Francis P. Sempa, "US National Security Doctrines Historically Viewed, A Commentary," http://www.unc.edu/depts/diplomat/archives_roll/2004_04-06/sempa_nsd/sempa_nsd.html.

The Value of American National Doctrines over Time

As Sempa has stated, "The evolution of (our) national security doctrines demonstrates that US policymakers repeatedly have reacted to immediate national security threats or challenges with far-sighted, long term but pragmatic doctrines that have helped them steer the ship-of-state through the troubled and uncertain waters of international politics."[3]

For instance, under the Monroe Doctrine in the mid-1800s, there were a number of equally powerful players attempting to gain dominance over a single, large area—the Western Hemisphere. In this case, the United States was not the dominant player, but was attempting to outline the rules of engagement with much larger nation-states with varying degrees of interest, including England, France, Spain, and the Netherlands. Although the United States did not have technological or numerical advantages over these nations, it publically declared the protection of the Western Hemisphere as part and parcel of its national security.

As we approached the mid-19th century, America also made clear to European powers, in the Doctrine of Manifest Destiny, that it would claim its rights and control over the middle portion of the North American continent—again, asserting its intent to lead the international arena rather than have someone else's will imposed upon it. It would do so through diplomatic and military actions over the next thirty years.

Within the twentieth century, we were guided by the Doctrine of Containment in the "Cold War." Promulgated by senior State Department official George Kennan in his 1947 "Long Telegram," and adopted by fifty years of United States leadership, America would not stand for the expansion of Communism beyond its current borders. Containment entailed a worldwide commitment of America's diplomatic and military resources, taking up the gauntlet of leadership of the world's democracies.

The Doctrine of Containment focused our resources—diplomatic, military, intelligence and even law enforcement—against a worldwide enemy who represented an existential threat to our survival. It focused our citizens on the danger they faced, and informed and hardened them to the decisions they needed to support at home to support success abroad. It allowed for argument over tactical execution in a framework that prevented the scattershot and unexamined to rule.

---

3.   *Ibid.*

Since the fall of the Soviet Union, the United States has been a reluctant world leader. From the overarching search for a "peace dividend" in the 1990s, we have sought out multilateral partners to engage in various international crises and troubles around the world in order to share responsibility, rather than portray ourselves as the sole superpower. Regardless of the pros and cons of multilateralism, as a result, we as a nation have not created a national-level doctrine that addresses the new realities of the twenty-first century nor our role in them. During the 1990s and continuing today, our strategies and policies have been more traditional and in reaction to world events, even as technology has quickly and profoundly altered our world environment.

As a result, nations such as Russia and China are re-emerging as peer competitors on the international stage. With continued adoption of cyber technologies and utilization of cyberspace, these and other nation-states, as well as non-nation-state actors, could eventually have the capacity and the ability to adjust balances of power politically within existing governments, economically, and militarily. Moreover, today's technologies, providing near-instantaneous interaction by individuals across the globe, enhance economic and personal freedoms to a point that has strained, and in some cases surpassed, government control. Given our reliance on these technologies for our nation's security, it is once again incumbent upon the United States to take a leadership role on an international scale.

Do Any Cold War Paradigms Translate?

As Dr. Joseph Nye, former Chairman of the National Intelligence Council (NIC) and former Dean of Harvard's John F. Kennedy School of Government, commented in a Winter 2011 Strategic Studies Quarterly article, "it would be a mistake to neglect the (nuclear lessons of) the past, so long as we remember metaphors and analogies are always imperfect. Nye quoted Mark Twain that "history never repeats itself, but sometimes it rhymes."[4]

As Nye implies, it is prudent to assess whether any of the Cold War paradigms translate to today's era. One of the most salient points of the Cold War was the eventual development of the ultimate existential threat—the total destruction of the United States and possibly the rest of the world. As the threat developed over time, it moved from one of a slow-rising threat over weeks and months to one that could take place in less than fifteen minutes.

---

4.   Joseph S. Nye, Jr., "Nuclear Lessons for Cyber Security?," *Strategic Studies Quarterly,* Winter 2011.

A current threat in cyberspace is far more relatable to the period of the 1940s and early 1950s, where the immediate threat was likely to be slower and more diverse in terms of action. However, by the late 1950s and early 1960s, the existential threat of total destruction became more of a reality, and although Containment itself was not changed as a doctrine, the underpinning strategies and tactics were reworked in order to address the new technological threat.

In the cyber world, we are currently dealing with less of an immediate existential threat, yet one that could take place over time—maybe even without our immediate knowledge. This threat could represent a "death by a thousand cuts" rather than one large, massive "industrial" strike, as was possible at the height of the Cold War. However, the cyber threat we are currently experiencing matches well with the Cold War period of 1946 through the early 1950s, prior to the buildup of a Soviet nuclear stockpile.

Cyber today, from a nation-state standpoint, represents one arrow in the quiver of military response. It can be used to blind and disrupt our military services, industrial base, and business sectors, and it also can be used in a covert way to undermine our ever-expanding knowledge bases and ever-expanding consumer-to-business sector. As with the period of the late 1940s, the United States Government today does not have a doctrine to deal with this space, and is inclined toward the use of tactics tactical strategies in an attempt to "answer the mail" during this period of time. This form of "answering the mail" has led to confusion within the government and the private sector, as well as misaligned resources, manpower, and spending.

As the Cold War developed, and both sides gained large nuclear stockpiles that could be delivered in a very short period of time, the concept of Mutually Assured Destruction (MAD) introduced the idea that the use of such weapons was unpalatable. This did two things: one was essentially to stop any potential use of nuclear weaponry, thus affecting both military and diplomatic tactics and strategies, and two was to create a hierarchy of tactical and strategic moves that both sides used against one another up to the level of a nuclear engagement. In an odd way, these provided leaders on both sides with a certain amount of flexibility in their response and prevented them from engaging in the kind of actions that would have led to precipitous disaster.

At the moment, MAD does not exist in the cyber domain. This is, in part, due to the nascent stage of the cyber world. It is also due to a lack of a doctrine, on our part, that explains how we intend to deal with challenges presented to us. One interesting aspect of the cyber world, which makes it like the world of chemical and biological weapons, is the potential for inadvertent blowback.

In fact, many believe that the nature of a cyber attack is more akin to the effects of a biological weapon. Although the results are not yet fully understood, media reporting suggests that the use of cyber weapons such as Stuxnet may have produced results unintended by the original attack, spreading far beyond the initial engagement.

We are still in the early stages of cyber world development, however, and cannot exclude the possibility that MAD may represent a responsible, indeed necessary, strategy going forward. What would constitute MAD in the cyber world is, as yet, unclear. For instance, would it be kinetic action involving conventional weapons in response to a Stuxnet-like attack? Could it involve a counter-Stuxnet-like attack? The situation lends itself to the development of a Herman Kahn "Ladder of Escalation" for the cyber world.

Attribution: Ambiguity as a Constant

During the Cold War, there was a certain amount of ambiguity in both the diplomatic and military areas of challenge between the United States and the Soviet Union. Each side engaged in varying levels of hiding and otherwise moving about their strategic and tactical nuclear weapons to promote their security. The finest example of this is the so-called "triad" of air, land, and sea platforms for delivery of nuclear weapons. Over the period of the Cold War, we developed a reasonably extensive and relatively effective set of detection systems that would help determine, with some precision, the development, location, and potential use of these weapons.

In the cyber era, this determination of the identity of the attacker and weapon is more difficult. Not unlike the initial period of the Cold War and the vastness of the Russian homeland, cyberspace allows for many places to hide. Additionally, unlike the Cold War, it also provides a strong level of anonymity. The complexity of cyberspace and its routers, addresses and other technologies represent a unique challenge for those seeking attribution. Today, this makes a response to a cyber act difficult and likely imprecise.

Continued Reliance on Intelligence

During the Cold War the United States developed a vast, extensive, and fairly precise intelligence system to root out motivation and understanding of the tactics and strategies of its enemies. Human Intelligence (HUMINT), in particular, was used as a way of determining not only motivation, but the understanding of potential strategic and tactical strategies in the minds of the Soviet leadership. In the cyber age, intelligence is faced with a far greater challenge. We are playing chess on multiple boards at multiple levels. We must not only understand motivations, intentions and capabilities of nation-states we also have to deal with non-nation-state players with a potentially vast international reach, including within our continental borders.

The Intelligence Community (IC) now must also understand motivations and capabilities of non-nation-state players as diverse as Anonymous, LulzSecs, and Al Qaeda. Given the ability to hide in the jungle of cyberspace, these non-nation-states are particularly dangerous, and require more granular collection of intelligence on a consistent basis. In particular, we find that human intelligence will likely remain the primary determinant of what we know about these enemies. This will require highly agile and technically trained HUMINT officers who thoroughly understand the aspects of cyberspace.

Retaliatory Equivalency

When dealing with the Soviet Union, a scientifically developed nation-state like us, with similar military, intelligence and diplomatic structures, was quickly able to establish a level of retaliatory equivalency. Both sides were aware that if someone took action X, response Y would take place. Neither side was prepared to engage in actions that would release full-scale retaliatory strike. Thus, when it came to retaliatory equivalency, we were in many ways one and the same with our Soviet adversaries.

In the cyber world, there are no rules. There is no version, yet, of retaliatory equivalency. We are still feeling our way toward that goal. The questions remain: should we treat a non-nation-state the same as a nation-state? The same as a cyber flash mob? Does an attack by a nation-state on America's cyber soil constitute an attack on the nation that deserves a military response? If so, would that response include the use of kinetic weapons, or would it be limited to a cyber or a diplomatic response?

As for non-nation-states, who have no defined territory, retaliatory equivalency could perhaps take place with the use of counter-cyber weapons, with the recognition that attribution is an ambiguous constant. We would also need to determine whether or not a non-nation-state attack would fall in the realm of a law enforcement counterattack. Would we attempt arrests unilaterally, or would we seek out the help of other nation-states? If so, would we need to establish some form of international laws regarding such behavior, or would they be tried under American law?

Preemption

The Doctrine of Containment in the Cold War provided the United States definition its world leadership. In that definition, we positioned ourselves not only as leaders of the free world, but also as seekers of peace. Despite the eventual production of fifty thousand-plus nuclear weapons, the United States made it an official strategic policy not to engage in first strike. The Soviet Union, in turn, said that they would not resort to a first strike strategy. Both sides, however, were willing to engage in preemptive strikes on more tactical levels.

The concept of preemption in the cyber world, with its multitude of players, is much more problematic. At this early stage of development, we are hampered by the ambiguity of the effects of cyber weapons, as evidenced by the supposed unintended effects on non-targeted nodes by Stuxnet (as media reporting suggests). Still, as the sophiscation of cyber weapons grows, the United States should not foreclose a cyber preemptive option.

Civil Defense

In the 1950s and 60s, with the knowledge that the entire nation was under threat of imminent nuclear strike, the government sensitized the public to the need for Civil Defense and to their roles and responsibilities therein. This reflected the American experience of national threat during World War II and was embraced wholeheartedly by the American population from the 1940s through the early 1970s. The system was premised on providing resiliency in a post-nuclear exchange period. Because of this, the American populace had a feeling of ownership of their nation's security.

The United States in the cyber period has yet to sensitize or rally the population around the roles and responsibilities of individuals in their nation's cybersecurity. With an American populace twice the size of the 1950s and far more diverse in background, the concept of cyber civil defense is more difficult. Still, America should develop some form of cyber civil defense that will rally a public to action. Given our vulnerabilities and the many vectors available to exploit them, the stakes are surely as high.

Arms Control and International Norms

The United States and Soviet Union, over a fifty-year period of time, developed an intricate set of international norms and arms control negotiations, agreements, and treaties governing their diplomatic and military behavior. These covered various weapons, from conventional forces to intercontinental ballistic missiles, and included bans on the proliferation of these technologies. The idea was to maintain some form of equal balance between the two nation-states, to increase transparency and confidence aimed at ensuring the nuclear weapons would not be used, and, ultimately, to decrease the arsenals on each side.

Given the number and diversity of players within cyberspace, the establishment of norms and "arms control" options are far more difficult and, due to the ambiguity of the cyber domain, may not be necessarily advantageous to the United States. Unlike the period at the end of the Cold War where the impact of each side's nuclear arsenals were roughly equivalent, the United States seemingly holds a technological advantage over most, if not all, countries that intend inclusion of cyber weapons in their military arsenals. Thus, there could be scenarios whereby norms and agreements could put us at a strategic disadvantage. Although there likely is value in exploring multilateral talks and agreements, without a stated doctrine governing the goals the United States seeks to achieve, it can ensure neither the viability nor the advantage of such agreements at this point.

Roles of Government, Academia, Business and the Individual

From the end of World War II to the end of the Soviet Union, the United States Government directed doctrine, strategy and tactics at all levels to deal with the Cold War. The government also, in large part, directed the research and development of technologies specifically slated toward our national security, both internal to the government and with business and academic partners. As importantly, the United States Government led the free world in implementing the Doctrine of Containment.

Although the private sector composed two-thirds of the United States economy, it was expected to, and did, work closely with the United States Government on all issues affecting national security. Indeed, businesses were willing partners with the government in development of technologies—often paid for by the government. They cooperated with Federal law enforcement authorities in ensuring that their efforts in developing Federal projects were secure. Businesses viewed these responses as part of their patriotic duty to the government and people of the United States. During this period, innovation was both driven and developed by the United States Government to meet the Cold War threat. In today's cyber age, the opposite is true. Private industry tends to lead in terms of developing new and different technologies, which in turn are adopted (albeit, arguably, at a snail's pace) by the Federal

Government. For private industry, the consumer market largely tends to drive technology development, rather than government security needs.

The individual during the Cold War, though not often having a direct role, embraced their participation as American citizens in the defense of their country. This meant active participation in civil defense, support of United States strategy and tactics overseas, and the willingness to allow more law enforcement capabilities within the United States. That said, from the beginning of the Cold War to its end, the involvement and the attention of the American public waned. The government was seen as the protector and the individual's personal role and responsibility diminished.

In the cyber era, the ready access to advanced technologies places responsibilities on the individual citizen that have not yet been realized. A growing sense of individualism combined with a lack of shared purpose with the government, makes cybersecurity and defense more difficult and, seemingly less consequential today.

Information, Speed, and Gratification

The 1940s through the 1990s saw a sharp rise in the ability of mankind to communicate and travel across nation-state borders. This exchange led to an unprecedented increase in volume of information received by individuals across the planet. For some nations (especially those whose governments are non-democratic) control over information and content, as well as the speed with which that information provided, was of paramount importance. Especially in the Soviet Union, people were forced and then conditioned by their government to repress immediate gratification of their private needs in lieu of the needs of the state. For the United States, whose generations lived in a society based on the shared experiences from World War II, the spread of information, enshrined in the First Admendment, continued to be seen as advantageous to all, while still sharing a sense of shared responsibility with our government regarding our security. Consequently, immediate gratification was less of a factor.

In the early twenty-first century, with advanced search engines, "smart" mobile devices, and access to seemingly unending volumes of information, the trend toward immediacy has simply skyrocketed. We are filled with information and starved for wisdom. A nation-state's ability to react to information in a timely manner has simply been overwhelmed. Non-nation-state players are becoming more agile in their ability to put out information. Today, social networks are every bit as powerful as a designed, state-sponsored propaganda or public diplomacy campaign. This immediate gratification makes it increasingly difficult for nation-state governments to lead their people without being able to clearly articulate the advantage to their individual citizens.

The Players Today

Our Government

The government of the United States came into its own during the mid-twentieth century. A product of World War II and the Cold War, it compartmentalized activities by function. Individual agencies and departments were responsible for specific matters of national and international interest. Although they operated within the framework of a single doctrine, they each had individual, and relatively clear-cut, responsibilities and different capabilities to carry out their respective missions. For example, the State Department was responsible for diplomacy; the Department of Defense (DoD) was responsible for employment of military capabilities.

Of specific note was the creation of the Office of Strategic Services (OSS), and later the Central Intelligence Agency (CIA), that established a formal government intelligence apparatus. Due to our foundational fear of government intrusion in our personal lives, combined with concern not to repeat the Nazi example of a Gestapo-like function, we crafted rules, regulations, and laws that provided specific and separate authorities to intelligence, law enforcement, and DoD organizations and military services. Although there was overlap and friction between these elements of our national security structure, prior to the information age, the "lanes in the road" were understood and we became comfortable with them.

At the end of the Cold War, the United States became a reluctant leader internationally and attempted to pull back from being a sole superpower, relying instead on consistent multinational, shared leadership and responsibility approaches for security on an international front. Unconstrained by the previous geopolitical structure, several regional incidences quickly placed the military at the forefront of foreign policy, often including diplomatic as well as military actions. Regional commanders-in-chief were thrust into positions akin to Roman proconsuls, with concerns and interactions in their areas of responsibilities that were well beyond military readiness and defense. Moreover, technological advancement in kinetic weaponry further refined our ability to engage in "sanitary" military actions. We could launch a cruise missile to make a diplomatic point.

Given the success of America in the Cold War, we have in the cyber era continued to rely on the technical prowess of the DoD in cyberspace. This has put the DoD in the position of being the lead component in "providing for the common defense" in cyberspace. As cyberspace leads into both business and individual lives, the traditional lines between the military, law enforcement, and intelligence are blurring, presenting legal and, potentially, constitutional issues.

At the same time, we searched for a "peace dividend," deciding to significantly scale back our military and intelligence resources in the belief that there was no peer competitor nor major national security threat. As a result, we were generally ill-equipped and ill-prepared for dealing with the assumptive threat of terrorism in such a fashion that would have prevented the actions on September 11, 2001. Moreover, the terrorists effectively utilized the segregation of responsibilities of our government structures against us.

As we enter the twenty-first century, however, this "staff and line chart government" seems increasingly unable and ill-suited to effectively deal with twenty-first century cross-border problems, such as cyberspace. As a consequence, the Federal Government has difficulties responding to cyber threats because of the numerous agencies involved with the process and their numerous jurisdictionsional interests.

Moreover, given the state of the economy today, there is now serious discussion of deeply cutting government spending, especially within defense. Although the rationales in reducing government spending today are different from those of the early 1990s, without careful consideration, the effects on our security could be the same, especially considering the overwhelming need for sustained intelligence capabilities and the increasing number of threats that are developing in cyberspace. In this era of austerity, the United States Government must seek cooperation of the academic and private sectors and individuals to help deal with the increasingly difficult issues in cyberspace. Effective use of academia and businesses will provide the United States Government a force multiplier for its limited resources. The issue is how best to engage.

Government regulation of business from the New Deal onward has been fairly extensive. Generally, business was willing to accept government as the senior partner, in areas related to national security. Today, business is now dominated by Internet-related companies far less willing to accept government regulation. The Internet itself was founded on the ethos of minimal restrictions and no regulations. Today, Internet entrepreneurs believe their proven success would be hampered by government regulation. Additionally, the rules of the road have changed for governance in the private sector, because it has become increasingly hard to tell which companies are "American" and which "international."

The pace of technological change and decision making is also a key factor in the government's inability to cope. In the cyber world, this means an amazingly fast speed of change. New technologies and new systems develop within months, and those capitalizing on the cyber capabilities have adopted a Moore's Law pace to their operations and acquisition models. For example, the use of the Internet for commercial purposes was virtually nonexistent in the late 1990s; today, it's a virtual cornerstone of most American businesses; each with a website and an ability to purvey goods online anywhere in the world.

On October 1, 2011, Google head Eric Schmidt noted in comments to the *Washington Post*, that given the slow speed of government reaction to change versus Silicon Valley, cyberspace can literally be nine times faster in its decision making than the US Government. In all, this means that the US Government as currently constructed is in a difficult position to deal with the massive and swift changes in cyberspace.[5]

Business—Self-protection and Regulation

Because technology and control of cyberspace rest largely in the hands of business, business is assuming a much more significant role in policy and international governance, akin to the period where Lloyd's of London significantly controlled the interests of Britain through insuring the shipping industry. As a result, it would seem incumbent upon business to seek out constructive avenues of cooperation with government, taking into account national security considerations alongside the need of business to serve its shareholders.

Business (whether a multinational corporation or a "mom-and-pop" store doing business extensively on the Internet), however, is oriented towards successful engagement in the marketplace. The private sector has reservations about government involvement: it feels the government doesn't understand the marketplace and that its motives are different. Although the government seeks to address concerns of the whole nation, the private sector is principally responsible to its own concerns and those of its shareholders. The two

---

5.   "Google's Eric Schmidt Expands on His Senate Testimony," *Washington Post*, 1 October, 2011, Lillian Cunningham (reporter).

actors, accordingly, see the problem through their respective lenses. Business fears that government regulation only encourages compliance-based security rather than technical-based security. This is important when an assessment emerges that government and its regulations cannot keep pace with technological change.

Government has few levers that allow it to guide business, especially when dealing with non-US companies. Government believes regulation is needed; private sector wants expanded dialogue. At the end of the day, this is not a question of either information sharing or regulation: both are necessary to ensure sound cybersecurity.

The Individual's Role

The individual citizen of the United States, although he or she may be cyber savvy, has yet to develop a sense of shared responsibility with government. The Internet has gone from being a novelty to almost a necessity in less than a decade, becoming the means by which people communicate with friends, do business, do their banking, and do their shopping. They are, however, almost universally unaware of the depth of the potential vulnerabilities on the Internet in relation to our nation's security. Few are aware of the level of security that is needed on their own access points. Fewer still are aware that one can be unknowingly "used" on the Internet, with their computers serving others' means and purposes.

Across generations, an expectation of government's benign presence on the Internet is widespread. In many respects, cyberspace has now become a utility. At the same time, an era in which the Internet is our critical infrastructure is foreseeable. Those who came of age in the early 2000s view the Internet as a place of individual freedom, unlimited access to free information, and as a normal extension of daily life. In short, for many, the Internet is a blind item of many positives and few negatives.

Roles in a Cyber Era: The Shifting Spectrum of Responsibilities

The Federal Government

The Executive Branch: More than any of the three branches of government; it is incumbent upon the Executive Branch to set the course for the development of American doctrine in cyberspace. In addition, it must set the tone for the relationship of government, academia, business, and individuals within the context of national cybersecurity. Moreover, the Executive Branch must clearly articulate the doctrine publically and ensure that the strategies and activities of the government, nationally and internationally, drive toward meeting the objectives of the stated doctrine. It is critical that the Executive Branch review existing laws and regulations to ensure that the stated doctrine can be executed and that the government can function to its maximum capability within the cyber arena. This may mean a fundamental re-thinking of previously legislated parameters such as, for example, United States Code, Title 10 and Title 50, that may no longer apply to a twenty-first century cyber world.

One of the most difficult challenges for the Executive Branch is to be understanding and agile enough to know when and how to deal with business in a lead role or a supporting role. At times, the US Government must rely on businesses, such as those in the Defense Industrial Base (DIB), to take the lead in national security. At other times, government must lead, especially in times of national crisis. However, at all times national security is the responsibility of the US Government. The obvious "wild card" is the fact that many US Companies are multinational and all not domestic institutions. This makes government's relationship to those businesses that are "United States" companies a critical factor in our security.

Too much of the current debate rests on the false choice of regulation versus information sharing. Some believe that setting cybersecurity standards ensures greater security, while information sharing of any consequence jeopardizes tenuous cyber tools and technologies that, once released, will allow a would be attacker to understand how they have been detected and to design around that collection capability and to build different capabilities to penetrate American cyber defenses. Others encourage a more open and constructive dialogue between business and government, so threats can be evaluated against security systems and a more robust cost benefit analysis of steps that need to be taken can be accomplished. Business believes that regulation results in a "compliance" mentality by both those being regulated and those regulating, and that this would inhibit the agility and ability of business to keep pace with the technologies for attack and defense. The problem is that both sides are right and a debate between these points does not enhance our security. Both sides must seek balance and work together to a common purpose that a national doctrine can provide.

One additional factor that government must consider is that the principal developers and stewards of cyber technologies are companies that have an increasing level of worldwide presence and influence. In this development, American companies—especially those within the defense industry—have become specific targets of penetration, exploitation, and theft of sensitive materials and intellectual property. Those "attacking" these companies range from hackers to foreign governments. In many cases today, these companies are significantly advancing their ability to understand information on the attackers and are increasingly developing capabilities to respond. In the future, as threats increase, should government utilize a company's capabilities differently to do its bidding? Is it possible that some day the government would consider issuing Letters of Marque and Reprisal?

The Legislative Branch: It is incumbent upon Congressional Leadership to reach out to the public and the Executive Branch to put together sensible and effective laws that can provide security to the cyber world while ensuring access to that cyber world. At this juncture it is critical that this be done within the overall framework of a national doctrine, rather than engaging in interest-dominated legislation. The Legislative Branch, the Executive Branch, and the business community must come together to create laws and regulations that enhance America's cybersecurity and support its cyber doctrine. Again, a holistic approach to review and identify laws that may be problematic in protecting our interests might be a good first step, albeit one that is not simple. Although leery of commissions, we believe that representation from all three branches of government and business would be valuable to such a process. The group noted that changing laws is not something to be done without careful consideration; likewise, this is not best done in the heat of the aftermath of a crisis, when government writ large feels compelled to act to show the public that it is responsive. Nor is this a simple or quick process. Debate is critical and compromise and balance are necessary. To be effective to our nation's security in a cyber era, there must be an understanding of our overarching goals—as expressed in a doctrine—with debate and action to that end. Though well meaning, current legislative efforts address symptoms more so than underlying national security objectives.

The Judicial Branch: The judiciary operates best when operating on precedent. Unfortunately, the cyber era—complete with its built-in ambiguity—potentially creates precedent at a rapid rate. Like the Executive and Legislative Branches, it is also incumbent upon the judiciary to obtain a greater understanding of this increasingly complex domain and to look at an effective role of engagement with the other Branches during and throughout the process to ensure that our overall objectives are achieved without undercutting our constitutional ideals.

State and Local Governments: Along with the three branches of the Federal Government in the American Constitution, the Founding Fathers wrote extensively about the rights and responsibilities of local authorities. After the terrorist attacks of September 11, 2001, the Executive Branch took great pains to assess State and Local responsibilities for security, as opposed to those of the Federal Government. The roles and responsibilities of State and Local Governments have evolved, due to the nature of the terrorist threat, resulting in a more dynamic interaction of State and Local Governments in our national security process. One example is the evolving role of the New York City Police Department and its view of its responsibility to protect the city, vis a vis Federal responsibilities to counter terror. Especially in a cyber era, these lines continue to blur, and it is incumbent upon State and Local authorities to work with the Executive Branch to definitively address the roles and responsibilities of each in carrying out our national doctrine.

Business: American businesses must acknowledge and participate in the execution of a national doctrine. Understanding that the incentives for security will often differ between business and government, in carrying out a national doctrine it is equally incumbent upon business to find better avenues for communication and cooperation with the Federal Government. Equally important is business's role in jointly pursuing legislation and regulations that effectively allow for the execution of doctrine. Business's role may well be most significant on an international scale, and must presuppose some responsibility for our overall national interest.

Academia: The academic and public policy communities need to apply their considerable energy and skills to develop the technical and policy-based knowledge, techniques and general understanding of options that can help governments to formulate a national doctrine. Academic computer scientists explore methods of violating computer security and disrupting networks as well as techniques to better protect both. Historically, useful and relevant academic research has been translated into products. It follows that effective communication between academia and business needs to be encouraged. Policy formulation in the cyber arena is best done with the participation of computer scientists. At times the latter can help find technical solutions to difficult policy questions and to anticipate issues that will need policy solutions. Academics were key players in science diplomacy in the nuclear age, building trust between nations. Today, American think-tank scholars, employees of ISPs, and academic computer scientists all maintain contacts with their international counterparts. Collectively they build a basis for trust for government-to-government contact.

Our Educational System: In the Cold War era, the American educational system was included as part of the public outreach by the Federal Government, as it explained the importance of the citizen in national security. The teaching of civics—putting into context America's role in the world and an individual's rights and responsibilities from and to the government to bolster that role—was part and parcel of our upbringing. Over the intervening years, that connection has been lost. In the cyber era, it once again needs to be addressed. Our educational system, in cooperation with our Federal, State, and Local authorities, must devise an educational program that addresses cyber safety and how the young people of America can best conduct themselves in cyberspace. This outreach is crucial because the most prolific users of the Internet are people between the ages of 10 and 18. They are often the most vulnerable to criminals and other predators. They are, however, also the most educable part of our citizenry. The young people of America need to be taught about cybersecurity and to understand their role through cyber in protecting our national defense.

There are today, gaps in understanding technology, security, and civic responsibility. In the cyber era, this is important not only as a matter of security, but also to ensure that America's lead in understanding and developing cyber-related technologies can be maintained, as well as our economic process. In many countries today, basic typing and programming begins in elementary school and the availability of Internet access is nearly universal and seen as a distinct advantage for future generations, as well as for a nation's security. The United States appears woefully behind in our ability to provide access, priority, and understanding of both technical capability and civic responsibility for the next generations that will inherit the environment established by this national doctrine. The responsibility for supplying cyber education is jointly held by Federal, state and local governments, regardless of the broader context of educational policy. Cyber education must be a national priority.

Individual Responsibility: As part of their duty as citizens, Americans must understand that, as the Internet and our reliance on it continues to expand, protection of that Internet and also of our security lies in each of their hands.

In this age, Americans have become increasingly diverse and scattered in their interests and support. We have not had, since the terrorist attacks on September 11, 2001, a defining national event that has caused people to come together on any given issue. Cyber civil defense may be that issue. Almost every citizen engages the Internet every day. We must tap into that precious resource.

Historically, placing national-level interests ahead of individual pursuits has not been foreign to us. Well-articulated national-level campaigns such as "Only You Can Prevent Forest Fires," captured the American psyche by registering the individual gain to the common good. This has been effective in a variety of social and national security situations in our history. For instance, an issue once confined to the shadows and the backs of milk cartons, has been brought into the daily news, highway signs, and phone numbers to contact authorities, in the form of Amber Alerts, resulting in many successes. A version of this "See Something, Say something" policy must be considered part of your duty as a citizen of the United States. Cybersecurity cannot be the purview of Federal, State and Local Governments alone.

And the message must be addressable to multiple generations that do not have shared experiences like World War II. Our deliberations were enhanced by inclusion of nine graduate students who were invited to attend as rapporteurs. We took the occasion to invite them to speak as a group during one of our plenary sessions. These are citizens who have come of age in a cyber world, and their views were instructive. Generally, they see the Internet as a given. Most are very cognizant of the need for individual security measures as necessary to protect their individual information, but are generally not aware, or concerned, about broader, national-level security issues. Most see a role for government in protecting the Internet, but not at an individual level. "I want government not to intrude in my life, but to save me in a disaster," seemed to sum up a general belief. These individuals were strident in their views on free access to information, music, movies, etc., expressing rights but also acknowledging responsibilities to artists, for example. Some had "hackers" as friends, and did not view them as necessarily malicious. Several expressed concern related to the American education system regarding its ability to keep up in a cyber world, or to best prepare individuals to compete and thrive in this era, especially when compared to other nations. These bright, energetic citizens expressed a broader appreciation, because of the conference, of the issues involved in national-level cybersecurity and the importance of having a doctrine to provide a framework in which to work. Some also acknowledged that this would not occur to their friends, and likely not to their parents.

The Role of the President

Leadership and the Bully Pulpit

The President of the United States is the key player in the United States Government effort to protect America in cyberspace. There are no substitutes; no czar that can adequately articulate the national doctrine, nor engender and inspire the government, businesses, and citizens in achieving our doctrinal goals. The President is the only one to be elected by the whole nation, and the bully pulpit is his alone.

In previous eras, various Presidents, beginning with Washington, have set, led, and guided our doctrine. Overseas, the President and his appointed representatives are the government and people of the United States. Only the President can make treaties or commit to military action, with or against other nation-states. Along with those legal responsibilities, it is crucial that the President sets the tone of any effort, to show that he is willing to invest both time and political capital.

A national-level doctrine that encompasses the cyber era must be more than a policy or a strategy. Presidential leadership cannot be replaced by the individual responsibility of cabinet departments and agencies for the creation and support of an American "cyber" doctrine. A national level doctrine must transcend an Administration's policies and an Administration's strategies that execute that doctrine. For instance, Containment was maintained for nearly fifty years across eight different Presidencies. In that period, each President put forth strategies and tactics that he believed fit the current situation, but that were universally framed by the same doctrine. We must expect the same of all current and future presidents in the cyber arena.

Attributes of the Doctrine

History shows that enduring national-level doctrines are the product not of the Government alone, but also of those who understand the depth and implications of a given issue as well as, in many cases, sustained national-level debate. For example, simultaneous with the development by scholars and policy makers of the containment doctrine were the development of the theories and principles that postulated the use of nuclear technology and our diplomatic strategies that ultimately fed the development of Containment. These attributes of nuclear technology were not developed within government, but instead were developed by the scientists who were most familiar with the technology and best understood the potential implications of its use. Similarly, today it is incumbent upon scientists, engineers, and practitioners of cyber technology together with political scientists, economists, and social scientists to collectively develop the theories and principles that will lead to a national doctrine for the cyber era. It is for this reason that this project was begun, and that the conference attendees participated. This is very much a work in progress. That said, the participants have identified a broad framework from which a doctrine might be developed, which is described below.

1. The United States views the Internet as a critical component of its national security, and wishes to enforce a secure and peaceful cyberspace.
2. In doing so, the United States will take the lead internationally in cooperation with, but not subject to, other nation-states' desires.
3. The United States government, in cooperation with the private sector and individuals, will work to pursue a reasonable set of rules for safe use and development of cyberspace.
4. The United States will use all offensive and defensive means to protect its citizens and interests in cyberspace.
5. The government of the United States will work in cooperation with its academic and corporate sectors and citizens to establish a firm understanding of citizenship in the cyber age.

Battelle will continue with this effort over the next several months and looks forward to working with this and future Administrations in developing a doctrine that will endure for the betterment of mankind; one of Battelle's founding principles.

Conference Participants

CARRIE BACHNER
National Security Solutions
Chief Executive Officer
Mission Concepts
Alexandria, VA

RADM JAMIE BARNETT, USN (RET)
Senior Vice President
Potomac Institute of Policy Studies
Arlington, VA

**CASEY BASSETT
Institute of World Politics
Master's in Strategic Intelligence
Studies

DR. JAMES G. BELLINGHAM
Chief Technologist
Monterey Bay Aquarium Research
Institute
Moss Landing, CA

**AMY BHATIA
Virginia Tech
B.S. in Electrical Engineering
(magna cum laude 2012)

+SHARON L. CARDASH
Associate Director
Homeland Security Policy Institute
The George Washington University
Washington, DC

**PATRICK CHEETHAM
Research Assistant
Potomac Institute for Policy Studies
Arlington, VA

**JIEUN (IVY) CHOI
Virginia Tech
B.S. in Psychology

SHELBY COFFEY III
Vice Chair/Newseum
Senior Fellow/Freedom Forum
Newseum

DAVID FISHER
Vice President and Director
Battelle Cyber Innovations Unit
Battelle Memorial Institute
National Security Global Business
Arlington, VA

HONORABLE GEORGE W.
FORESMAN
Former Under Secretary of
Homeland Security
Charlottesville, VA

+RANDALL M. FORT
Director of Programs Security
Engineering, Technology and Mission
Assurance
Raytheon
Arlington, VA

ROBERT J. GIESLER
Special Advisory
Applied Physics Laboratory
John Hopkins University
Laurel, MD

JAMIL JAFFER
House Permanent Select Committee
on Intelligence
Washington, DC

**ADAM HUMAYUN
The George Washington University
B.A. in International Affairs,
Concentration in Conflict and
Security

**J. CUSHMAN LAURENT
Institute of World Politics
M.A. in Statecraft and National
Security Affairs,
Specialized in Intelligence

**KATERINA (KATYA) MARGOLIN
Lewis and Clark College
B.A. in International Relations

+RONALD A. MARKS
President
Intelligence Enterprises, LLC
Washington, DC

PHIL MCKINNEY
President and Chief Executive Officer
Cable Labs
Washington, DC

HONORABLE ALDEN V. MUNSON JR.
Senior Fellow and Member,
Board of Regents
Potomac Institute for Policy Studies
Arlington, VA

**JACK NELSON
Miami University of Ohio
 B.A. in International Studies

JOHN NELSON
President and Chief Executive Officer
Zeta Associates, Inc.
Fairfax, VA

**TRAVIS RUMANS
Project Manager
The Institute of World Politics
Washington, DC

EDWARD D. NEUMEIER
Screen Writer
Pasadena, CA

+BARRY PAVEL
Director and Arnold Kanter Chair
The Brent Scowcroft Center on
International Security
Atlantic Council
Washington, DC

STEPHEN L. PETRANEK
Editor in Chief
Weider History Group
Leesburg, VA

ELIZABETH (BETSY) PHILLIPS
President
Old Town Creek Consulting
Washington, DC

BGEN DAVID G. REIST, USMC (RET)
Vice President of Strategy and
Planning
Potomac Institute for Policy Studies
Arlington, VA

+ALFRED ROLINGTON
Consultant
E-Side Publishing
UK

CHRISTOPHER J. ROULAND
Chief Executive Officer
Endgames
Chantilly, VA

THOMAS J. SACKIE
Chief Executive Officer and Principal
The LaConia Group
Reston, VA

+TIMOTHY R. SAMPLE
Vice President, Special Programs
Battelle Memorial Institute
National Security Global Business
Arlington, VA

JOHN SAVAGE
Ang Wang Professor
Department of Computer Science
Brown University
Providence, RI

ALEX SORIN
Special Assistant- Deputy Program
Manager
Edge 360
Herndon, VA

+MICHAEL S. SWETNAM
Chief Executive Officer and
Chairman
Potomac Institute for Policy Studies
Arlington, VA

MICHELLE VAN CLEAVE
Jack Kemp Foundation
Washington, DC

+RICHARD WEITZ, PH.D.
 Senior Fellow and Director,
Center for Political-Military Analysis
Hudson Institute
Washington, DC

LINTON WELLS II, Ph.D.
Director, Center for Technology
and National Security Policy
National Defense University
Washington, DC

**AMANDA WILLIAMS
Institute of World Politics
M.A. in Strategic Intelligence Studies

+KATHRYN SCHILLER WURSTER
Chief of Staff
Potomac Institute for Policy Studies
Arlington, VA

+Contributors
** Rapporteur

About Battelle

Battelle has been advancing scientific discovery and application for more than 80 years. Today, it is the world's largest independent

Battelle

research and development organization, providing innovative solutions to a variety of industry and government clients and partners. Headquartered in Columbus Ohio, Battelle is a charitable trust organized as a Section 501(c)(3), non-profit corporation.

Steel industrialist Gordon Battelle provided for the Battelle Memorial Institute in his 1923 last will and testament after a career devoted to the idea that science and research can solve problems in business and society as a whole. His vision became the Institute's mission when it opened its doors six years later. Today, Battelle's shared values are founded on the belief that superior business performance and high ethical and community standards can go hand-in-hand.

Clients appreciate our independent, candid and innovative approach to solving problems. Employees value our commitment to diversity, professional development and the notion of unity without uniformity. And the communities we live and work in benefit from our philanthropic and volunteer activities. Throughout Battelle and our people is a belief that no business objective is worth achieving at the expense of our integrity and ethics.

Battelle actively supports educational initiatives nation-wide that measure student achievement, assists with professional development for teachers, and promotes inquiry-based learning, especially in the science, technology, engineering, and mathematics (STEM) disciplines.

About Battelle's Cyber Innovation Unit

Battelle's Cyber Innovation Unit is a transformational business unit in Battelle's National Security Global Business. The Cyber Innovation Unit brings a new dimension of scientific engagement and client focus to cyber challenges in both commercial and governmental sectors.

Battelle offers a full-range of capabilities aimed at meeting the current and future needs of our customers. To truly address most cyber threats, we believe you must take a "silicon to satellite" approach to the problem and have depth from the hardware in a device, through the applications that run on them. We take a multi-disciplinary approach to our solutions and are focused in three areas:

- Cybersecurity
- Cyber Operations
- Mobile and Embedded Systems

The challenges we face are larger than any one organization can address on its own. With this as a core premise, Battelle has developed and follows a "Connect & Innovate" model for advancing the research, development and operational deployment of solutions to address the rapidly growing and vast array of cyber threats we face. To that end, we are focused by design on how we partner in a mutually beneficial way with industry, academia and government to make more rapid advancements than any one organization can on its own.

About Potomac Institute for Policy Studies

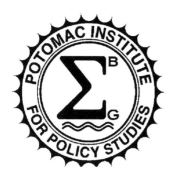

The Challenge: In the 21st century, technology is becoming increasingly pervasive. Communications, medicine, biotechnology, synthetics, robotics, composite materials, pharmaceuticals, energy sources, and transportation are just a few of the fields that technology is rapidly changing. These changes will have an enormous impact on our lives.

New cutting-edge technologies present challenges to our society. Reliable and familiar processes are often replaced by more complex systems, procedures, techniques, and equipment that have the potential to cause repercussions on a scale much larger than the technology itself. New markets open daily and established markets change or die. Workers are often displaced. Employees with different skills are needed.

Understanding the proper roles of industry, and local, state, and federal governments in relationship to these changes is a primary objective of the Potomac Institute for Policy Studies.

Our Mission: The Potomac Institute for Policy Studies is an independent, 501(c)(3), not-for-profit public policy research institute. The Institute identifies and aggressively shepherds discussion on key science, technology, and national security issues facing our society, providing in particular, an academic forum for the study of related policy issues. From these discussions and forums, we develop meaningful policy options and ensure their implementation at the intersection of business and government. The Institute's current endeavors include: Science and technology policy; National security; S&T forecasting; Operational research; Terrorism and asymmetry; Emerging threats and opportunities; Cybersecurity; and Neurotechnology and ethics.

Our Philosophy: The worthy and difficult functions stated in our mission can be met only through a consistent and continuing regard for two basic principles. First, we fiercely maintain objectivity and credibility, remaining independent of any federal or state agency, and owing no special allegiance to any single political party or private concern. This dedication to fierce objectivity is evident in our motto, Integrum Se Servare. We make every attempt to ensure that our work is conducted in an unbiased manner, regardless of the opinions of sponsors, or even self-interest. This often enables fruitful inquiries into issues that might otherwise be difficult to assess.

Second, we seek extensive collaboration with similar organizations, as well as with industry, academia, and government, and we work closely with Congress and the Executive Branch. We believe that the study of today's complex issues demands a wide variety of contributions from various perspectives, each of which add to the needed holistic understanding. But, even if the Institute possessed that understanding, a collaborative approach would be necessary. This is because, by their nature, solutions and strategies to solve significant problems at the national and international level are disruptive, tend to consume large resources, and challenge existing organizational structure and established jurisdiction. All of this results in difficulty in implementing recommendations, which otherwise profit from achieved consensus. For these reasons, Institute work typically involves experts in a variety of disciplines and includes leaders from business, government, and academia to create an environment that promotes exchange of information and analytical development.

 Potomac Institute Press

About The Founders Inn

The Founders Inn and Spa is named after the Founding Fathers who drafted the Constitution in 1787. Though built in 1991, The Founders Inn and Spa was built Georgian in design. This period is associated with the years between the accession of George I in 1714 and the death of George IV in 1830. The period's varied styles in British architecture, interior design and decorative arts are echoed throughout the property. Traditional in its origins, design and architecture, the hotel features captivating Grand Georgian and period antique furnishings. A well-manicured English garden centered among 26 landscaped acres surrounds the buildings creating a retreat from the sounds of distant rushing traffic and quietude of the mind. The spacious interior—240 generous guest rooms, wide hallways, high ceilings, a natural light atrium and 25,000 square feet of state-of-the-art meeting space—imbues a sense of space and efficiency.

Adjacency to Regent University—nationally recognized for its law school and doctoral programs—affords options to expand meeting venue space, content and technology via a 700-seat theatre and mock moot courtroom. The artwork, displayed prominently in some locations and subtly in others, complements the interior design with historic dignity and the impressionistic expertise of artistic masters. Portraits of the first four United States presidents hang on either side of the entrance to the Gallery: George Washington by James Peale, 1795; John Adams painted by John Trumbell, 1799; Thomas Jefferson by Rembrandt Peale, 1803 and James Madison by John Vanderlyn, 1812. Magnificent millwork is noted throughout the property, particularly at the arch of the Atrium, and the Chippendale railing. Having an expertise in millwork, interior designer, Mary Stone, of Austin, Texas, took great pains to assure that the Federal Style dentil work was authentic to the Georgian period of the building.

Index

A

Abu-Hassan, Ahmed Chazali, 36
academia, role of, 267–268
accountability, *vs.* attribution, 14–15
active defense
 capacity for, 170–171
 cyber exploitation in, 170–175
 in layered defense, 60–61
 legality of, 172–175
 permissible, 87
 by private sector, 80, 87
acts of war, in cyberspace
 identifying perpetrators of, 15
 Obama administration on, 231–232
 shades of gray in, 57
 status of, 166
Advanced Research Projects Agency
  (ARPA), in origin of
  cyberspace, 18
Afghanistan, military action in, as
  justified, 86–87
Afghanistan International Security
  Assistance Force, 194–195
aggression, defining, 179–180
Albright Commission, 198
Alexander, Keith
 on cost of cyber crime, 238–239
 on current threats, 138
 on cyber espionage, 110
 on information war, readiness
  for, 4
 on legal frameworks, 158
 on offensive capabilities, 170
 on proactive defense, 74

alliances
 in cyberspace, 9
 eternal, 193–194
 limits of, 200–203
 necessity of, 194–197, 203
 peacetime, 192
al Qaeda, cyber attacks by, 113
American Civil Liberties Union
  (ACLU), in regulation of
  cyberspace, 220
analysis, in defense, 43
anonymity, 40, 242–243
Anonymous
 major attacks by, 113
 objectives of, 186
anticipatory self-defense. *See*
  preemptive strike
Anti-Counterfeiting Trade Agreement
  (ACTA), 148
Antiochus IV (king of Seleucid Syria),
  101
Arab Spring
 Internet in, 224
 social networks in, 146
arms control, in cyber space, 57–58,
  258–261
ARPANET, 18
assassination, 165
assets
 cyber technology in protecting,
  230
 intangible, value of, 91
 in retribution, 186–187
The Atlantic (magazine), 87–88

attribution
    accomplishing, 27–29
    vs. accountability, 14–15
    ambiguity as constant in, 256
    analysis in, 43
    attacks in establishing, 16
    certainty in, 13, 17–18, 166
    challenges in, 6–7
    by corporations, 239–240
    in cyber coercion, 86
    cyber weapons in, 17
    definition of, 15
    in deterrence, 118–119, 180–
        183
    difficulty of
        authentication in, 22–23
        design of cyberspace in, 13–
            14, 19–22
        identification in, 22–23
        implementation of
            cyberspace in, 14
    doctrinal ramifications of, 29–30
    duck theory of, 130
    inaccurate, 182
    international legal frameworks
        in, 16
    nature of, 15–18
    network addresses in, 24–27
    perpetrators in, 15
    processes in, 14
    public discussion of, 132–133
    of remote attacks, 37–38
    in responding to attacks, 53, 87–
        88, 118–119
    standards for, 130
    technologies in, 14
    victims in, 17
Aucsmith, David, 6–7, 13–14
Aum Shinrikyo, 113
Aurora experiment, 107–108, 180

Australia, cyber policy in, 141
authentication
    in attribution, 22–23, 28–29
    bases for, 23
    DCHP allocation and, 24
    definition of, 23
authoritarian regimes, authentication
        used by, 28–29
authorization, laws of, 155, 155n7,
        156–157
awareness, in defense, 43

B
background checks, in assertions of
        identity, 22–23
Baker, Christopher, 171
Baran, Paul, 18–19
Battelle Doctrine Project report,
        245–271
Bay, Austin, 178
Big Brother, 219
binding, of IP addresses, 25–26
biometrics, in authentication, 23
Blueprint for a Secure Cyber Future
        (DHS), 62
borders, in cyberspace, 51, 153–158
Borg, Scott, 111
botnets. See also Stuxnet worm
    advantage of, 161
    Russian use of, 55–56
British Empire, 214
British National Physical Laboratory,
        18
Budapest Convention, 202–203,
        204–205
Bush, George W.
    on deterrence, 163
    on preemptive use of force, 163
businesses. See private sector
business processes, risks to, 92–93

C

cameras, in law enforcement, 241–242

Cardash, Sharon, 7, 49

Caroline Incident, 162–163

Carr, Bob, 94

Carr, Jeffrey, 86

Cartwright, James, 60, 64

catalytic war, 182

Cerf, Vint, 224, 235–236

certainty

    in attribution, 13, 17–18, 166, 182

    in liability, 155

Chabinsky, Steven, 174

Chamber of Commerce, in regulation of cyberspace, 220

channels, in cyberspace, 20

Chemical Facility Anti-Terrorism Standards (CFATS), 96–97

Chertoff, Michael, 54

Chief Information Security Officers (CISOs), cooperation among, 77

child pornography, international cooperation in prosecuting, 195–196

China

    alliance with, 201–203

    capabilities of, 57–58, 183

    censorship by, 239

    characterization of cyber attacks from, 127

    cyber doctrine and, 65

    cyber national security in, vision for, xiii

    espionage by, 52–53, 54, 110, 127–128, 133, 241

    Google attacked by, 174

    identifying attackers from, 53

    information control in, 234

    on laws of armed conflict, 78–79

    private sector of, 241

    as state sponsor, 186

    in supply chain, 111

Churchill, Winston, 11

Cilluffo, Frank, 7, 50

civil defense, 249, 258

civilians, rules of war on, 228

Clapper, James, 70

Clarke, Richard, 112–113

clearing house, for information sharing, 77

Clinton, Hillary, 135, 141, 147

coalition warfare, 44

Coldebella, Gus, 8, 153

Cold War

    acts of war defined during, 57–58

    deterrence during

        Mutually Assured Destruction in, 101–102, 169, 255–256

        objective of, 106

    government role in, 261–262

    parallels to, 6, 8, 254–256

    private sector in, 259–260

    security focus during, 211–212

collateral damage, 79

combat, in distinguishing war, 50

commercial hardware, using, 45–46

commercial organizations

    cyber attacks on, attribution of, 16

    defense industry compared to, 34t, 35

    government enlistment of, 46

commercial software, using, 45–46

cooperation among, 46
defense strategies of, 43
investment in cyber, 33
lack of agility in, 33–35
problems facing, 46
responsibility for justice, 39
secrecy of, 143
talent and, 35
The Greenbrier, 1
Gulf of Tonkin, 144–145, 145n10

H
hactivist movement, 38, 88
hard powers, 135
hardware
    commoditized, using, 45–46
    introduction of, control over, 45
    modification of, 41
    updated, 44–45
Hayden, Michael
    on need for cyber doctrine, 5–6,
        107, 246
    on Stuxnet worm, 55
Healey, Jason, 119, 132, 198
Heartland, 94
Henry, Shawn, 110
Holder, Eric, 165
Hoover, J. Edgar, 219
hostile acts
    cyber attacks defined as, 80–81
    defining, 54–55
hotline, 65
Huawei Technologies Co., Ltd., 141,
    241
Human Intelligence (HUMINT),
    256–257
human rights, online, 235
Hydraq, 174

I
identification
    in attribution, 22–23, 28–29, 256
    in authentication, 23
    of Chinese hackers, 53
    in deterrence, 115
    establishing, rigor in, 22–23
    methods of, 181
    as risk for attacker, 40
identity, in cyberspace, information
        as, 8
incentives
    in private sector, uses of, 88
    for security implementation,
        90–91
individuals
    as attackers, 184, 185
    role of, 264, 268–269
industrial age, 33, 224
industrial control system attacks,
        definition of, 126
infiltration, definition of, 125
information
    freedom of, 234–237
    in immediate gratification, 260–
        261
    as national asset, 234–236
    reliability of, 236–238
information age, obsolescence in, 33
Information Operations (IO), 51–52
information sharing, as defense
        strategy, 73, 75–77
Information Sharing and Analysis
        Centers (ISACs), 77
information war. See also cyber
        conflict
    development of, 4–5
    lack of framework for, 4

Iran-Contra scandal, 230
Iraq, in USS *Stark* attack, 15
Iraq War
    false intelligence in, 144–145
    Internet used in, 51
isolated systems, 43n12
IT department, as scapegoat, 42

J
Judicial Branch, role of, 266

K
Kagan, Donald, 99–100
Kahn, Herman, 8
Kant, Immanuel, 42
Koh, Harold, 164–165
kto kogo, 35
Kugler, Richard L., 115–116

L
Lacedaemonius, 100
law and legislation
    in copyright protection, 148
    information sharing in, 73, 75–
        76
    pending, 72–73, 84–85
    physical location and, 154
    reactive, 250
    regulation in, 73–75, 95–97
    traditional, application of, 166
law enforcement
    in attribution, 28
    cameras in, 241–242
    in cyber defense, 61
    international cooperation among,
        195–196, 204
    sovereignty in, 157
laws of armed conflict (LOAC), 78–
    79
layered defense, 60–62

leaders, in cybersecurity, 88–89
legal frameworks
    in attribution, international, 16
    consensus on, 155–156
    for cyberspace, 8
    purposes of, 155, 155n8
Legislative Branch, role of, 266
Letter of Marque and Reprisal, 240
Lewis, James A., 110, 171
liability
    certainty in, 155
    laws of, 155, 156–157
Libicki, Martin, 104, 106
Libya, cyber attack on, 51
Lieberman, Joel, 85
Lieberman-Collins bill, 73
limitation, laws of, 155, 155n7,
    156–157
Lipan, David, 178
Lisbon Summit, 198–199
Liscouski, Robert, 7–8, 83
Liwicki, Martin, 182
Lloyd's of London, 144
local data, in cyberspace structure,
    21
local governments, role of, 267
locations, of cyber attackers, 37
logging
    of system usage, 46
    volume of data and, 25–26
logic bombs, 173–175
low intensity conflict, 213
Lynn, William, 54, 70, 113, 162

M
Mahan, Alfred Thayer, 212
maintenance, *vs.* innovation, 33
Manifest Destiny, 253
manipulation, definition of, 126
Marks, Ronald, 9, 207

licensing of cyberspace, 128–129

remote attacks, attribution of, 37–38

Republican Party, approach to cybersecurity, 96

reputation, as asset, 90–95

resilience
  after cyber attacks, 59, 136
  market reactions and, 94

responsibility
  of Federal Government, in cyberspace, 9
  identity as assertion of, 22
  for infrastructure, of private sector, 69
  of nations, 119, 126–127, 128, 205

retaliation
  in deterrence, 104, 116
  disproportionate, 181, 187–188
  in equivalence doctrine, 177–179, 257

retribution, for cyber attacks, 37

risk
  to business processes, 92–93
  in defining aggression, 180

rogue actors, acts of war by, 15

Rolington, Alfred, 8, 137

Roman Empire, 101

routing
  ephemeral data in, 25–26
  historical learning in, 20–21
  IP addresses in, 24
  in network computing, 19
  in surveillance, 233

Russia, 187–188
  alliance with, 201–203
  botnet attacks from, 55–56, 118
  capabilities of, 183

characterization of cyber attacks from, 127

clandestine espionage ring of, 173

cyber doctrine and, 65

Georgia attack and
  attribution of, 118
  as hybrid war, 187–188
  as model of cyber warfare, 55–56
  state sponsors in, 186

information control in, 234

Russian Business Network, 32, 186

Rustock botnet, 240

S

Sample, Timothy R., xiv–xv, 1, 221

satisficing, 213, 218

scale, of attack, significance of, 40

scapegoat, IT department as, 42

Scheier, Bruce, 168–169

Schelling, Thomas, 102

Schmidt, Eric, 263

Schmidt, Howard, 202

Scipio, Publius Cornelius, 101

secretaries, 225

"Securing Cyberspace for the 44th Presidency," 160–161

security
  business case for, 89–90
  as business process, risks to, 93
  during Cold War, 211–212
  cost of, 218
  diplomatic discussions on, 142–143
  incentives in, 90–91
  investment in, sufficiency of, 93–95
  lack of development in, 85
  leaders in, 88–89

Sutton, Willie, 32
Swetnam, Michael S., xiv, 222
Sybota, Battle of, 99–101

T
talent
    globalization of, 35
    private use of, 33
Taliban government, military action
        against, as justified, 86–87
targeted marketing, data in, 236
targets
    reconnaissance on, 38
    subornation within, 41
TCP/IP, in cyberspace structure, 24
technology
    changes in, paying attention to,
        45
    emerging, private sector *vs.*
        government, 70
    growth of
        private sector in, 69
        speed of, 82, 263
    revolutionary changes from, 225
telegraph, wartime use of, 145
telephone system
    cyberspace compared to, 142
    universal service, 235
terrorist groups
    cyber attacks by, 113, 183–185
    data tracking of, 243
    preemptive use of force on, 163–
        164
theft, targets for, 32
thermonuclear war, escalation steps
        to, 8
threat, determination of, 7–8
Thucydides, 100
Titan Rain, 138n2
tokens, in authentication, 23

Total Information Awareness (TIA)
        Program, 243
traffic, lack of regulation of, 127
translation table, for NAT addresses,
        25
Trojan Horse attack, on Google, 174

U
undetectability, as objective of attack,
        40
United Nations
    laws of armed conflict, 50
    on preemptive strike, 163–164
"Unrestricted Warfare" (Liang and
        Xiangsui), 53
USA PATRIOT Act, surveillance
        under, 232–233
US Cyber Command
    formation of, 215
    scope of, 216
    surveillance by, 232–233
USS *Stark*, attack on, 15

V
Vatis, Michael, 182
verification principle, 57
Virtual Cybe Discussion, 149
Virtual Embassies, 148–149
viruses, enhancement of, 85–86

W
Walt, Stephen, 169, 197
war
    catalytic, 182
    cyber component in, 51, 225–
        226, 228–230, 248–
        249
    cyber war as, 227–228
    definition of, 16, 50–51
    friction in, 43–44

300